毕加索在街上跳舞，胡安莱潘，1920 年夏，被认为是奥尔加・毕加索拍摄
国立巴黎毕加索博物馆，APPH6535
Picasso dancing on a street in Juan-les-Pins, summer 1920.
Attributed to Olga Picasso, Musée national Picasso-Paris. APPH6535.

"重要的不是艺术家在做什么，
而是他是谁。"

"It is not what the artist does that counts,
but what he is."

毕加索坐在克里希大街 11 号的工作室的沙发上，手里抱着一只猫，1910 年 12 月，巴黎，
佚名，翻底片，国立巴黎毕加索博物馆，MPPH15301
Picasso sitting on a couch holding a cat in his studio on 11 Boulevard de Clichy, December 1910, Paris.
Anonymous, print internegative, Musée national Picasso-Paris. MPPH15301.

毕加索语，转引［希］克里斯蒂安・泽尔沃斯：《与毕加索交谈》，
载《艺术手册"毕加索 1930—1935"》，巴黎，1935 年。
Remarks by Picasso reported by Zervos, Christian.
"Conversation avec Picasso." *Cahiers d'art "Picasso: 1930-1935."* Paris, 1935.

毕加索
一位天才的诞生
Picasso
Birth of A Genius

本展览由 UCCA 尤伦斯当代艺术中心与国立巴黎毕加索博物馆联合举办
Exhibition organized by UCCA in collaboration with the Musée national Picasso-Paris

尤伦斯当代艺术中心
Center for Contemporary Art

MuséePicassoParis

文化艺术出版社
Culture and Art Publishing House

目录　Contents

前言

洛朗·勒邦

馆长
国立巴黎毕加索博物馆

落成于 1985 年的国立巴黎毕加索博物馆拥有世界上最重要的巴勃罗·毕加索 (1881—1973) 作品的收藏。这些藏品主要来自 1979 年巴勃罗·毕加索继承人和 1990 年杰奎琳·毕加索继承人的两次代税捐赠。得益于私人捐赠和毕加索档案的补充，如今我们的藏品包括五千多件作品以及数万件档案。

不论从质量、规模，还是从其所代表艺术领域的多样性来看，国立巴黎毕加索博物馆都是世界上唯一能够囊括毕加索所有类型和时期作品，包括绘画、雕塑、雕版和素描的公共收藏。与此同时，大量草图、习作、速写、素描本、不同阶段的版画、照片、图册、影片和资料，让我们得以再现这位艺术家的创作历程。

“毕加索——一位天才的诞生”基于国立巴黎毕加索博物馆的馆藏，是迄今为止在北京举办的最重要的巴勃罗·毕加索展览。这意味着我们推行的国际合作政策走进了一个全新的阶段，毕加索的作品将在中国大放光彩，我为此感到十分欣喜。

我由衷感谢为此次项目成功实现而付出努力的所有人。

田霏宇

馆长与 CEO
UCCA 尤伦斯当代艺术中心

展览“毕加索——一位天才的诞生”的举办，对于 UCCA 尤伦斯当代艺术中心有着里程碑式的意义。这是机构自成立以来首次举办现代艺术大师展，不论从制作投入还是影响力方面上看，这都是 UCCA 最具野心的一个展览项目。这也契合了 UCCA 致力于将艺术带入中国当代生活，扩展观众的艺术视野，促进中国与世界交流的全新使命。我们始终坚信，中国观众应有机会欣赏最高水平的展览，这些展览所引发的交流与讨论，也将成为这个特定历史情境中的文化风向标。此次为 UCCA 与中国观众量身打造的展览，呈现了毕加索创作生涯的前几十年，让我们得以了解其独特的艺术力量与创作视野的塑造过程。这位伟大的艺术家，通过不断的实验、即兴与创新而开辟自身艺术道路的过程——正所谓“摸着石头过河”——也呼应着这个国家与这座当代艺术机构的发展历程。

此次展览得到了众多合作者的支持。首先，我想要由衷地感谢国立巴黎毕加索博物馆的馆长洛朗·勒邦对 UCCA 的信任，让如此珍贵的藏品来到北京展出。我还想要诚挚地感谢此次展览的策展人，毕加索博物馆藏品总监艾米莉娅·菲利普，她以新颖、敏锐的视角发掘馆藏作品之间的全新关联与叙事线索。包括苏菲·哈塔扎克、苏菲·达伊尼 - 迪阿罗和莱斯利·勒舍瓦利耶在内的国立巴黎毕加索博物馆团队，感谢你们为推动这一项目所付出的努力。阿德里安·卡迪工作室为展览提供了精致的空间设计方案，让作品在展厅里大放光彩。感谢吴雪杉教授为展览图录贡献了一篇关于毕加索与现代中国历史的精彩论文。感谢 Doors 门艺文化公司的黎静、零零及其团队，从项目的最初酝酿到最终成型，每一步都离不开你们的帮助与支持。这本图录的成功出版得到了文化艺术出版社杨斌社长的帮助与支持，同时也感谢本书的设计师，来自 26 Studio 的杨绍谆与冷静。此外，我还想对整个 UCCA 团队致以诚挚的谢意，在各个部门同事的共同努力之下，我们完成了这个在几年之前根本不敢想象的展览项目。

感谢摩根士丹利、苏富比以及玛丽黛佳对此次展览提供的大力支持，展览的儿童教育项目由英氏婴童用品有限公司及英氏儿童成长基金会提供慷慨支持。明基 BenQ 为展览提供影像解决方案。本次展览的住宿与相关活动由北京诺金酒店倾情支持，展览出行由谛珞轲旅游咨询有限公司支持。感谢 UCCA 战略合作伙伴阿那亚对展览的支持。

我们为能够向北京的观众呈现这样一场展览而倍感荣幸也充满喜悦，由衷地希望每一位来到 UCCA 参观展览的观众都能从中汲取全新的艺术热情，并加深人们对个体才能禀赋之力量的信念。

Forewords

Laurent Le Bon

President
Musée national Picasso-Paris

Inaugurated in 1985, the Musée national Picasso-Paris conserves the most important collection of works by Pablo Picasso (1881-1973) in the world. Its collection originated in two major donations granted to the state through gift-in-lieu, respectively, by the heirs of Pablo Picasso in 1979 and by the heiress of Jacqueline Picasso in 1990. It is supplemented by donations from private collections and Picasso's archives, and it currently holds more than five thousand artworks and tens of thousands of archival materials.

Due to its quality, size, and diversity of artistic fields represented, it is the only public collection in the world that allows for an exploration of all of Picasso's practice, whether painting, sculpture, engravings, or drawings. It clearly evokes–across sketches, studies, drafts, drawing notebooks, successive stages of etchings, photography, illustrated volumes, films, and documents–the creative processes of the artist.

Realized exclusively from museum's collection, "Picasso – Birth of a Genius" is the most important Picasso exhibition ever to take place in Beijing. I am delighted by this new stage in the museum's policy of international cooperation that allows the artist's works to shine in China.

I warmly thank all those who have made this event possible.

Philip Tinari

Director and CEO
UCCA Center for Contemporary Art

The exhibition "Picasso – Birth of a Genius" marks a milestone in the history of UCCA Center for Contemporary Art. The first time since its founding that the institution has explored a figure of the modern period, the exhibition is also the most ambitious project UCCA has ever undertaken in terms of both resources required and influence achieved. It speaks to a renewed commitment to our mission to bring art into the public life of contemporary China, to expand our audience far beyond the narrow purview of the art world, and to promote cultural exchange between China and the wider world at the highest levels. We firmly believe that audiences in China deserve exhibitions of the highest caliber, and that the conversations and dialogues nurtured by such exhibitions create the cultural tenor of their specific historical moment. Telling the story of how Picasso's uniquely powerful voice and vision took shape throughout his first decades, this exhibition, curated specifically for this context, speaks to a country and an institution that, like the great artist, have forged a path forward through experimentation, improvisation, and innovation—or as the aphorism says, "crossing the river by feeling the stones."

This exhibition bears the contributions of many. First and foremost, the Musée national Picasso-Paris has entrusted us with jewels of its collection, for which we are grateful to its president Laurent Le Bon. Emilia Philippot, head of collections, has curated the show with a fresh and piercing eye, tracing new connections and forging new narratives from the work at hand. The MnPP team, including Sophie Ratajczak, Sophie Daynes-Diallo, and Leslie Lechevallier have worked to further our collaboration. Studio Adrien Gardère has provided a precise and exquisite scenography in which the works can truly shine. Wu Xueshan has contributed a beautiful essay situating Picasso in the history of modern China. Crucially, Bérénice Angremy and Victoria Jonathan, along with their colleagues at Doors Art & Culture Agency, have contributed to every step of this project, from its initial conception to its final execution. The catalogue would not have been possible without Yang Bin, director of Culture and Art Publishing House, as well as its designers Yang Shaozhun and Leng Jing of 26 Studio. Finally, our team at UCCA, across all departments, have come together to realize a project that would have been unthinkable here even a few years ago.

The exhibition is made possible by Morgan Stanley, Sotheby's, and Marie Dalgar. The children's educational programs for this exhibition are made possible by Asia Ying's Baby World Limited and YeeHoO Children Growth Foundation. BenQ provides film projection support. Accommodation and event support come from NUO Hotel Beijing and transportation support comes from D-LUX Travel. The catalogue is published by Culture and Art Publishing House. UCCA thanks its strategic partner, Aranya, for supporting the exhibition.

We are honored and elated to present this exhibition to our audience in Beijing. We hope that it may inspire a renewed love of art and a deepened confidence in the power of individual talent among all those who see it.

毕加索——一位天才的诞生

艾米莉娅·菲利普

国立巴黎毕加索博物馆藏品总监

“（天才）也就是个性加上一点才华，从平凡中跳脱出来的错误。例如在美术馆中，只有失败的画作……现在被我们视为‘杰作’的，都是一些远离当时大师之规的作品。那些最优秀的作品也最清晰地揭示出创作者身上的烙印。”[01]

就毕加索而言，天才也许首先是一种特殊个性的体现，这种个性与其所属时代的艺术惯例格格不入。毫无疑问，从这个角度上看，没有什么比“天才”这个词更适合形容这位 19 世纪之子，他再创造的能力让他不断背离所有同时代的创作教条。拥有难以置信的生命力，毕加索是真正意义上的现代艺术先锋，其生活与作品密不可分，共同造就了他的非凡形象。甚至连他出生的故事也好似英雄传奇：助产士本以为这个新生儿已经死亡，但是毕加索当医生的叔叔唐·萨尔瓦多对着他的脸吹了一口雪茄的烟气，然后他就复活了。那些用来塑造毕加索神话的小逸事更是层出不穷：据说他会说的第一个字是“piz”，[02] 该词是西班牙语“lapiz”的缩写，意思是铅笔，这早早就显露了他的未来志向；再如，他 14 岁时就成功地被巴塞罗那的隆哈美术学校录取，年龄比其他考生要小得多，而且他只花了 24 小时准备入学考试作品，而不是学校规定的一个月。[03] 艺术家自己也曾经讲述过，[04] 他的父亲是一位画家同时在美术学院担任老师，在他 13 岁那年的某一天，父亲交给他任务，让他帮自己完成一幅作品，为画上的鸽子添上爪子。当父亲看到毕加索的才华时，大吃一惊，随即决定放弃自己的绘画事业，毕加索寥寥数语描绘了当时的场景，“他把自己的画笔和颜料交给我，从此以后再未执笔作画”。[05] 这一象征意义上的父亲之死，发生在毕加索走上命中注定的艺术道路之初，将在他的创作中留下一个决定性的标记：摆脱学院传统和规范，或者更广泛的层面上，通过表现主题和造型方式，不断质疑人们习以为常的经验和边界。

毕加索从未写过关于个人创作的理论性文章，只是零散地表达过自己的想法，这些片段之间没有明显的逻辑性，更多是跳跃性的观点。他的整个创作表达也是如此，充满了断裂、转向、闪现、渐进以及不同道路的相互交织与承接。在被毕加索比喻为“实验室”的工作室中，尤其可以感受到他作品中的那股勃勃生机[06]、在场感和独特力量。

国立巴黎毕加索博物馆拥有世界上最重要的毕加索收藏，其中大部分通过 1979 年和 1990 年的代税捐赠进入博物馆。这批“毕加索的毕加索”收藏，直接出自艺术家工作室，艺术家和它们共同“生活”多年，在世时一直将它们保存在身边，人们因而得以通过这些藏品深入大师的创作内核。它们既是独一无二的见证，也是人们对毕加索的天赋不断提出新问题的思考之源。从这位艺术神童早年求学期间以精湛技艺绘制的古典雕塑石膏像临摹习作，到晚年全身心投入创作的绘画和雕版画作品，从技术的再创造到主题的突破，国立巴黎毕加索博物馆的藏品构成了独一无二的作品库，让人们全面了解艺术家其人和其作品的复杂性。

从 1895 年前后毕加索的求学时期，到 20 世纪 20 年代初的“古典主义”黄金时期，展览“毕加索——一位天才的诞生”贯穿了毕加索的蓝色和粉色时期，并且通过众多杰作，展现了他在原始主义和立体主义时期不同阶段的创作。通过一系列重要绘画、雕塑和纸本作品，展览体现了这位艺术奇才如何在极短的时间内，吸收古代艺术的精华，掌握同时代艺术家的最新风格，同时发展出立体主义——这个全新的创作手法对传统的艺术表现形式提出了深刻质疑。

我们之所以选择专注于毕加索创作生涯的前 30 年，是因为这个时期所奠定的艺术实践基础彻底革新了 20 世纪的艺术，并且让这位西班牙年轻人成为古典世界与现代世界之间为数不多的联系人。与惯常将毕加索的艺术生涯简化为一系列严格定义和相互封闭的创作时期的策展方式有所不同，此次展览在不同时期保留

01. 毕加索语，转引［西］吉米·萨巴尔特：《毕加索，肖像与回忆》，巴黎，路易·卡雷与马克西米利恩·沃克斯出版社 1946 年版，第 219 页。

02. “他的母亲很喜欢提起毕加索会说的第一个词就是‘piz，piz’，他着急地要铅笔（lapiz）。”［英］罗兰·潘罗斯：《毕加索》，1958 年，雅克·夏维，保罗·佩尔勒瓦德译，法译本，巴黎，弗拉马里翁出版社 1981 年版，第 25 页。

03. “……巴勃罗当时只有 14 岁，尽管没有到达入学年龄，在他父亲的坚持下，校方同意让他跳过枯燥的准备期，直接参加高级班《古代，自然，人体模特与绘画》的考试。结果让人大吃一惊。他只花了一天时间就完成了人体模特素描考试，而不是学校所规定的一个月，而且质量非常高。很多有经验的学生都难以画出高水平的画作，毕加索由此证明了自己的水平已经超过了他们”。同上书，第 47—48 页。

04. “一天晚上，天气稍微没那么阴沉，他向儿子布置了一个任务，然后就沿着阿尔梅达街道散步。街上到处都是漫步的行人，他走在人群之中，希望缓解一下自己悲伤的情绪，洋金花散发出浓浓的香气，它们的模样就好像是挂着的白色灯笼。当他回到家的时候，发现鸽子的脚已经画完了，如此栩栩如生，唐·何塞一时难以控制住感情，突然把自己的调色盘、画笔和颜料都塞给巴勃罗，他说儿子才华横溢，其实已经超越了自己，所以他不会再继续画画”。同上书，第 33 页。

05. 韦特·英格·F：《世纪天才，1881—1973》，科隆，梅迪亚出版社 1986 年版，第 8 页。

06. “他梦想举办展览时，能像在工作室那样展示他的画作——工作室里的作品才是鲜活的。”［法］伊莲娜·帕姆兰：《毕加索之旅》，巴黎，罗伯特·拉封出版社 1980 年版，克里斯蒂安·布尔乔亚 1994 年版，第 49 页。

07.《藤椅上的静物》，绳框蜡布面油彩，29x37cm，国立巴黎毕加索博物馆，毕加索代税捐赠，1979年，MP36

08.［美］罗莎琳德·克劳斯，《毕加索的纸》，1998年，让-路易·欧德宾尼，苏菲·耶尔辛·勒格朗译，法译本，巴黎，马库拉出版社2013年版，第31页及之后。

了开放性和穿透性的视角，由此强调毕加索身上多种看似矛盾的艺术语言的共存。秉持同样的理念，展览以艺术家1927年至1972年较为晚期的一系列杰出的绘画和雕塑作品作为结尾，勾勒出贯穿他创作生涯的主题和基本原则。他尤为关注对创作行为提出质疑和思考的自画像体裁、在不同媒介间展开持续的对话、热衷于探索形体的变化。正是这些不同的方面，构成了天才毕加索的整体创作。

展览选取了一个独特的视角，即从艺术和理论，而不是从个人传记或历史的视角，来突出毕加索的天赋构成。如此非凡的创造力是在什么时候，又是如何表现出来的？哪些线索能够让我们更好地理解并定义毕加索作品千变万化而又不可分割的特殊性？

在形式跃然纸上之前，我们从毕加索的表现手法和创作意图中，就能够感受到这位现代领航者的过人禀赋；这不仅体现在他留给后世的作品中，也体现在他一生留下的为数不多的文字和声明中。这些不时相互矛盾的话语为我们展现出这位人物的多面性，其天赋是两个方面的结合：对技术炉火纯青的掌握，并将其应用到极富野心的项目之上；不断革新、富有远见的创作理念，造就了他“野蛮”的眼力。从很年轻的时候起，毕加索就不满足于画得“像拉斐尔一样”，哪怕这意味着非凡的技巧、对绘画和艺术再现的深刻理解。他几乎立刻就熟练掌握了这一传统，并迅速扩大了自己对形式和风格的参考范围，交替地从同时代艺术（巴塞罗那先锋派、象征主义、后印象主义、塞尚、安格尔、马奈或是雷诺阿的绘画）、地中海文化（古典时代、伟大的巴洛克绘画传统、伊比利亚塑像、庞贝绘画）、或近（报纸、戏剧、斗牛、诗歌、马戏团和杂耍艺人）或远（非洲雕塑、大洋洲艺术，甚至日本版画）的当代民间文化中汲取灵感。

同样地，毕加索抓住周围环境的一切元素来构建他的作品，从未将自己限定于单一技术之中——尽管他的绘画技艺精湛——而是不断地，以一种自然而轻松的方式，从绘画过渡到雕塑、从素描过渡到雕版画，甚至参与戏剧创作，以及后来的电影领域！这是一种在所有媒介中表达自我、并将一个媒介中所掌握的经验转移到另一个媒介的能力，这也是毕加索天赋的另一个重要特征。对材料的精妙理解和对实验的兴趣，让他无拘无束地跨越传统艺术体裁的分类。这在立体主义时期表现得尤为明显，他采用三维的绘画方式，带来了媒介之间的相互渗透性和物体的不确定性，这深刻地改变了我们的观看方式。从1910年开始，毕加索致力于在平面画布上复原现实的复杂性。创作出来的人和物仿佛经过了特定感知方式的蒙太奇处理：简化体积、以连续平面切割表面、沿棱边打开形体、透明的平面、突出或图示化的内在结构、被分解为小平面的体积。一些大幅单色调油画，以《弹曼陀林的男子》（1911—1913）为例，这幅作品中黑色、白色和不同程度的灰色调起到了示范作用，确定了立体主义的全新造型原则。创作于1912年的《藤椅上的静物》[07]则是一件复合材料作品，毕加索将错视画、绘画与缆绳结合在一起，由此创作了现代艺术上的第一幅拼贴画。壁纸、织物、印刷字体，这些风马牛不相及的物品被他引入构图之中，在空间中组成了无数的实验，引入了第三维度，扰乱了人们对真实的感知。作品从此不再是“再现”，而变成“表现”。在这些画作、结构、素描或拼贴画中，洋溢着毕加索以马拉美的方式将造型符号与印刷符号相结合，由此而带来的诗意。

在《毕加索的纸》这部著作中，[08]罗莎琳德·克劳斯（Rosalind Krauss）借助语言学和符号学理论，对立体主义拼贴和毕加索在拼贴画中剪取的报纸进行了精彩的分析。在她看来，每一个拼贴元素都在他的作品中发出丰富多样的声音，毕加索没有做任何删除，尽管如此，也没有任何一个元素能够保留原初的性质。历史学家在这里想要突出的是“符号的传播”，即通过剪报和拼贴所带来的符号传播，这也正是她专著中第一章的标题。毕加索仿佛宣称自己在拼贴画这种新媒介的陪伴之下，就可以进入一个新的空间，符号在这里不再拥有相似的固定性，而是玩起了不断向象征性开放自身意义的游戏。拼贴画的起源——将类似于报纸这种无法长久保存的材料拼贴在一起——可以说是不值一提的，但是我们并不能因此忽略它为创作者和观众带来的重要范式转变，这是一种真正意义上的革命手法，将在20世纪的艺术中留下深刻的烙印。

毕加索一方面掌握扎实、渊博且令人敬佩的专业技能，另一方面拥有空前自由的眼光，他吸收一切，没有阶级或等级之分；这两个方面并不协调，他却将它们结合在一起，这正是他创作方法的真正基石，同时也奠定了他的过人天赋。精湛的技术加上狂野的创造力，精彩地造就了毕加索顽强的艺术独立性：“我把所有我喜欢的一切都放进画里。那也没办法，这些东西只能在画面里自己互相协调了。”[09]

毕加索的天才是何时，又是如何觉醒的呢？在他的求学时期，在他第一次巴黎之旅之后，还是在他发明立体主义的时候？毕加索在多年之后回顾自己职业生涯的缘起，当时他已经是一位前途无量的艺术家，他似乎佐证了自己“成为毕加索”的概念：“我小的时候，我妈妈曾对我说：‘如果你当士兵，你会成为将军。如果你当修道士，你会成为教皇。’我本想成为画家，然而却成为了毕加索。”[10] 我们也许可以试图推测，1901 年正是毕加索成为真正毕加索的转型期：因为他在画中的签名，从“巴勃罗・鲁伊斯・布拉斯科”变成“P. 鲁伊斯・毕加索”，然后再变成简短的“毕加索”。逐渐转变的签名揭示了这个特殊的艺术家身份的构建过程，当时毕加索正进入蓝色时期，即第一个他真正的个人风格。与此同时，采用这一新的签名，体现了另一层面上的决定：放弃名字带来了两个结果，一是改变姓氏的地位，二是将个人身份变为创作实体。自此以后，画家与他作品的统一性取代了他的个人和生平起伏。这个统一性不仅存在于他的整体作品之中，并且在他的作品和本人之间的关系中也得到确认：“每一幅画都是一个装满我血液的小瓶子，都是我的心血之作。”[11] 这也是毕加索天赋的另一个典型的标志。

09. 毕加索语，转引［希］克里斯蒂安・泽尔沃斯：《与毕加索交谈》，载《艺术手册“毕加索：1930—1935”》，巴黎，1935 年，第 37 页。

10. 毕加索语，转引［法］弗朗索瓦丝・吉洛：《与毕加索一起生活》，巴黎，加尔曼 - 勒维出版社 1965 年版，第 50 页。

11. 毕加索语，转引［英］彭罗斯・罗兰：《毕加索》，弗拉马里翁出版社 1982 年版，第 472 页。

Picasso – Birth of a Genius

Emilia Philippot
Head of Collections
Musée national Picasso-Paris

(Genius). It is personality with a little bit of talent, the error that emerges from the ordinary by chance. In museums, for example, there are only failed paintings [...] What we now see as "masterpieces" are those that most departed from the rules dictated by the masters of their time. The best ones reveal most clearly the stigmata of the artist who painted them.[01]

If we believe Picasso, genius is, above all, the assertion of a singular personality that breaks with the artistic conventions of its time. In this regard, undoubtedly no other term would be more appropriate to describe this child of the nineteenth century, whose capacity for reinvention constantly pulled him away from contemporaneous creative dogma. Possessed of an incredible vitality, Picasso is indeed the trailblazer of modern art, whose life and work, inseparable, express an identity outside of the ordinary. Even the tale of his birth borders on heroic legend: believed to be dead by the midwife, the infant is revived by his uncle, a doctor named Don Salvador, who blows cigar smoke into the newborn's face to bring him back to life. There are a plethora of anecdotes that later contributed to shaping the Picasso myth: from the first word Picasso supposedly babbled, "*piz*"[02]–the diminutive of *lapiz*, Spanish for pencil–a sign of his early vocation, to the dazzling success of his admission into the La Lljotja school in Barcelona, where he passed the entrance exam at only fourteen years old, far younger than the other candidates, and submitted his work within twenty-four hours instead of the month allotted.[03] One also recalls Picasso's terse comment describing how, at the age of thirteen, his father, a painter and professor at the School of Fine Arts, made the decision to abandon his career. He was astounded by the talent of his son, to whom he had entrusted the completion of one of his paintings by finishing the talons of a pigeon.[04] "He gave me his paints and his colors, and he never painted again."[05] This symbolic death of the father, who intervenes very early on in the predestined path of the artist, signals one of the definitive characteristics in the making of Picasso: the liberation from codes and traditions passed on from the academic world and, more broadly, a constant questioning of acquired knowledge and accepted boundaries, both in the subjects represented and in their formal treatments.

If Picasso never wrote theoretical texts on his work, he expressed himself in fragments, moving from one idea to another with no apparent logic. His entire creative process is found within the image, made of ruptures and returns, of flashes and slow progressions, of paths that intersect and succeed one another. In his studio, which he compares to a "sort of laboratory," his works are alive,[06] invested with a singular presence and power.

Because Picasso chose to retain them throughout his life, and because they mostly "lived" by his side, the works in the collection of the Musée national Picasso-Paris–acquired primarily through gifts-in-lieu in 1979 and 1990–allow one to delve into the heart of the artist's creative process. The world's leading collection of his masterworks, these "Picassos of Picasso," coming directly from his studios, are at once an exceptional testimony and a source for renewed examination of the Picassian genius. Spanning his very first years of training, in which the young prodigy brilliantly executed copies of plaster casts of antique marbles, to the final seasons of his life, marked by an intense practice of painting and engraving–straddling his reinventions of technique and transgressions of subject–the collection of the Paris museum constitutes a unique corpus that allows audiences to approach the man and his work in all of their complexity.

01. Picasso cited in Sabartés, Jaime. *Picasso. Portraits et souvenirs*. Paris: Louis Carré and Maximilien Vox, 1946, p. 219.

02. "His mother liked to say how the first word he could pronounce, "*piz, piz*," was an imperative demand for a *lapiz*, a pencil." Penrose, Roland. *Picasso*. 1958. Translated into French by Chavy, Jacques and Peyrelevade, Paul. Paris: Flammarion, 1981, p. 25.

03. "Pablo was scarcely fourteen, but although he was below the required age, at the insistence of his father he was allowed to skip the boring preparatory stages and take the entrance examination for the higher class, 'Antiquity, Nature, Live Models, and Painting.' The results were remarkable. He completed the test, for which one month was prescribed, in exactly one day, and so successfully that in his live model drawings, he was more advanced than the more experienced students, who often found it difficult to meet the required standards." Ibid, pp. 47-48.

04. "One evening, when the weather was less depressing, he gave his son a task and went out for a stroll along the alameda. Among the crowds passing slowly up and down, under the heavy scent of the datura flowers hanging like white lanterns, he aired his melancholy. On his return, the pigeons were finished, and so lifelike were their talons that Don José, in a burst of emotion, suddenly gave Picasso his palette, brushes, and colors, saying that his son's talent was now mature, in fact already greater than his own, and that he himself would never paint again." Ibid, p. 33.

05. Walther, Ingo F. *Picasso. Le génie du siècle. 1881-1973*. Cologne: Médéa, 1986, p. 8.

06. "He dreamed of exhibitions where the paintings were shown as in the studio–that is where they are alive." Parmelin, Hélène. *Voyage en Picasso*. Robert Laffont, 1980. Christian Bourgois, 1994, p. 49.

Exploring the period that spans the training of the artist circa 1895 to the golden age of Picasso's Classical style at the beginning of the 1920s, the exhibition "Picasso – Birth of a Genius" covers the Blue and Rose Periods and considers, through numerous masterpieces, the Primitivist Period and the different phases of Cubism. Through an important selection of paintings, sculptures, and graphic artworks, the exhibition illustrates how the young prodigy, in record time, succeeded not only in assimilating the lessons of ancient art and absorbing the latest expressions of his contemporaries, but also and especially in managing to develop, with the invention of Cubism, a new approach that deeply questioned the art of traditional representation.

The reason we have chosen to concentrate on the first thirty years of Picasso's creative output is that during this period, the foundation was laid for an artistic practice that would revolutionize the art of the twentieth century, and would make the young Spaniard one of the rare intermediaries between the classical and modern worlds. While nuancing a vision that reduces his works to a succession of strictly defined and delimited periods, the proposed path contains openings and points of view that cross from one period to another, reaffirming the coexistence, in Picasso, of several seemingly contradictory languages. In the same vein, the exhibition concludes with an exceptional collection of later paintings and sculptures, from 1927 to 1972, which reflects the continuity of subjects and foundational principles implemented very early on in his work. Among these, notably, are the genre of the self-portrait, which questions and puts into perspective the creative act, and the constant dialogue between different mediums, or even a penchant for the metamorphosis of forms: facets of Picasso's genius that nourished all of his work.

The purpose of the exhibition is thus to adhere to a singular perspective: to highlight the formation of Picasso's genius, not so much from a biographical or historical point of view, but rather from an artistic and theoretical perspective. In which moment and through what means did this abnormal creative force express itself? What are the contours that enable a better understanding and definition of the exceptional character of this protean and indivisible work?

The remarkable aptitude that characterizes this figurehead of modernity implicates both the facture and the intent that determine the emergence of forms. It is manifest not only in the items that Picasso bequeathed to posterity, but also in the rare texts and statements that the artist delivered throughout his life. Put in this perspective, these sometimes contradictory words outline a multifaceted character whose genius is expressed in the convergence of an exceptional technical mastery, which was applied in service of the most ambitious projects, and a constantly renewed inspiration—a visionary who cultivated the savagery of his eye. Although very young, Picasso did not let himself be restricted by his famous gift for drawing "like Raphaël," which referred both to his extraordinary skill and to his deep understanding of painting and the art of representation. With this inheritance that he acquired almost immediately, he quickly widened the field of his formal and stylistic references, drawing by turns on the art of his time (the Barcelona avant-garde, Symbolism, Post-Impressionism, and the paintings of Paul Cézanne, Jean-Auguste-Dominique Ingres, and finally Édouard Manet and Pierre-Auguste Renoir), the Mediterranean (classical antiquity, the great Baroque painterly tradition, Iberian statuary, Pompeian painting), and contemporary popular culture from both near (newspapers, theater, bullfights, poetry, the circus, and traveling performers), and far (African sculpture, Oceanic art, and Japanese prints).

In the same way that he grasped all that surrounded him to form his works, Picasso did not limit himself to a single technique—as virtuosic as he is at painting—but rather constantly passed, with ease and clear naturalness, from painting to sculpture, from drawing to engraving, and even to the theater and, later on, cinema! This capacity to express himself in all media, and to transpose the lessons learned from one onto the other, is another characteristic of the Picassian genius. It evinces a profound understanding of materials and a taste for experimentation that is deliberately liberated from the traditional categories of genre. Particularly significant in the Cubist Period, during which Picasso adopted a three-dimensional approach to painting, the permeability of media, and the indeterminacy of objects thereby shaped, profoundly renewed our way of seeing. From 1910 onward, Picasso strove to restore the complexities of reality on the plane of the canvas. He presented a figure, an object, as a montage of specific perspectives: simplified volumes, surfaces cut up through consecutive planes, objects opened along their edges, transparent planes, highlighted and schematized internal structures, and volumes deconstructed into facets. The monochrome of large canvases like *Man with a Mandolin* (1911-13), with their blacks, whites, and shades of grey, played a didactic role in affirming the new formal principles of Cubism. With *Still Life with Chair Caning* in 1912,[07] a composite object combining a *trompe l'œil* canvas, painting, and string, Picasso created the first collage of modern art. Wallpaper, fabrics, typographical lettering–the most heterogeneous of objects are brought into his compositions, which constitute experiments in space where the introduction of the third dimension disturbs our perception of reality. They are no longer works of "representation," but of "presentation." In these canvases, constructions, drawings, and papiers collés, the poetic spirit of Picasso, which connects formal and typographical signs to the Mallarméan mode, is found throughout.

In *The Picasso Papers*,[08] Rosalind Krauss applies linguistics and semiotics to brilliantly analyze the Cubist collages and the newspaper clippings chosen by Picasso in his papiers collés. Each reveals a multitude of voices, none of which are censored by the artist, yet neither are they authentically his own. What the historian brings to the fore, and the title of the first chapter of her publication, is "the circulation of the sign" elicited by the use of cut and pasted newspaper clippings. It is as if in these collages, Picasso claims that with this new medium he has entered into a space where the sign no longer has the fixity of resemblance, but is instead an unending game of open meaning. Through the trivial act of cutting and pasting such perishable materials as newspapers, the papiers collés are nonetheless, by the paradigm shifts they imply for both the creator and the viewer, true revolutionary acts that go on to profoundly mark the art of the twentieth century.

The true basis for Picasso's creative process is the jarring marriage of an enlightened, cultivated, and respected savoir-faire and the unprecedented freedom of a vision that absorbs everything, regardless of class or rank. This is undoubtedly the very foundation of the artist's genius. Picasso is at once an unparalleled technical master and a wild creative force, which affirms, with panache, his inveterate artistic independence: "I put everything I love on my canvases. So much worse for the things; they have only to arrange themselves with one another."[09]

When and how was the genius of Picasso born? With his academic training? After his first journey to Paris? With the invention of Cubism? Recalling the origin of his vocation, Picasso himself seemed to confirm the notion, several years later, of a moment when, as an aspiring painter, he "became Picasso": "When I was a child, my mother said, 'If you become a soldier, you will be a general. If you become a monk, you will end up as pope.' I wanted to be a painter, and so I became Picasso."[10] Yet it was in the year 1901, one is tempted to say, that Picasso truly became Picasso: on his canvases, Pablo Ruiz Blasco gave way to P. Ruiz Picasso, then to Picasso for short. The shifting signature indicates the gradual construction of a singular artistic identity at the moment when the painter enters his Blue Period, his first authentically personal mode. At the same time, the adoption of this new signature reflects a decision of another order: abandoning the first name has the effect of changing the status of the moniker, transforming the identity of the individual into a creative entity. From then on, the painter and the unity of his work supplant his person and the vicissitudes of his biography. This unity is affirmed not only in his art as a whole, but also between the work and Picasso himself: "Each painting is a vial full of my blood. That is how it was done."[11] Another mark of the Picassian genius, par excellence.

07. *Still Life with Chair Caning*, oil and oilcloth on canvas framed by rope, 29 x 37 cm. Musée national Picasso-Paris / Pablo Picasso gift-in-lieu, 1979. MP36.

08. Krauss, Rosalind. *The Picasso Papers*. 1998. Translated into French by Houdebine, Jean-Louis and Legrand, Sophie Yersin. Marcula, 2013, p. 31 and later instances.

09. Remarks by Picasso reported by Zervos, Christian. "Conversation avec Picasso." *Cahiers d'art "Picasso: 1930-1935."* Paris, 1935, p. 37.

10. Remarks by Picasso reported by Gilot, Françoise. *Vivre avec Picasso*. Paris, 1935. Calmann-Lévy, 1965, p. 50.

11. Remarks by Picasso reported by Penrose, Roland. *Picasso*. Paris: Flammarion, 1982, p. 472.

毕加索在中国：1917—2019

吴雪杉

中央美术学院人文学院 教授

20 世纪初期，中国开始有意识地引入西方艺术，西方古代及现当代著名艺术家在中国逐渐得到广泛而全面的介绍。然而，名声家喻户晓的不过寥寥数人而已，其中就有毕加索。毕加索生前得享大名，早在 1910 年代，他的名字就已传入中国，并逐渐成为中国人心目中艺术天才的代表。在这近百年的传播史与接受史中，毕加索获得了鲜花和掌声，也遭遇过批评与批判。在所有西方艺术家中，毕加索作为艺术家的形象与中国自身历史发展脉络紧密结合在一起，历经大起大落，最为跌宕起伏。毕加索在中国的接受过程是中西方文化交流的一个缩影；“毕加索”在中国的形象演变，在某种意义上，也成为中国自身的一面镜子。

01. 在中国的早期传播

1917 年，姜丹书在上海商务印书馆出版的《美术史》里提到了“立方体派”，该书是为师范学校编写的教科书，也是中国最早的美术史著作之一，内容比较简略。对于“立方体派”（“立体派”早先的译名）为何物，只惜墨如金地说了一句：“研究物象之体积，欲于画面上表体积之感。”[01] 1918 年，姜丹书又编辑出版了《美术史参考书》，作为前一年《美术史》的辅助读物。这本书以词条说明的形式对中外重要画家、流派和术语进行讲解，“立方体派”条下增补了新内容，提到了毕加索：

> 最近起于巴黎之一画派。此派之主张，反抗印象派新印象派之光线本位色彩本位，而由于动学说的思想，讲而研究物象之体积，欲将体积之感，表出之于画面之上。无论画线画面，皆用立体，交错难辨，不肖自然。初颇受人非笑，近渐见许于识者矣。现代画家昆迦叔（Picasso，Pablo 西班牙人住于巴黎）为此派之首领。[02]

这是毕加索最早见于中文著述中的一例。毕加索在后世的主要形象——立体派的创始人——此时已经确立下来。这也是该书所提供的关于毕加索的主要信息。

吕澂于 1922 年出版的《西洋美术史》开始比较详尽地介绍立体派的各个代表人物，尤其是毕加索：

> 立方主义自昆迦梭（即毕加索，1881）之作品创之。昆氏禀性好奇，初时模仿各家，均随即废弃。及见斐洲土人之雕刻品，多用单纯之立方形，遂易其画法，欲以种种几何形体，别求自然之实际。其影响所及，乃有立方派 Cubists。[03]

吕澂以法国人赖那克（Salomon Reinach）的《阿波罗艺术史》的英译（*Apollo*：*An Illustrated Manual of the History of Art Throughout the Ages*）为蓝本，不过该书只写到 19 世纪。吕澂又参考了多种著作，增补了 20 世纪的欧洲艺术史。[04] 在毕加索的部分，吕澂说他“禀性好奇”，受非洲黑人艺术启发开创了“立方主义”。值得一提的是，《西洋美术史》也是由上海的商务印书馆出版，这家出版社对于西方美术在中国的译介居功甚伟。

从 1918 年的《美术史参考书》以后，绝大部分在中国出版的西方美术通史类著作都遵循了一个惯例：将毕加索放在立体派名下。梁得所 1929 年编译出版的《西洋美术大纲》（1929），第 21 章用来介绍“后期印象派立体派与未来派”（“立体派”这个译法得到流行和确立），毕加索继续以“立体派”发明人的形象出现。[05] 这本《西洋美术大纲》以英国人威廉·奥宾（William Orpen，1878—1931）《艺术概论》（*Outline of Art*，1924）一书为蓝本增删而成。奥宾的《艺术概论》出版于 1924 年，收录 300 多张作品插图，其中

01. 姜丹书：《美术史》，商务印书馆 1917 年版，第 82 页。姜丹书将“Picasso”译作“昆迦叔”，与今天通行的“毕加索”相去甚远。这是外国名人传入中国后都会遇到的问题，往往要历经多年之后，才能获得一个公认的译名。毕加索的名字前前后后有十余种译法，后文不再赘述。

02. 姜丹书：《美术史参考书》下编，商务印书馆 1918 年版，第 29 页。

03. 吕澂：《西洋美术史》，商务印书馆 1922 年版，第 153—154 页。

04. 关于 20 世纪的部分，吕澂说他“参用 R.Muther 及日人黑田重太郎之说尤多”。参见吕澂《西洋美术史》“述例”，第 1 页。

05. 梁得所编译：《西洋美术大纲》，良友图书印刷公司 1929 年版，第 209—211 页，图版第 257、258。

06. [英] 爱伯：《现代绘画论》，刘海粟译，上海商务印书馆 1936 年版，第 20—25 页。

07. 倪贻德：《西洋画派解说》，商务印书馆 1937 年版，第 132—133 页。

08. 陈士文：《比加索》，《艺风》1933 年第 1 卷第 5 期，第 25 页。

09. [日] 外山卯三郎：《现代绘画概论》，倪贻德译，开明书店 1934 年版，第 183—186 页。

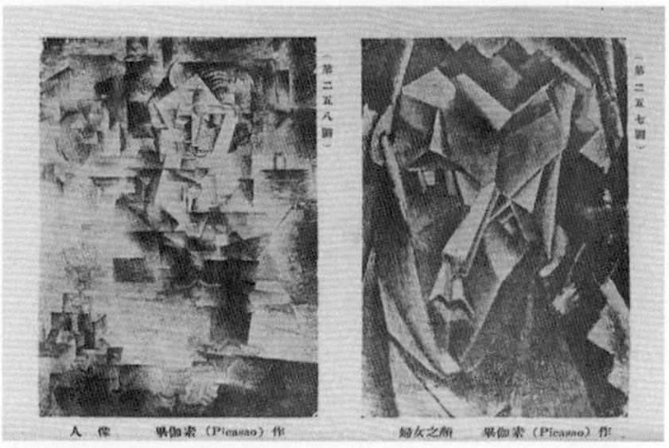
梁得所编译《西洋美术大纲》选用的插图

24 张彩印。主持良友图书印刷公司的梁得所发挥他在出版方面的优势，中文版里的所有图版都用铜版纸印刷，彩图选印 10 张，制作极为精良，很可能是民国时期最奢华的艺术史书之一。书中收录毕加索三件作品，是该书待遇最高的艺术家。

民国早期的西方艺术通史大多是编译欧洲或者日本学者著作，这些著作将毕加索放入立体派进行讲述的叙事框架限定了中国对于毕加索最初的理解。相应的，毕加索立体派时期的作品得到较多介绍。随着毕加索本人在欧洲艺术界地位的提升和风格的持续变化，这种情况也逐渐得到改变。

1930 年代之后出版的西方艺术史书开始对毕加索的艺术风格做出更为细致的划分，讨论毕加索在立体派之前和立体派之后各阶段的差异。1936 年，刘海粟翻译出版了英国人爱伯（T. W. Earp）的《现代绘画论》（*The Modern Movement in Painting*），对毕加索立体派之前的“青色时代”“赤色时代”和受黑人艺术影响阶段的绘画都做了介绍。[06] 倪贻德则在《西洋画派解说》（1937）里提到毕加索在“青的时代”“赤的时代”“立体派时代”之后的“新古典主义时代”。[07]

毕加索“蓝色时期”的作品为他赢得了关注底层人民的名声。很多中国评论文章都会谈到毕加索这个时期的特点，甚至据此将毕加索称作“绘画上的列宁”。曾去过巴黎的陈士文 1933 年发表一篇文章专论毕加索，讲述他看过毕加索原作后的感想：

> 以立体派的作品为多，最可爱的是他的希腊雕刻，作风和他的表现平民阶级一类的画，他的雄伟的气概，高远的格局，强烈的色彩，适宜的组合，在近代画家中很少有人可以比拟。就是同时在 L’Orangerie 开百年纪念展览会的 Manet，我觉得也不及他。他是 Cezanne 以后影响最大的画家，称他是绘画上的列宁或是 Phidias 都没有什么不确当。[08]

列宁在中国一直拥有崇高声望，“绘画上的列宁”能够使毕加索在特定历史情景中获得更加正面的形象，不仅是艺术上的，还有政治上的。

到了 1930 年代，中国出版物中对毕加索的评价也越来越高。日本人外山卯三郎原著，由倪贻德翻译的《现代绘画概论》（1934）一书里列举出“现代十大画家”，排在第一的是“首领马蒂斯”，第三位则是“奇才僻卡索（即毕加索）”。这本书将毕加索到巴黎后的艺术发展分为几个阶段，先是带有格列柯和野兽派影子的一批忧郁的、青绿色彩的绘画，之后是塞尚影响下的静物，再往后是黑人雕刻影响下的“立体主义时代”，到了 1917—1918 年，毕加索转回到新古典主义；而在“最近”，毕加索似乎又显露出超现实主义的倾向。由于毕加索在艺术领域中不断取得进展，毕加索得到了“善变”（“豹变”）的名声。[09]

1933年，倪贻德在《西洋画概论》里将毕加索列为“现在为全世界知名”的画家。[10] 到1946年作的《画室随笔》中，倪贻德给出了更有力的评价：“毕加索是20世纪画坛上最伟大的巨人，也是最善于豹变的怪杰”，“可说是达到了世界艺术水准的顶点，人类最高的智慧的结晶。”[11]

不过，也并不是所有介绍者都一定喜欢毕加索或者理解毕加索的艺术。例如著名文学家、美术史家和画家丰子恺对毕加索就有一个从全盘接受到逐渐怀疑的过程。丰子恺于1928年根据日本人一氏义良的《西洋美术的知识》节译出《西洋美术史》一书，书中将毕加索奉为“立体派的首领”、绘画中“现代的建设的表现的第一人”。这是沿袭了日本学者的叙述。[12] 到1930年出版的《西洋画派十二讲》里，丰子恺用一讲专论立体派，又用近半篇幅对毕加索的绘画条分缕析[13]，所以丰子恺对毕加索的绘画应该有比较深入的了解。但在1931年《西洋名画巡礼》一书中，丰子恺无意中泄露了他对毕加索的质疑：

　　无论何等复杂的物象，总不过是有许多的四方形、三角形、圆形、锥形等的凑合而成的。故描画须从物象中分解出这等原形，把它们重新组织起来，组成一幅绘画。所以他的画中，不见物体的形状，而只见种种的几何形体。人们看了都不懂。[14]

“人们看了都不懂”这个评语，多少显露出丰子恺对毕加索的调侃与不满。在1935年出版的《绘画概说》一书里，丰子恺更直接表达了他对毕加索的批评：

　　此种画风现在普遍地弥漫在世间。但多用以作装饰，如商店的样子窗，建筑物及家具的模样，广告的图案等。然而除少数特殊画家以外，绝少有爱用几何形体作画，或爱看这种玄妙的画的人了。听说比卡字（即毕加索）现在亦已不再作那种画，有许多同派的画家已舍弃画笔，去作电影事业了。[15]

这时的丰子恺对毕加索作品中人物画里不见人物，静物画里不见静物的情况持否定态度，更以艺术家们对立体派风格的放弃为依据，暗示立体派已经失去了生命力。

丰子恺对毕加索的批评在于“看了都不懂”。关于毕加索绘画的难以理解，在中国流传着一个笑话，虽然很难确定这个笑话最早的出处。1946年《明朗周报》刊登了这一则名为《毕加索怨贼蠢》的小故事：

　　一天，西班牙名画家毕加索的居室被窃。匪徒们翻箱倒箧，把屋子弄得一团糟，文件散满一地，写字台上还给枪打了一个洞。

　　“强盗偷走了贵重的东西么？”朋友问。

　　“就是拿了几件衬衣。”画家答。

　　“那么，你为什么动气呢？”

　　“我气的是他们竟蠢得不拿我的画！”[16]

以上批评和关于毕加索的笑话表明，在1920—1940年代，虽然一批专业画家和学者已经认同毕加索是当时最伟大的艺术家之一，但公众对毕加索的了解程度可能并不高，对毕加索艺术的认同就更低了。

02. 毕加索风格的接受与效法

在20世纪上半叶，能够真正看到毕加索原作，对毕加索有深入了解的应该是到欧洲学习艺术的中国留学生，尤其是到巴黎学习的那些中国画家。1931年到巴黎的秦宣夫回忆当时的情形：“学院之外就是现代派的汪洋大海：最新的东西是超现实主义，立方派、野兽派已经是强弩之末，但毕加索、马提斯仍然是许多青年的偶像。”[17]

方干民，《秋曲》，1931年

10. 倪贻德：《西洋画概论》，现代书局1933年版，第303页。

11. 倪贻德：《画室随笔》，《胜流》1946年第4卷第4期，第106页。

12. 丰子恺：《丰子恺全集》第7卷，海豚出版社2016年版，第101页。

13. 同上书，第281－287页。

14. 丰子恺：《丰子恺全集》第8卷，海豚出版社2016年版，第105页。

15. 丰子恺：《绘画概说》，亚细亚书局1935年版，第115页。

16. 纭：《毕加索怨贼蠢》，《明朗周报》1946年第2卷第1期，第7页。

17. 秦宣夫：《吕斯百油画作品展览观后》，《新华日报》1961年8月4日，第三版。

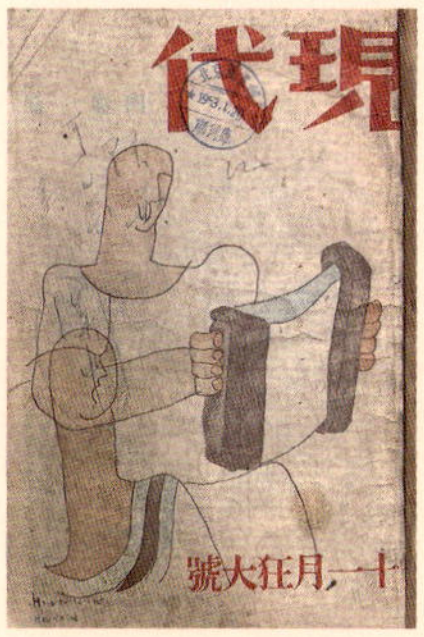

庞薰琹，《构成》，1933 年 11 月《现代》杂志封面

李桦，《生命》，1934 年

阳太阳，《海边裸女》，《新垒》1934 年第 4 卷第 5 期

1925 年底到法国留学的方干民一度沉迷于立体派，认为印象派、野兽派、巴黎画派和立体派的艺术才是“真正揭示了时代的美感”。[18] 通过临摹塞尚、马蒂斯等人的画作，方干民掌握了现代派的绘画语言。回国之后，方干民到国立杭州艺术专科学校任教，在 1930 年代创造了一批带有鲜明立体派色彩的作品，如《白鸽》《秋曲》《西湖》等。[19] 在中国画家里，方干民可能是模仿立体派风格进行创作的最为典型性的画家。方干民的学生闵希文评价说，方干民这类风格的绘画是“中国化了的立体作品”。[20]

1925 年来到巴黎的庞薰琹也很喜欢毕加索。在他存世作品中也能看到一点毕加索的痕迹。如他为《现代》杂志 1933 年第 11 期封面作的《构图》，用线手法和人物造型都有毕加索新古典主义时期绘画的风采。对于毕加索的认同与接受，不一定直接来自他的作品本身，还可以来自毕加索的艺术态度。庞薰琹回忆他在巴黎的学习体会时说：

在现代的一些画家中，我佩服毕加索，他的作品有的我喜欢，有的我不喜欢，因为我看不懂。但是，我佩服毕加索的探索精神。在巴黎，找不出第二个人敢于这样地变，大胆地变，不断地变。出名的画家中，很少人敢于改变自己的作风，抛弃自己所熟悉的一套办法。像马蒂斯、雷诺阿等都没有这样的勇气，都没有这样的才华，都没有这样的气魄！毕加索是一个真正的艺术家，他的一生是在艺术上不断探索的一生！[21]

毕加索的善“变”往往给中国画家留下深刻印象，关于毕加索的介绍里也经常特意强调这一点。庞薰琹即便不能接受毕加索的某些风格，但毕加索勇于探索、大胆改变的作风依然予他以启迪，促使他努力寻找属于自己的艺术道路。

没有去过欧洲的画家也能通过图册和作品图像的传播，吸收毕加索的一些艺术元素。李桦在 1930 年代的部分版画看起来就很“毕加索”。他作于 1934 年底、1935 年初的《李桦色刷木刻十帧》，几乎完全是毕加索影响下的产物。例如这部木刻集的第一幅作品《生命》，女人拉长的脖子、身体结构近乎随意的组合，以及梦幻般的背景处理，都有毕加索新古典主义时期的影子。

还有一批在 1930 年代崇尚西方现代主义风格的油画家，在当时人们心目中被视为毕加索的追随者，例如决澜社的阳太阳和杨秋人。倪贻德于 1935 年指出，杨秋人和阳太阳学的是毕加索：

那么杨秋人和阳太阳可说是一对广西人的伙伴。他们也是具有清新的头脑和优秀的画才的青年作家。因为时常在一起共同研究，他们的作风是有些相近的，他们都在追求着毕加索和契里珂的那种新形式，而色彩是有着南国人的明快的感觉。[22]

他们当时创作的作品留下得不多，只能从一些杂志印刷品上获得印证，其中一部分确实有毕加索新古典主

18. 闵希文：《中国早期油画的奠基人：记第一代油画家方干民先生》，见郑胜天编：《方干民》，台北，加拿大亚太国际艺术顾问公司 1996 年版，第 9 页。

19. 郑胜天：《文化交错：游荡者没有档案》，中国美术学院出版社 2013 年版，第 133—134 页。

20. 闵希文：《中国早期油画的奠基人：记第一代油画家方干民先生》，第 9 页。

21. 庞薰琹：《就是这样走过来的》，生活·读书·新知三联书店 2005 年版，第 86 页。

22. 倪贻德：《艺苑交游记》，良友图书印刷公司 1936 年版，第 10 页。

义阶段的特色，如阳太阳1934年的作品《海边裸女》。总体来说，1930年代的中国油画家对毕加索那些兼顾写实与变形的作品似乎更感兴趣。

1930年代，中国艺术家对毕加索的热爱最集中地体现在1937年《美术杂志》第五期的“辟卡梭（即毕加索）特辑”，其中刊登收录梁锡鸿、林镛、赵兽、陈抱一四位画家的文章，以及日本画家藤田嗣治和英国批评家赫伯特·里德（Herbert Reed）的两篇译文（陈抱一和施蛰存译）。[23] 这几位画家不一定在自己的绘画里直接体现出毕加索的风格元素，但都是毕加索的仰慕者。在他们眼中，“凡他所研究的艺术无一不达到最高的程度”。[24]

当然也有不喜欢毕加索的画家。崇尚学院写实的画家们多半对毕加索缺乏好感。例如徐悲鸿。就像丰子恺反复强调毕加索喜欢用“三角形”来画画一样，徐悲鸿对毕加索的总结是“三角板”，而徐悲鸿提到“三角板”时，也总是充满了不屑：

故法国近代塞尚、马蒂斯、勃纳儿、又毕加索、大冷、于脱理窝之辈，并日本人嗣治等，皆受该类商人庇护，大享其名，其作品皆狗矢之类。故至世界经济恐慌 Georges Petit 首先倒闭，毕加索见事不佳，极改作风，向日之三角版今亦不用，而好言恩葛尔矣（古典主义之 origrine）。[25]

作为20世纪中国学院艺术最著名的代表，徐悲鸿对西方现代绘画的厌恶众所周知。和丰子恺一样，徐悲鸿也用毕加索本人1920年代前后一度转向古典主义画风作为佐证，说明“三角板”缺乏艺术的价值。活动在上海的画家胡金人也对毕加索不以为然，把那些效法毕加索的中国画家视为“画鬼作家”，毕加索则是“画鬼画家”们哄骗艺术青年的幌子：

青年艺人们有如火的热情，纯洁的心灵，他们不满意现实，常常幻想新奇，可是他们缺乏严格的训练，修养不足，认识不清，为了要趋新，要炫奇，不免想利用小聪明取巧，结果把热情和勇敢完全用在盲目的“画鬼”上面，而“画鬼作家”竟认为“吾道不孤”，就有意赞扬他们：“呵，你的作风是近于毕迦索（即毕加索）的，呵，你的笔调是近于……”可怜这些青年们在“受宠若惊”之余，就拼命做了毕迦索（即毕加索）或其他奴隶，同时也做了赞扬他人的奴隶而不自知。[26]

尽管胡金人对毕加索略有微词，却也无意中承认，艺术青年被夸作“毕加索”时便会生出“受宠若惊”之感。民国时期的油画领域，崇尚写实的画家和崇尚现代主义的画家之间聚讼不休，互有攻讦，无论对毕加索推崇还是贬损、效法抑或排斥，“毕加索”都已经成为他们抒发个人艺术主张的一个“媒介”。毕加索不仅进入中国，还变成了中国艺术话语和评价体系中重要的一环。

03. 毕加索、共产党与和平鸽

在毕加索的生平事迹中，毕加索于1944年10月4日加入法国共产党一事对毕加索在中国的形象塑造影响深远。实际上，入党这件事改变了所有共产主义国家对毕加索的认识。由于画家拥有的巨大声望，毕加索加入共产党成为共产主义巨大魅力的证明。毕加索加入共产党的第二天，法国共产党机关报《人道报》在头版位置做了报道。同样，在第二次世界大战还没有结束的中国，《解放日报》也进行了报道。

大约在1944年底，毕加索加入共产党的消息传到中国延安，延安的艺术家们欢欣鼓舞，马上于1945年元旦在延安鲁迅艺术学院举办了一个毕加索“画展”。这时的延安不可能有毕加索原作，陈列的应该是毕加索画作的印刷品。[27] 随后，1945年1月11日《解放日报》发表了胡蛮（笔名：祜曼）《庆祝名画家皮卡索（即毕加索）加入共产党》一文，评价说：“皮卡索（即毕加索）最近加入法国共产党，不只在我们美术界是一件大事，而且在人类文化史上，也是一件大事。”[28] 胡蛮的文章高度肯定了毕加索的进步政

23.《美术杂志》1937年第1卷第5期，第117—129页。

24. 梁锡鸿：《辟卡梭艺术的阶段》，《美术杂志》1937年第1卷第5期，第119页。

25.“于脱理窝”即郁特里罗。徐悲鸿：《悲鸿漫谈》，见《徐悲鸿文集》，第71页。

26. 胡金人：《略谈上海洋画界》，《上海艺术月刊》1941年创刊号，第5页。

27. 祜曼：《名画家皮卡索加入共产党》，《解放日报》1945年1月11日，第4版。

28. 同上。

世界和平大会宣传海报 1949 年

巴勃罗·毕加索，《鸽子》，1949 年 1 月 9 日
锌版上水墨，56.7 x 76.2 cm
国立巴黎毕加索博物馆，MP3414

中国代表团接受鲜花后在世界和平大会会场门口留影，1949 年 4 月，捷克，布拉格，石少华摄影

治倾向，以及他在作品中体现出的对底层人民的关注。不过这个马克思主义的阐释视角并没有得到所有人的认可，很快有读者给《解放日报》写信表达不同意见，主张更应该从纯形式的角度来理解毕加索，而非仅仅从社会学角度。1945 年 3 月 18 日的《解放日报》刊登了这封来信，并请胡蛮写了一篇回应文章。胡蛮仍坚持认为政治倾向是毕加索艺术成就的重要方面。[29] 毕加索加入共产党这一事件本身可以有不同解读，既可以是政治进步与艺术个性的并存，也可以是艺术家追求进步的体现。[30] 活跃在延安的艺术家们最终认可了后者。或者说，正是毕加索的政治身份使他在延安获得了合法性，而从毕加索的艺术作品里寻找政治正确的部分，不仅顺理成章，也并不困难。为了强化毕加索在政治上的身份，同一版《解放日报》还刊登了毕加索的文章《我为什么加入共产党》。编者按再次强调："名画家皮卡索（即毕加索）加入共产党的消息，对于全世界文化界的影响，是很大的。"[31]

1949 年到 1952 年，毕加索三次为世界和平大会创作和平鸽。这几只鸽子使毕加索的名字传遍共产主义世界的每个角落。毕加索为 1949 年巴黎和布拉格召开的世界和平大会制作的和平鸽是一幅石版画，创作于 1949 年 1 月。和平大会召开的前一天中午，毕加索的朋友、诗人、共产党员阿拉贡从毕加索画室选出了这幅石版画。当天下午，这只鸽子就变成了和平大会的标志，出现在巴黎的街头巷尾。据说毕加索本人对此颇不以为然，他曾说："再也没有更残忍的动物了。我这里就养着几只（鸽子），它们把另一只可怜的小鸽子啄死了，因为它们不喜欢它。它们先是啄出它的眼睛，然后再把它撕成碎片，实在可怕。这怎么可以成为和平的象征？"[32] 毕加索的个人看法并不妨碍这只鸽子从巴黎飞向五大洲，让毕加索本人在全世界人民心目中获得了"和平卫士"的形象，也不妨碍他 1950 年被授予斯大林奖。不过，毕加索也因此引发美国政府的不满，即便在美国举办毕加索的个人展览，他本人也被拒绝进入美国。[33]

1949 年 4 月，在布拉格参加世界和平大会的中国代表团见到了毕加索的和平鸽。随后，这只和平鸽飞到了北京。1949 年 10 月 2 日，北京举办了"中国保卫世界和平大会"，朱德、高岗、陈毅、林伯渠、董必武、郭沫若、邓小平等出席大会。《人民日报》10 月 3 日的报道特别指出："大会会场布置庄严朴素，主席台正中悬挂着毕加索的名画——象征世界和平的鸽子。"[34] 10 月 4 日《人民日报》再次发文记述这一大会，描述了主席台上出现的图像："斯大林和毛泽东的画像高悬台上，毕加索的名画《鸽子》从主席台上放射着和平的光辉。"[35] 毕加索的鸽子与斯大林、毛泽东像同时出现在主席台上。自然，这一"名画"应该是根据和平大会宣传品制作的复制品。

1950 年 11 月，第二届保卫世界和平大会召开，毕加索又创作了一幅鸽子作为大会的标志。《人民日报》1950 年 11 月 17 日在报头位置刊登了这只鸽子的图像，注明这是"第二届世界保卫和平大会招贴上的和平鸽图，法国名画家毕加索作"。报头另一侧用一篇短文揭示了毕加索前后两只"和平鸽"象征意义的变化：1949 年，"献给第一届世界和平大会的是画了一只恬静又洁白的鸽子，它表示出千百万人民纯朴的尊严，和他们反抗黑夜与死亡的斗争。它坚持光明和正义反对黑暗的世界"；1950 年，"又画了一只鸽子，这

29. 周爱民讨论了这一争论，见周爱民：《延安木刻艺术研究》，河北教育出版社 2009 年版，第 121—121 页。

30. 蔡涛：《1938 年：国家与艺术家——黄鹤楼大壁画与抗战初期中国现代美术的转型》，中国美术学院 2013 年博士论文，第 120 页。

31.《解放日报》1945 年 3 月 18 日，第 4 版。

32. ［美］阿丽娅娜·斯塔希诺普勒·霍芬顿：《毕加索传——创造者与毁灭者》，刘建军、贾琦译，上海文艺出版社 1991 年版，第 299—300 页。

33. David Craven, "When Picasso was Feared by the US Government", in Jonathan Harris with Richard Koeck (ed.), *Picasso and the Politics of Visual Representation: War and Peace in the Era of the Cold War and Since*, Liverpool, Liverpool University Press, 2013, pp.109-112; 李有观：《毕加索与共产党》，《世界文化》2017 年第 3 期，第 14 页。

34. 新华社：《全国各界代表千余人集会首都，保卫世界和平大会揭幕》，《人民日报》1949 年 10 月 3 日，第 1 版。

35. 张沛：《东方和平堡垒外岁！记中国保卫世界和平大会》，《人民日报》1949 年 10 月 4 日，第 3 版。

世界和平大会宣传海报
1950 年

人民日報

和平鴿子在飛翔

電賀二屆世界和平大會

《人民日报》1950 年 11 月 17 日第一版报头

世界和平大会宣传海报
1952 年

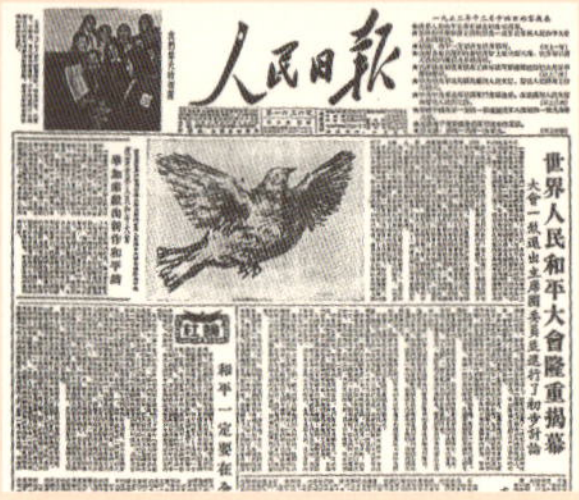
人民日報

世界人民和平大會隆重揭幕

《人民日报》在 1952 年 12 月 14 日头版

鸽子仍然保有使得千百万人民的心灵感到如此亲切的那种风格，但是这鸽子现在已经不是停在那里，它正展翅高翔，这位艺术家对他从前大作已赋予了新的感情，他表示出和平人类已经获得的进展和胜利以及未来的胜利”。[36]

《人民日报》为毕加索的第二只鸽子赋予了一个明确的象征意义：鸽子在飞翔，和平在前进。毫无疑问，这个象征意义就成为这只鸽子在中国唯一具有合法性的解释。《人民日报》1950 年 12 月 18 日《关于国际和平奖金》里提到毕加索时，再次提到：“去年四月，毕加索献给第一届世界和（平）大（会）一幅画，用一只恬静洁白的鸽子表示出亿万人民纯朴的尊严和他们争取和平的愿望。今年他又画了一只正在展翅高翔的鸽子（见人民日报十一月十七日第一版）献给在华沙召开的第二届世界和大，它象征和平正在前进，和平人类已经获得进展和胜利以及未来的胜利。毕加索获得 1950 年度国际和平奖金的作品就是他第一幅和平鸽。”[37]

1952 年，为庆祝维也纳召开的世界人民和平大会，毕加索又画了一只和平鸽。这只鸽子也在展翅飞翔，《人民日报》在 1952 年 12 月 14 日头版刊登了这第三只鸽子，并继续为它赋予更新的意义：

> 它仍然保持着使一切爱好和平人民的心灵感到极为亲切的一种风格，但是现在的这只鸽子，翅膀展开得更大了，羽毛更丰满了，它正向着更高的地方飞去。这只鸽子的整个形象，使我们非常明显地感觉到它更加年轻，生命力无限充沛。它有力地表示着：在世界和平运动不断进展和已取得胜利的基础上，经过这次世界人民和平大会，世界人民争取与保卫和平的运动将向更高的阶段发展，取得新的伟大胜利。这只和平鸽今后必然要在全世界爱好和平人民的支持下，更勇敢地、更高更高地到处飞翔起来。[38]

这只不仅在飞翔而且翅膀张得更大的鸽子，就象征着和平正飞向更高的地方。

鸽子是毕加索绘画中一个常见母题，毕加索一生画过多幅鸽子或带有鸽子图像的作品，但为中国所熟知的，主要是上述三次用于和平大会宣传的鸽子图像。朱伯雄在一篇 1980 年发表在《人民日报》上的文章里说：“新中国成立后的一些年月，我国广大人民群众对他先后所画的三只‘和平鸽’，也是印象深刻的。”[39] 所谓的“三只‘和平鸽’”，就是前文提到的三只。

继加入共产党之后，和平鸽进一步改变了毕加索在中国乃至社会主义国家的形象。1953 年 6 月 21 日的《人民日报》发表了苏联作家爱伦堡（Ehrenburg）的文章《毕加索与和平》，文中一方面承认说，毕加索的作品和“新社会”（大约是指社会主义国家）还有很大距离；但同时，每个人又都能从毕加索身上看到“一个有力量而又异常真诚的艺术家”，他的名字也被千百万普通人所认识，因为他的鸽子飞翔在世界五大洲的上空：“一个获得世界荣誉、原作被银行家太太和部长的情妇们贪婪地搜求着的艺术家转变到了人民这

36. 新闻摄影局：《毕加索的新献礼：和平鸽子在飞翔》，《人民日报》1950 年 11 月 17 日，第 1 版。

37. 何育滋：《关于国际和平奖金》，《人民日报》1950 年 12 月 18 日，第 4 版。

38. 《人民日报》本报讯：《祝贺世界人民和平大会，毕加索献出新作和平鸽》，《人民日报》1952 年 12 月 14 日，第 1 版。

39. 伯雄：《毕加索的怪癖与遗产》，《人民日报》1980 年 6 月 23 日，第 7 版。

吴作人等，《让帝国主义者在全世界人民的面前发抖吧！》，1951 年

张怀江、张慈中，《团结起来，保卫和平》，1952 年，76 x 53.5cm

一边。”[40] 因为画家为世界和平奉献的鸽子，银行家太太所青睐的毕加索现在变成了“人民”的一员。这一叙述暗示了毕加索阶级身份的转换：从一个为资产阶级服务的艺术家，转变成了一个无产阶级艺术家。这一改变能够发生，很大程度上就是因为毕加索的鸽子成为世界和平的象征。

毕加索的和平鸽在中国传播极广，人们不免关注这只鸽子的来历，尤其第一只和平鸽的来历，毕加索的朋友潘罗斯在他 1958 年出版的毕加索传记里说它看起来就是毕加索在他画室笼子里养的那一只。[41] 但在中国，这只鸽子还有更动人的故事：德国占领巴黎之后的某一天，毕加索隔壁房屋的看门人密许老爹来拜访毕加索，告诉毕加索，他在 1915 年和德国的战争中失去了一条胳膊，他的儿子约翰在不久抗击德国的战争中牺牲，而在前一天，他的孙子鲁西恩在阁楼上用一面红旗召唤鸽子时，被两个德国士兵从楼顶推下摔死。德国士兵离开前还拧断了刚被召唤回来的这只名叫萧莱士的鸽子的脖子。老人说他有孙子的照片，现在恳求毕加索将这只死去的鸽子画下来作为纪念。于是毕加索画下“一只冠毛丛丛和美丽蓝眼睛的白鸽”，“但它没有死，而活泼生动，是生命本身的象征，是快乐、阳光与和平的象征”。1949 年，世界和平大会在巴黎召开的时候，毕加索想到了密许老爹、约翰还有鲁西恩，于是凭着回忆，再次画下那只名叫萧莱士的鸽子，并且“将这幅画献给那些和平战士”，“从他们的心中，在这为世界和平而斗争的年代里，千百万只白鸽正向萧莱士一般在鼓翼向前飞着”。[42]

这个故事的源头出自 1952 年《世界知识》刊登的一篇文章《毕加索的和平鸽》，原文作者是捷克斯洛伐克人古伯卡（Frantisek Kubka）。这篇文章原先刊登在伦敦出版的杂志《新中欧观察家》（*The New Central European Observer*），后来被《世界知识》发现，译作中文刊载。这个故事如此动人，就不免被反复讲述，被当作毕加索创作和平鸽的、令人信服的原因。例如 1990 年 7 月 8 日《人民日报》刊文《鸽子为何是和平的象征》依然在重复这个情节。[43] 毕加索与鸽子的故事还被转化为图像，如《美术大观》1998 年发表了连环画《毕加索与和平鸽》。在连环画中，有些细节被改写得更加煽情，例如老人的儿子和儿媳加入反法西斯游击队战死，德国士兵用手枪杀死了老人的孙子，鸽子受伤后未死，在毕加索的画案上“扑楞着带血的翅膀，艰难地站了起来”，直到毕加索画完最后一笔才最终倒下。[44] 这些故事赋予毕加索更加光辉的形象，因为他所描绘的不再是一只普通的鸽子，而是受到法西斯迫害的、无辜死去的鸽子；随着鸽子死去的，还有豢养它的、法西斯的受害者与反抗者。毕加索描绘这只鸽子本身就成为画家反抗法西斯的证明。这是一个政治正确的故事，而且变得越来越正确。

毕加索的鸽子后来被很多 20 世纪五六十年代拥护和平、反对战争的绘画所“转引”，成为那个时代最常见的“元图像”之一。比较早的例子，是 1951 年由吴作人、张光宇、蒋兆和、韦启美、叶浅予、罗工柳、胡一川等当时任教于中央美术学院的著名画家合作绘制的大型宣传画《让帝国主义者在全世界人民的面前发抖吧！》，画面刻画了各国人民举着各自国家的旗帜迈着整齐的步伐向着帝国主义者走去，而最前面的一面旗帜上，描绘的是毕加索 1949 年的那只和平鸽。

40. [苏联] 爱伦堡：《毕加索与和平》，《人民日报》1953 年 6 月 21 日，第 3 版。

41. [英] 罗兰德·潘罗斯：《毕加索生平与创作》，周国珍等译，人民美术出版社 1986 年版，第 404 页

42. [捷] 古伯卡：《毕加索的和平鸽》，寿华译，《毕加索的和平鸽》，《世界知识》1952 年第 12 期，第 21 － 22 页。

43.《鸽子为何是和平的象征》，《人民日报》1990 年 7 月 8 日，第 8 版。

44. 毕子编文、刘志刚绘画：《毕加索与和平鸽》，《美术大观》1998 年第 1 期，第 40 － 42 页。

巴勃罗·毕加索，《解放的公鸡》
1944，布面油画，100.33 x 80.65 cm
密尔沃基艺术博物馆

张仃，《公鸡与小鸡》，1960 年代
纸上彩墨，46 x 35 cm，私人收藏

张仃，《大公鸡》，1960 年代
纸上彩墨，69 x 46cm，私人收藏

1950 年的鸽子出现在张怀江、张慈中绘制的宣传画《团结起来，保卫和平》里，画中各国人民高举毕加索 1950 年的和平鸽，手挽手向前进。鸽子上还配有说明文字：“亚洲及太平洋区域各国人民团结起来，加强和扩大保卫和平运动！”该画于 1952 年 9 月由人民美术出版社制成印刷品发行。这类“转引”毕加索 1949 年和 1950 年和平鸽的宣传图像持久地传播和增长了毕加索在中国的名声。

1950 年代，中国对现代主义的态度还相对宽松。1956 年 11 月 10—25 日，中国美术家协会举办过一个“法国现代美术作品展览会”，展出毕加索、摩利斯·郁特利罗、拉奥·杜飞、乔治·鲁奥、亨利·马蒂斯、让·吕尔萨、披爱尔·勃那尔、马尔盖、费尔南·雷瑞等艺术家的绘画复制品。[45] 1961 年，毕加索 80 岁时，《美术》杂志发表了《中国文学艺术界联合会主席郭沫若给毕加索的贺信》，祝贺毕加索 80 岁的寿辰：“祝贺你，你英勇地向弗朗哥、希特勒纳粹分子进行了斗争，捍卫了人民的正义的事业。祝贺你，你积极地参加了反对侵略战争、保卫世界和平的神圣事业。祝贺你，你的艺术创造对世界的艺术宝库增加了光彩。祝你长生不老。”[46] 同一期《美术》又发表了艾中信的文章《祝毕加索八十大寿》，简要介绍了毕加索的艺术经历，重点谈了毕加索 1937 年的《格尔尼卡》（文中译作《基尼卡》）、1951 年的《在朝鲜的兽行》和毕加索的《和平鸽》。[47]

与此同时，中国又接受了从苏联传入的、对现代艺术的批判。普列汉诺夫在《艺术与社会生活》一文将立体派归入资产阶级现代派艺术，认为立体派否定艺术是现实生活的再现，因为立体派画家把“我”当作“唯一的现实”，除了“我”之外再没有任何现实的东西，结果使得“在绘画中也像在任何地方一样，就可以畅所欲为了”。[48] 普列汉诺夫把现代派“为艺术而艺术”归结为“资产阶级衰落时期的极端个人主义”，它堵塞了艺术家的真正灵感，“使艺术家看不见社会生活中所发生的一切，并使艺术家无谓地纠缠于毫无内容的个人体验和荒诞到病态地步的臆造”。[49] 所以在这个意义上，毕加索的绘画又是资产阶级腐朽艺术的一部分。

这一时期的中国，能够公然效法毕加索的艺术家可能只有张仃和受他影响的学生。张仃当时是中央工艺美术学院副院长，又曾有在延安参加革命的工作经历，个人创作上受的约束相对较小。1960 年前后，张仃直接临摹了毕加索的多件作品，例如毕加索《解放的公鸡》（1944），还把毕加索的形式手法转用到自己的创作里，创作出类似《公鸡》（约 1961 年）这样的作品。华君武因为这批作品，说张仃就是“毕加索加城隍庙”。这个评价流传很广。

张仃从读书时期就对毕加索情有独钟。1932 年，张仃考上北平美术专科学校国画系，开始从图册里接触到毕加索，对毕加索蓝色时期的绘画感触颇深。[50] 1956 年，张仃到法国参加一个国际博览会的展览设计工作，随同一个到访法国的中国文化代表团去拜访毕加索。代表团成员中只有张仃对毕加索艺术比较熟悉，因此

45. 新华社：《法国现代美术作品展览会》，《人民日报》1956 年 11 月 14 日，第 7 版。

46. 郭沫若：《中国文学艺术界联合会主席郭沫若给毕加索的贺信》，《美术》1961 年第 5 期，第 45 页。

47. 艾中信：《祝毕加索八十大寿》，《美术》1961 年第 5 期，第 45—46 页。

48. ［俄］普列汉诺夫：《普列汉诺夫美学论文集》，曹葆华译，人民出版社 1983 年版，第 877—878 页。

49. 同上书，第 879 页。

50. 张仃与毕加索的关系，见李兆忠：《它山之石——张仃与毕加索》，《名作欣赏》2016 年第 3 期，第 127—132 页。

51. 同上，第 130 页。

张仃与毕加索的合影，1956 年

毕加索给张仃画的和平鸽，1956 年

与毕加索交流的任务也主要由张仃承担。张仃后来回忆：

> 那是一天的下午，我们来到了毕加索的工作室，是在海边的一所别墅。当时毕加索睡完午觉，从楼上走下来，热情地欢迎我们的到来。他领着我们先参观了他的工作室，……他的工作室里，所有的墙上、地上都挂满、摆满了大量新作。可以想象到，他的全部注意力、思想、感情、心灵和生命都投入到艺术的世界中去了。他惊人的艺术劳动和异常旺盛的精力，十分令人佩服。[51]

张仃不仅在此次会面中看到毕加索的最新作品，还收到毕加索赠送给他的由文学家、批评家让·卡索（Jean Cassou）撰写的《巴勃罗·毕加索》（*Pablo Picasso*）。毕加索在这本书的扉页上写下张仃的名字，并且画上他著名的和平鸽。

1966年之后的十年，毕加索在中国美术领域成为禁忌。1966年《人民日报》上刊发的文章《周扬的“自由化”毒化了中央美术学院》里，宣扬毕加索成为周扬的一个罪状：

> 在周扬等一伙提出了这个彻头彻尾的修正主义文艺纲领之后，文艺界出现了资产阶级自由化的倾向。在美术学院，形形色色的资产阶级、封建阶级艺术大泛滥，过去不敢拿出来的毒草，统统奉为鲜花。在版画系画室中，公开贩卖马蒂斯、毕加索的野兽派艺术。在画室外又成立小沙龙，以 20 世纪没落的资产阶级艺术为追求的榜样。一整套资产阶级的教学方向，教学体制，教学内容，教学方法，在周扬等提出“稳定教学秩序”的指示下，一点也不能更改。他们对中央美术学院，实行了资产阶级专政。[52]

即便共产党员身份与和平鸽也不能将毕加索从“资产阶级艺术”和“毒草”中挽救出来。直到 1980 年，这种情况才得到彻底扭转。

04. 20 世纪 80 年代以后

1979 年 11 月，“星星”美展在中国美术馆的外举办，参展艺术家们提出两点诉求：1. 艺术家介入社会，2. 探求新的艺术形式。又将这两点总结为一个口号：“珂勒惠支是我们的旗帜，毕加索是我们的先驱”。[53]“星星”美展艺术家的诉求在 1980 年《美术》杂志第 3 期上得到介绍，批评家栗宪庭在文章中提到：“要像毕加索那样，探索永无止境。”[54] 毕加索再次进入中国的艺术话语。毕加索的艺术精神，而非毕加索的艺术形式，再次成为激励中国艺术家前行的榜样。

大约在 1980 年，毕加索的名誉在中国得到正式恢复。《人民日报》1980 年 6 月 19 日发表了邹荻帆的现代

52. 中央美术学院版画系革命师生：《周扬的“自由化”毒化了中央美术学院》，《人民日报》1966 年 7 月 16 日，第 3 版。

53. 栗宪庭：《关于“星星”美展》，《美术》1980 年第 3 期，第 9 页。

54. 同上，第 9 页。

诗《鸽子》，其中说道：

和平鸽是修正主义的象征？
修正主义就等于和平？
只顾自己有土豆烧牛肉
实可憎恨，
有必要连鸽子也杀绝斩尽？

呵，白玉石的鸽子，
银灰色的鸽子，
你飞吧！
在毕加索的笔下，
你栖息在人们的囟门，
起飞自人们的头顶，
我知道了和平有一双翅膀：
安定团结的双翼下，
哺养着汽笛的电力，
禾苗的乳浆，
学校的琅琅书声……
飞吧，飞吧，鸽子，
和平，和平……[55]

也是在 1980 年以后，中国才开始出版关于毕加索的专著。1982 年，吴步乃选出毕加索作品若干，编成《毕加索》一书，由人民美术出版社出版。[56] 之后，毕加索的各种图册由不同出版社大量印行。对于毕加索生平和艺术的系统介绍则是来自翻译。1986 年，英国人罗兰特·潘罗斯（Roland Penrose）的《毕加索生平与创作》中文译本由人民美术出版社出版，该书之后两次再版；[57]1990 年，美国人阿莲娜（Arianna Stassinopoulos Huffington）的《毕加索传：创造者与毁灭者》中译本由人民美术出版社出版[58]，之后又有两个出版社重新出版了这本书。这两册译著成为中国艺术爱好者了解毕加索最常见的文本来源。在艺术之外，毕加索丰富多彩的个人生活也开始为人所津津乐道。到 2018 年，用中文出版的、以毕加索为主题的各种类型的著作、图册已有三百多种。

在所有毕加索的作品中，《格尔尼卡》（1937）取代“和平鸽”，成为最受关注的作品。这件作品具有人道主义关怀，蕴含了对战争的控诉与和平的渴望，在中国被视为毕加索一生中成就最高的作品。《人民日报》多次报道了这幅画作。1985 年中国美术馆举办“前进中的中国青年美展”，王向明、金莉莉《渴望和平》[59] 是最受关注的作品之一，画中漂浮着一个巨大的画框，穿插描绘了西方艺术家“反对战争、描绘和平的众多画幅”，其中最醒目的就是毕加索的《格尔尼卡》。这一展览的另一件参展作品《孩子们安慰毕加索的鸽子》则以轻松的笔调调侃了和平鸽，用当时一篇评论文章的话来说：“1953 年毕加索为世界和平大会创作的和平鸽曾翱翔高空，飞跃四大洋五大洲，然而现在它已经……轮到孩子们为它演奏音乐了。”[60] 在这个抒情性的画面里，和平鸽不再咄咄逼人。毕加索艺术与人生更多的面相开始浮现出来，他可以是受人尊敬的艺术大师，也可以成为幽默的调侃对象。

毕加索的艺术还以更直接的方式与中国发生关联，他的绘画原作开始进入中国，以展览的方式呈献给公众。1983 年 5 月，中国美术馆举办了“毕加索绘画原作展览”，展览图册由中国展览公司出版，收录作品 33 幅。[61] 这是最早一次在中国举办毕加索的个展。当时正在中国访问的法国总统密特朗出席了开幕式，中国文化部副部长周巍峙和法国负责文化事务部长级代表雅克·兰在开幕式上讲话。[62] 这次展览固然是艺术的交流，同样也是中、法两国之间政治往来密切的象征。2011 年 10 月，“2011 毕加索中国大展”在上海世博园

王向明、金莉莉，《渴望和平》，1985 年
布面油画，122 x 91.5 cm，中国美术馆

俞晓夫，《孩子们安慰毕加索的鸽子》，1985 年
160 x 169 cm，布面油画

55. 邹荻帆：《鸽子》，《人民日报》1980 年 6 月 19 日，第 8 版。

56. 吴步乃编：《毕加索》，人民美术出版社 1982 年版。

57. ［英］潘罗斯：《毕加索生平与创作》，周国珍等译，人民美术出版社 1986 年版；1987 年，人民出版社重印该书；2002 年，广西师范大学出版社再版该书。

58. ［美］阿莲娜 · S. 哈芬顿：《毕加索传：创造者与毁灭者》，弘鉴等译，人民美术出版社 1990 年版；1991 年，上海文艺出版社重译出版（[美] 霍芳顿：《毕加索传：创造者与毁灭者》，刘建军、贾琦译）；2007 年，金城出版社再次重译出版此书（[美] 雅瑞安娜·哈芬顿，《毕加索：创造者与毁灭者》，陈子慕译）。

59. 王向明、金莉莉：《我们与〈渴望和平〉》，《美术》1985 年第 7 期，第 45 页。

62. 张蔷：《艺术断想录——观“前进中的中国青年美展”》，《美术》1985 年第 7 期，第 25 页。

61. 米歇尔 · 里歇编：《毕加索绘画原作展览》，中国展览公司 1983 年版。

62. 新华社：《毕加索绘画原作展览在京开幕》，《人民日报》1983 年 5 月 7 日，第 3 版。

中国馆开幕，作为第十三届中国上海国际艺术节的重要展示项目，展出毕加索62件原作；2014年3月，由西班牙官方信贷局、西班牙驻华大使馆、西班牙国际合作发展署与中国国家博物馆等共同组织的“毕加索：沃拉尔系列版画展”在中国国家博物馆举办，展出毕加索20世纪30年代的版画100幅，作为中国与西班牙建交40周年的系列活动之一。2018年1月，法国总统马克龙访华时表示，希望更多的法国重要美术馆到中国举办展览。部分是作为这一愿望的结果，UCCA尤伦斯当代艺术中心于2019年6月举办展览“毕加索——一位天才的诞生”，展出法国国立巴黎毕加索博物馆的103件藏品。毕加索作品具有极高的价值（在文化和经济双重意义上），又是中国家喻户晓的名人，他的作品出借到中国展出，自然更能成为国家与国家之间友谊的体现。从艺术传播的角度来说，这类活动自然多多益善。在不出国门的情况下，中国人有越来越多的机会接触到毕加索的原作。

到1996年，中国的博物馆机构终于有了毕加索原作收藏。1996年3月，德国收藏家路德维希夫妇捐赠给中国美术馆82位欧美艺术家的89件作品，包括毕加索的《人物形象》(1967)、《抽烟斗的男人》(1969)、《带鸟的步兵》（1972）、《花瓶边的男人和女人》（年代不详）四幅画作。同年，中国美术馆举办了路德维希夫妇捐献作品展，将这些作品展示给公众。2011年11月，中国美术馆把其中两件毕加索作品送到湖南湘潭齐白石纪念馆参加第三届中国（湘潭）齐白石国际文化艺术节系列主题艺术作品展，将它们与4件齐白石作品摆放在一起，使观众能够面对面地比较中西两位艺术大师；2018年，中国美术馆又以“中国美术馆藏国际艺术”的名义展出了它们。路德维希夫妇的捐赠为中国收藏毕加索拉开了帷幕。未来也许还会有更多毕加索的作品从世界艺术市场进入中国的美术馆和博物馆。

结语

毕加索成名很早，艺术生命又足够长久，他在中国的介绍与传播几乎与他本人的成长同步。从1917年起，毕加索就作为西方艺术历史发展中的一个重要环节传入中国，他的新作不断被刊登到中国报刊之上，作为一个活着的大师为人所称道，同时也不免引发批评与争议。

1944年毕加索加入共产党之后，他的政治身份和政治倾向成为判断毕加索艺术的一条核心指标。1949年新中国建立后对毕加索的认同，很大程度来自他的政治立场，以及他作为世界和平卫士的正面形象。但同时，毕加索那些倾向于抽象形式的绘画作品又是颓废的资产阶级艺术代表。这两种形象不断拉锯，最终还是后者占据上风，以致在1966年到1980年之间，毕加索成为一个禁忌的名字。

到1980年以后的中国，毕加索又恢复了作为世界一流艺术家的名誉。他的天才和成就激励了无数艺术青年，他的作品成为国家之间往来的文化载体，他的名声不仅响彻中国艺术界，还为广大民众所熟知。在今天的中国，毕加索和达·芬奇、凡·高一样，已经成为最为中国人所熟知的外国艺术家。毕加索的名字已经成为传奇，而对于他的作品——尤其是原作——中国还需要更多更深入的了解。

Picasso in China: 1917-2019

Wu Xueshan

Professor, School of Humanities,
Central Academy of Fine Arts

Western art first entered China in the early twentieth century. During this period, classical and modern artists from the West were circulated widely and comprehensively. However, only a few foreign painters became household names. One such artist was Pablo Picasso. Picasso achieved tremendous fame in his lifetime, and by the 1910s, his reputation had reached China. There, he gradually became an icon of artistic genius. In this hundred-year history of circulation and reception, he earned both high praise and harsh criticism. Picasso's image as an artist was closely linked to the historical context of China's development. Among all Western artists, his trajectory in China hewed closest to the radical changes that the country underwent. The history of Picasso's reception serves as a microcosm of cultural exchange between China and the West; in a sense, the evolution of Picasso's image in China was a mirror onto the nation itself.

01. Early Circulation in China

In his 1917 book *Art History*, published by Shanghai Commercial Press, Jiang Danshu raised the topic of Cubism. The publication was a textbook used in teaching colleges, and it was one of the first art history books written in China. The content was relatively simple and concise. In defining Cubism (*li fang ti pai*, an early translation of the now standard *li ti pai*), Jiang spared only one sentence: "It researches the volume of images to express a sense of volume on the picture plane."[01] In 1918, Jiang edited another publication, his *Art History Reference Book*, as a supplement to the previous year's *Art History*. This book featured encyclopedic entries that introduced important artists, movements, and technical terms from China and abroad. The entry on Cubism included new content and mentioned Picasso:

A new movement that has emerged in Paris. This movement opposes the primacy Impressionism and Neo-Impressionism give to light and color; instead, it researches the volume of images. Its aim is to express a sense of volume in the picture plane. Both the lines and the planes are represented cubically, creating interlocking structures that are hard to distinguish from one another and do not resemble natural appearances. At first glance, they seem quite laughable, but of late they have gradually been accepted by scholars. The modern painter Pablo Picasso (a Spaniard living in Paris) is the leader of this school.[02]

This is the earliest mention of Picasso in a Chinese text. The dominant image of Picasso that would last for generations–the founder of Cubism–was first established here. This was the main information the book provided about Picasso.

Lü Cheng's 1922 book *Western Art History* included a comparatively detailed introduction of Cubism's key figures, first and foremost Picasso:

Cubism originates with the work of Pablo Picasso (1881). Picasso is a naturally curious artist, who began by imitating different artists, then abandoning them. He saw that native African sculptures often used cubic forms, which he then adapted to his painting technique. He wanted to use various geometric shapes, unconcerned with the realism of nature. Those he influenced were called Cubists.[03]

01. Jiang Danshu. *Art History*. Shanghai: Shanghai Commercial Press, 1917, p. 82. Jiang Danshu translated Picasso as *pijiashu* 毘迦叔, quite different from *bijiasuo* 毕加索, which is used today. This is a problem all famous foreigners face when entering China–they do not get a standardized Chinese name until many years after they first arrive. Picasso's name has been translated in more than a dozen different ways, but they will not be discussed here.

02. Jiang Danshu. *Art History Reference Book* volume 2. Shanghai: Shanghai Commercial Press, 1918, p. 29.

03. Lü Cheng. *Western Art History*. Shanghai: Shanghai Commercial Press, 1922, pp. 153-54.

04. In the section on twentieth-century art history, Lü Cheng notes that he "primarily referenced R. Muther [Richard Muther] and Jutaro Kuroda from Japan." Lü Cheng. *Western Art History*. "Explanatory Examples," p. 1.

05. Liang Desuo ed., trans. *An Outline of Western Art*. Shanghai: Liangyou Book Company, 1929, pp. 209-11, images 257 and 258.

06. Earp, T. W.; Liu Haisu trans. *The Modern Movement in Painting*. Shanghai: Shanghai Commercial Press, 1936, pp. 20-25.

07. Ni Yide. *An Introduction to Western Schools of Art*. Shanghai: Shanghai Commercial Press, 1937, pp. 132-33.

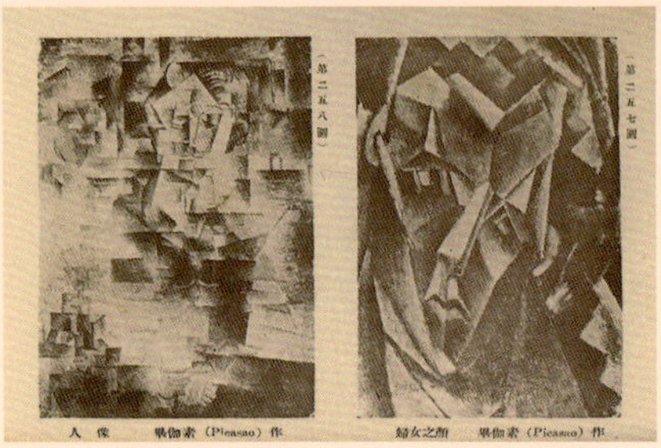

The Picasso illustrations Liang Desuo selected in *An Outline of Western Art*.

Lü Cheng based his work on the English translation of the French author Salomon Reinach's *Apollo: An Illustrated Manual of the History of Art Throughout the Ages*, but this book only covered works created before or during the nineteenth century. Lü also referenced many other texts, supplementing his book with twentieth-century European art history.[04] In the section on Picasso, Lü wrote that Picasso was "naturally curious," and that he created Cubism after being inspired by African art. It is worth noting that *Western Art History* was also published by Shanghai Commercial Press—this publishing house played a pivotal role in translating Western art resources into Chinese.

After the 1918 publication of *Art History Reference Book*, the vast majority of overviews of Western art history followed the same convention: Picasso was discussed under the heading of Cubism. The 21st chapter of *An Outline of Western Art*, compiled by Liang Desuo and published in 1929, introduces "Late Impressionism, Cubism, and Futurism" (by now, the translation of Cubism as *li ti pai* was well established and in popular use). In this book, Picasso continued to be described as the creator of Cubism.[05] *An Outline of Western Art* is a modified version of *The Outline of Art*, a 1924 book by the English author William Orpen. *The Outline of Art* compiled more than 300 artwork illustrations, including 24 color plates. Liang Desuo led the Liangyou Book Company, and he used his publishing role to his advantage: all the pictures were printed on coated paper, there were ten color images, and the production value was excellent. It was one of the most extravagant art history books published during the Republican Era in China. The volume features three of Picasso's works, making him the most prominently featured artists in the book.

Early overview publications of Western art history were mostly translations of European and Japanese scholars. These works introduced Picasso only in the context of Cubism, and this narrative framework limited Chinese understanding of the artist. Accordingly, Picasso's Cubist works were introduced more thoroughly than his others. However, as Picasso's position in the European art world ascended and his style continued to evolve, this situation also gradually began to change.

Books about Western art history published after the 1930s began to make more subtle artistic distinctions, discussing the differences between Picasso's various pre- and post-Cubist periods. In 1936, Liu Haisu translated English scholar T.W. Earp's *The Modern Movement in Painting*. This book mentioned several phases of Picasso's work before Cubism, including the Blue Period, Rose Period, and African-influenced Period.[06] Ni Yide's *An Introduction to Western Schools of Art* (1937) also included the Neoclassical style that came after Picasso's Blue, Rose, and Cubist Periods.[07]

Picasso's Blue Period works earned him a reputation for his interest in the lower classes of society.

Many Chinese critical essays note this distinguishing feature, some even calling him the "Lenin of painting." Chen Shiwen, who had traveled to Paris, published an essay on Picasso in 1933 that recounted his thoughts upon seeing Picasso's work in the original:

Although most of his works featured here are Cubist, the loveliest are his Grecian sculptures. In his style here, and in those works that reflect the state of the common people, his lofty structures, strong colors, and relaxed compositions are without compare among modern painters. I believe that even Manet, who had a centennial exhibit at the L'Orangerie at the same time, cannot match Picasso. He is the most influential painter since Cézanne. It would not be wrong to call him the Phidias or Lenin of painting.[08]

Lenin has always been revered in China, so to be called the "Lenin of painting" imputed a positive image onto him within this specific historical context–not just artistically, but also politically.

By the 1930s, Chinese publications began to give Picasso higher and higher praise. In 1934, Ni Yide translated Japanese author Toyama Usaburō's *Survey of Modern Painting*. This book contained a list of "10 Great Modern Painters." Number one on this list was "The Leader, Henri Matisse," while number three was "The Genius, Pablo Picasso." This book divides Picasso's art after his arrival in Paris into a few periods. The first was a group of melancholy, blue and green paintings with shades of El Greco and Fauvism. The next was Cézanne-inflected still lifes, followed by the Cubist Period, during which Picasso was influenced by African sculpture. By 1917 and 1918, Picasso returned to Neoclassicism. And "recently," Picasso began to show an inclination toward Surrealism. This constant progression earned Picasso a positive reputation for his constant evolution (he "changed like a growing leopard," quoting an ancient text).[09]

Ni Yide refers to Picasso as a painter "known throughout the world" in his 1933 book *Survey of Western Painting*.[10] By 1946, he gave Picasso an even more definitive evaluation in his work "Notes from a Painting Studio": "Picasso is the greatest painter of the twentieth century. He is a *monstre sacré*, constantly evolving," and, "One can say that he has reached the summit of world art. He is the crystallization of humanity's highest wisdom."[11]

However, not everyone who introduced Picasso to China liked or understood his art. For example, renowned writer, art historian, and painter Feng Zikai at first wholeheartedly accepted Picasso, but he gradually began to doubt his work. In 1928, Feng released the book *Western Art History*, an abridged translation of Japanese writer Yoshinaga Ichiuji's *Information on Western Art*. The book enshrines Picasso as "the leader of Cubism" and "first in expressing the constructions of modernity" in painting.[12] In his 1930 book *12 Lectures on Western Paintings Schools*, Feng spends an entire lecture discussing Cubism, with half his time devoted to a detailed analysis of Picasso's paintings.[13] It is clear that Feng Zikai had a profound understanding of Picasso's works. However, in his 1931 book *A Survey of Famous Western Paintings*, Feng subconsciously reveals his doubts about Picasso:

No matter how complicated the image, it is never more than the assembly of many squares, triangles, circles, and cones. Hence, depiction must be broken down into these original shapes and reorganized into a painting. So in his [Picasso's] paintings, one does not see the form of the object, only these geometric shapes. When looking at a Picasso painting, no one understands what they see.[14]

The criticism "no one understands what they see" to an extent reveals Feng's dissatisfaction and light derision. In his 1935 book *An Overview of Painting*, Feng criticizes Picasso's Cubist works more directly: *This kind of painterly style pervades the world today. However, it is mostly used as decoration, like*

08. Chen Shiwen. "Picasso." *Yifeng* 1933 volume 1 issue 5, p. 25.

09. Toyama Usaburō; Ni Deyi trans. *Survey of Modern Painting*. Shanghai: Kaiming Bookshop, 1934, pp. 183-86.

10. Ni Yide. *Survey of Western Painting*. Shanghai: Xiandai Shuju, 1933, p. 303.

11. Ni Yide. "Notes from a Painting Studio." *Tides of Victory* 1946 volume 4 issue 4, p. 106.

12. Feng Zikai. *The Complete Works of Feng Zikai* volume 7. Beijing: Dolphin Books, 2016, p. 101.

13. Ibid, pp. 281-87.

14. Feng Zikai. *The Complete Works of Feng Zikai* volume 8. Beijing: Dolphin Books, 2016, p. 105.

in store window displays, on buildings or household items, or in advertisements. However, outside of a few special painters, you rarely find artists who like to use geometric shapes to make paintings, or people who like to look at these abstruse works. I have heard that Picasso also no longer makes these paintings. Many of the members of this movement have already tossed aside their paintbrushes and gone onto careers in filmmaking.[15]

This time, Feng disavows the lack of discernable figures in Picasso's portraits and discernable objects in his still lifes. Taking as evidence that some Cubists renounced painting, he implies that Cubism had lost its vitality.

Feng's criticism of Picasso is that people "do not understand what they see." A joke about the incomprehensibility of his work began to circulate in China, though it's hard to know its provenance. It makes an appearance in a brief story entitled "Picasso Complains that the Thief Is Stupid" in the publication *Bright Weekly* (1946):

One day, the Spanish painter Picasso's house was robbed. The burglars rifled through all the chests and cupboards, making a huge mess of the house. They scattered Picasso's documents all over the floor and even shot a hole in his desk.

"Did the thieves steal anything valuable?" Picasso's friend asked him.
"They just took a couple of shirts," the painter replied.
"So why are you so angry?"
"I'm angry that they were too stupid to take my paintings!"[16]

As the above criticisms and joke show, between the 1920s and 1940s, while many professional painters and scholars recognized Picasso as one of the greatest artists in the world, the public did not have a deep understanding of, and far less appreciation for, Picasso's work.

02. Reception and Imitation of Picasso's Style

During the first half of the twentieth century, it was primarily Chinese art students in Europe who had a deep understanding of Picasso's works, having seen the originals. This is especially true of a group of Chinese painters attending school in Paris. Qin Xuanfu, who arrived in Paris in 1931, recalled the situation at the time: "The world outside the academy is a boundless sea of Modernism. The newest thing is Surrealism; Cubism and Fauvism are already yesterday's news, but Picasso and Matisse are still the idols of many youths."[17]

Fang Ganmin, who arrived in France in late 1925, was enamored of Cubism for a time. His experience studying in Paris inspired a passion for Post-Impressionism, Fauvism, Cubism, and the School of Paris, believing that only such works "truly reveal the aesthetic of the era."[18] By imitating the paintings of Cézanne, Matisse, and others, Fang mastered the artistic languages and concepts of the Modernists. After returning to China, he taught at the National Hangzhou School of Art (now known as the China Academy of Art). In the 1930s, he created a series of clearly Cubism-inflected paintings, including, among others, *White Goose*, *Song of Autumn*, and *West Lake*.[19] Of all Chinese painters, Fang is the most characteristic example of an artist imitating a Cubist style in his works. As his student Min Xiwen commented, Fang's style of painting is "Sinicized Cubist work."[20]

Pang Xunqin, who went to Paris in 1925, also appreciated Picasso. Traces of Picasso can be seen in his surviving works. For example, *Composition*, used for the cover of the November 1933

15. Feng Zikai. *An Overview of Painting*. Shanghai: Asia Book Company, 1935, p. 115.

16. Multiple authors. "Picasso Complains that the Thief Is Stupid." *Bright Weekly* 1946 volume 2 issue 1, p. 7.

17. Qin Xuanfu. "Thoughts After Viewing the Lü Sibai Oil Painting Exhibition." *Xinhua Daily* 4 August 1964.

18. Min Xiwen. "The Founder of Early Chinese Oil Painting: Remembering the First Generation Oil Painter Mr. Fang Ganmin." See Zheng Shengtian, ed. *Fang Ganmin*. Taipei: Canada Asia Pacific Art Promotions Ltd., 1996, p. 9.

19. Zheng Shengtian. *Cultural Crisscross: The Flâneur Without Record*. Hangzhou: China Academy of Art Publishing House, 2013.

edition of the magazine *Modern Age*, employs brushwork and figuration reminiscent of Picasso's Neoclassical paintings.

Positive reception and approval of Picasso were not always rooted in his works themselves, but rather in his artistic attitude, as illustrated by how Pang once recalled his time studying in Paris:

Among modern painters, I respect Picasso. I like some of his pieces and dislike others, because I don't understand them. However, I respect Picasso's spirit of exploration. No one else in Paris dares to change the way he does–courageously and consistently. Very few famous painters are willing to change their style and give up the methods with which they are familiar. Even artists like Matisse and Renoir didn't have this kind of courage, this kind of talent, this kind of vision! Picasso is a true artist. His life is one of continuous artistic exploration![21]

Picasso's ability to change left a strong impression on many Chinese artists, and their descriptions of him often emphasized his adaptability. Although Pang couldn't accept some of his styles, his courage to explore different modes inspired Pang to find an artistic path of his own.

Painters who never went to Europe also adopted some Picasso-like artistic elements after seeing his works in catalogues and other images. Some of Li Hua's 1930s prints seem very Picassian. His "10 Color Woodcuts by Li Hua," produced in late 1934 and early 1935, seems to be entirely a product of Picasso's influence. For example, the first work in this collection, *Life*, depicts a woman whose elongated neck and bodily structure seem arbitrarily assembled against a dream-like background, all of which reflect Picasso's Neoclassical Period.

There was also a group of oil painters in the 1930s who idolized Western Modernist styles. At the time, these people were seen as followers of Picasso, including Yang Taiyang and Yang Qiuren of the Storm Society. In 1935, Ni Yide pointed out how the two learned from Picasso:

Yang Qiuren and Yang Taiyang are a couple of fellows from Guangxi province. They are clear-headed and talented young artists. Because they often do research together, their styles are similar. They both follow those new styles of Picasso and de Chirico, and their colors have the lively feel of southerners.[22]

Not many of their works from this period survive, but certain magazines and printed materials confirm that at least part of their practice, such as Yang Taiyang's *Nude Woman by the Sea* (1934), reflects some of the distinguishing features of Picasso's Neoclassical Period. Overall, Chinese oil painters from the 1930s seemed more interested in those Picasso pieces that balanced realism and exaggerated forms.

In the 1930s, the most prominent embodiment of Chinese artists' enthusiasm was a special Picasso edition of *Fine Arts Magazine*. The publication compiled essays by famous painters Liang Xihong, Lin Yong, Zhao Shou, and Chen Baoyi alongside texts by Japanese artist Tsuguharu Foujita and English critic Herbert Reed (translated by Chen Baoyi and Shi Zhecun).[23] Not all of these artists necessarily incorporated Picassian elements into their paintings, but they all were admirers of his work. In their eyes, "He reached the summit of every single art form that he explored."[24]

Of course, other painters disliked Picasso. Most artists who advocated academic realism, such as Xu Beihong, held no fond feelings for the artist. Just as Feng Zikai emphasized Picasso's use of "triangles," Xu summed up Picasso's work as "set squares," a term he used scornfully:

Fang Ganmin, *Song of Autumn*, 1931.

20. Min Xiwen. "The Founder of Early Chinese Oil Painting: Remembering the First Generation Oil Painter Mr. Fang Ganmin." See Zheng Shengtian, ed. *Fang Ganmin*. Taipei: Canada Asia Pacific Art Promotions Ltd., 1996, p. 9.

21. Pang Xunqin. *This Is How I Got Here*. Beijing: Life • Reading • Xinzhi Sanlian Life Bookstore, 2005, p. 86.

22. Ni Yide. Traveling Notes in the Garden of Art, Shanghai: Liangyou Book Company, 1936, p.10.

23. *Fine Arts Magazine* 1937 volume 1 issue 5, pp. 117-29.

24. Liang Xihong. "The Periods of Picasso's Art." *Fine Arts Magazine* 1937 volume 1 issue 5, p. 119.

25. Xu Beihong. "Utrillo." *The Informal Discourses of Xu Beihong*. From *The Collected Writings of Xu Beihong*, p. 71.

26. Hu Jinren. "Some Thoughts on the Western Painting World in Shanghai." *Shanghai Art Monthly* November 1941, inaugural issue, p. 5.

Pang Xunqin, *Composition*, on the cover of the November 1933 edition of *Modern Age*.

Li Hua, *Life*, 1934.

Yang Taiyang, *Nude Woman by the Sea* in *New Base* 1934 volume 4 issue 5.

Recently in France, the generation of Cézanne, Matisse, Bonner, as well as Picasso, Utrillo, Derain, and the Japanese painter Tsuguharu Foujita, enjoyed great fame under the patronage of those businessmen, even though their works are bullshit. When Galerie Georges Petit went bankrupt during the Great Depression, Picasso saw that things were not going well, so he dramatically changed his style. He no longer uses those set squares, but rather speaks highly of Ingres (the origin of Classicism).[25]

As the most famous representative of twentieth-century academic art, Xu expressed a distaste for modern Western painting that was widely known. Like Feng, Xu used Picasso's shift to classical painting in the 1920s as evidence that "set squares" lacked artistic merit.

Hu Jinren, an artist active in Shanghai, also took exception to Picasso. He saw the Chinese painters who modeled themselves after Picasso as "painting ghosts," and Picasso as a pretense to deceive artistic youths:

Young artists have fiery passions and pure hearts. They are unsatisfied with reality and often fantasize about novelty, but they lack serious training. They lack cultivation and clear understanding. They use clever little tricks to follow the trends and show off their uniqueness, with the end result being that they waste all their passion and courage on blindly "painting ghosts." Therefore, these "ghost painters" now think "I am no longer alone" and praise one another, saying, "Oh! Your style is similar to Picasso's! Oh! Your brushwork is just like…" The sad thing is that these youths, outside of this flattery, unwittingly use all their energy to be slaves to Picasso or some other, while also being slaves to praising other Picasso admirers.[26]

Although Hu Jinren offers veiled criticism of Picasso, he also unintentionally confirms that calling a young artist "Picasso" had already become a form of flattery.

During the Republican Era, painters who advocated realism and those who promoted Modernism endlessly debated and attacked one another. Whether they revered or denigrated Picasso, imitated or condemned him, in every case he was a vehicle to express their personal artistic visions. In the Chinese art scene, Picasso was a figure that everyone had to confront at some point, to the extent that he became an important node in the artistic discourse and critical system.

03. Picasso, the Communist Party, and the Dove of Peace

Of all the events in Picasso's life, joining the French Communist Party on 4 October 1944 had the greatest impact on his image in China. In truth, Picasso's membership in the Communist Party changed how all Communist countries understood the painter. Because of his outsize reputation, his membership served to affirm the allure of communism. The day after Picasso joined, *L'Humanité*, the official organ of the French Communist Party, ran a front-page article about the painter. At the same time in China, which was still in the throes of World War II, *Liberation Daily* featured a report on the same topic.

Around the end of 1944, news that Picasso had joined the Communist Party reached the city of Yan'an (then the base of the Central Committee of the Communist Party of China), and the artists encamped there were elated to hear this. They organized an exhibition of Picasso's "paintings" on New Year's Day at the Lu Xun Academy of Arts (now called the Lu Xun Academy of Fine Arts) in Yan'an. At the time, there were of course no original Picassos in Yan'an, so the works exhibited were likely printed materials.[27] After, on 11 January 1945, *Liberation Daily* published an essay by Hu Man entitled "Celebrating the Famous Painter Pablo Picasso's Enrollment in the Communist Party." In this essay, Hu writes that "Picasso's recent enrollment in the French Communist Party is not only an important event in the art world, but also an important event in the history of humanity."[28] In his essay, Hu thoroughly affirmed Picasso's progressive political leanings, as well as the interest in the proletariat manifest in his work. However, this Marxist interpretation was not supported by everyone. Soon after the article was published, a reader sent a letter to *Liberation Daily* expressing a different view. Instead, this reader advocated for understanding Picasso from a purely formal perspective, rather than only looking at his work from a sociological angle. *Liberation Daily* published the article in their 18 March 1945 edition and invited Hu Man to pen a response. Hu maintained that Picasso's political leanings were an important aspect of his artistic achievements.[29] There can be many different interpretations of Picasso joining the Communist Party, whether as a political progression that sits alongside aesthetic individuality, or as a reflection of an artist's pursuit of progress.[30] The artists active in Yan'an ultimately endorsed the latter. In other words, it was Picasso's political identity that gave him legitimacy in Yan'an, and therefore finding "politically correct" aspects in Picasso's work was not just rational, but also straightforward. To further stress Picasso's political identity, the same issue of *Liberation Daily* also featured Picasso's essay "Why I Joined the Communist Party." The editors emphasized the point further, saying, "The news about renowned painter Pablo Picasso's enrollment in the Communist Party has had a huge impact on cultural spheres around the world."[31]

Between 1949 and 1952, Picasso painted three doves of peace for the World Peace Council (then known as the World Congress of Partisans for Peace), spreading his name to every corner of the Communist world. In January 1949, Picasso created a lithograph of the dove of peace for the World Peace Council that would convene in Paris that year. Around noon the day before the conference, poet, party member, and friend of Picasso Louis Aragon selected the lithograph in the painter's studio. That afternoon, the dove became the symbol of the Council, appearing on countless streets across Paris. It is said that Picasso himself took exception to this, once noting, "There has never been a more wretched animal. I have kept a few of them as pets, and several of them worked together to peck a pitiful little one to death because they didn't like it. They first tore out its eyes and then shredded it to pieces–it was terrifying. How could an animal like this become a symbol of peace?"[32] However, Picasso's personal views did not stop the dove from flying from Paris to each corner of every continent on Earth, nor did they prevent Picasso from earning the mantle of "Defender of Peace" in the hearts and minds of people across the world. It did not even stop him from receiving the International Stalin Peace Prize in 1950. Picasso did not win favor in the

27. Hu Man. "Celebrating the Famous Painter Pablo Picasso's Enrollment in the Communist Party." *Liberation Daily* 11 January 1945, p. 4.

28. Ibid.

29. For more on this controversy, see Zhou Aimin. *The Art of Yan'an Woodcuts*. Shijiazhuang: Hebei Education Publishing House, 2009, pp. 121-21.

30. Cai Tao. "The Anti-Japanese Propaganda Mural in Huanghelou (1938) and the Turning Point of Modern Chinese Art." China Academy of Art doctoral dissertation, 2013, p. 120.

31. *Liberation Daily* 18 March 1945, p. 4.

32. Huffington, Arianna; Li Jianjun and Jia Qi trans. *Picasso: Creator and Destroyer*. Shanghai: Shanghai Literature and Art Publishing House, 1991, pp. 299-300.

Promotional material for the World Peace Council, 1949.

Pablo Picasso, *Dove*, 9 January 1949, ink on zinc, 56.7 x 76.2 cm, Musée national Picasso-Paris. MP3414.

After receiving bouquets of flowers, the Chinese delegation poses for a photograph in front of the conference hall of the World Peace Council, April 1949, Prague, Czechoslovakia Republic, photograph by Shi Shaohua.

United States, however—even when he held a solo exhibition there, he was barred from entering the country.[33]

In April 1949, the Chinese delegation to the World Peace Council in Prague saw Picasso's dove of peace, and later, this dove flew to Beijing. On 2 October 1949, the Chinese Conference for the Protection of World Peace was held in Beijing, with major figures like Zhu De, Gao Gang, Chen Yi, Lin Boqu, Dong Biwu, Guo Moruo, and Deng Xiaoping in attendance. In the 3 October edition of *People's Daily*, a report stated that "the decorations at the meeting site were stately and refined, and hanging from the center of the dais was Picasso's famous work—a dove representing world peace." [34] The next day, *People's Daily* published another article about the conference that described the images above the dais: "Portraits of Stalin and Mao Zedong hung above the stage, while Picasso's famous dove emanated a radiant light of peace."[35] In other words, Picasso's dove was featured alongside portraits of Stalin and Mao. Naturally, this "famous painting" was probably a copy based on the promotional materials for the World Peace Council.

The second World Peace Council was convened in November 1950, and Picasso again painted a dove as the symbol of the conference. This dove made an appearance on the front page of the 17 November 1950 edition of *People's Daily*, which noted that this was "the picture of the dove of peace featured on the poster for the 2nd World Peace Council, painted by the famous French painter Pablo Picasso." Another article on the front page described symbolic differences between Picasso's two doves: the 1949 dove was "presented as a gift to the first World Peace Council. It is a tranquil and pure dove that expresses the simple dignity of millions and millions of people, and their struggle against darkness and death. It persists in light and justice against the dark world." The 1950 dove "also warmed millions of hearts through its tender style, but this dove no longer just sits there—its wings are spread in flight. The artist imbues his old work with new emotions. He shows the progress and victories that humanity has achieved as well as the victories it will win in the future."[36]

People's Daily gave Picasso's second dove a clear symbolic meaning: the dove's wings are spread; world peace advances. Without a doubt, this symbolism became the only valid interpretation in China. When *People's Daily* mentioned Picasso in the article "About the International Peace Award" on 18 December 1950, the newspaper reiterated:

Last April, Picasso made a large painting for the first World Peace Council. He used a tranquil and pure dove to express millions of people's simple dignity and their wish to achieve world peace. This year, he painted another dove, this time with its wings spread in flight (see page one of the 17 November issue of People's Daily*) for the second World Peace Council in Warsaw. This dove*

33. Craven, David. "When Picasso Was Feared by the US Government." Harris, Jonathan and Koeck, Richard Koeck ed. Picasso and the Politics of Visual Representation: War and Peace in the Era of the Cold War and Since. Liverpool: Liverpool University Press, 2013, pp. 109-12.

34. Xinhua News Agency. "Over 1,000 Representatives from Across the Country Gather in the Capital for the Opening Ceremony of the Conference for the Protection of World Peace." People's Daily 3 October 1949, p. 1.

35. Zhang Pei. "Long Live the Eastern Fortress of Peace! Report on China's Conference for the Protection of World Peace." People's Daily 4 October 1949, p. 3.

36. Photojournalism Department. "Picasso's New Gift: The Dove of Peace Is Flying." People's Daily 17 November 1950, p. 1.

Promotional flier for the World Peace Council, 1950.

The front page of the 17 November 1950 issue of *People's Daily*.

Promotional flier for the World Peace Council, 1952.

The front page of the 14 December 1952 issue of *People's Daily*.

symbolizes peace advancing, the progress and victories that humanity has achieved, as well as the victories it will win in the future. Picasso won the 1950 International Peace Prize for his first dove painting.[37]

In 1952, Picasso painted another dove of peace to celebrate the World Peace Council being held in Vienna. This dove was also pictured in flight. The front page of the 14 December 1952 edition of *People's Daily* featured an image of the third dove and continued to endow them with new meanings:

The dove has a familiar style that warms the hearts and souls of all who love peace. However, this dove spreads its wings wider, its feathers are richer and fuller, and it is flying toward even higher reaches. The whole image of the dove clearly lets us know that the bird is younger, overflowing with limitless vitality. This image is a powerful expression of how, on the foundation of the continuous progress and victories that the world peace movement has already earned, the movement of peoples fighting for and defending peace will only develop further into a new phase and win even greater victories through this World Peace Council. With the support of all who love peace, this dove will courageously fly higher and higher.[38]

Not only is the dove flying, but its wings are spread wider, symbolizing the flight of peace to greater heights.

Doves were a common motif in Picasso's work. In his lifetime, Picasso painted many images that contained doves, but in China, only these three doves featured on World Peace Council promotional materials were well known. In an article published in a 1980 edition of *People's Daily*, Zhu Boxiong wrote, "In the months and years following the establishment of New China, the three 'doves of peace' that [Picasso] painted left a deep impression on the many citizens of our nation."[39] Of course, the "three 'doves of peace'" that he mentions are the same three discussed above.

After joining the Communist Party, the dove of peace continued to change Picasso's image in China and other socialist countries. The 21 June 1953 edition of *People's Daily* featured an article by the Soviet author Ilya Ehrenburg entitled "Picasso and Peace." On the one hand, he admitted that there was still some distance between Picasso's work and the "new society" (likely referring to socialist countries). At the same time, he noted that it was clear to all that in Picasso one sees a "powerful and exceptionally sincere artist," and that his name was known to millions of common people because his dove had flown to every continent on Earth. "An artist who earned glory around the world, whose original works were coveted by bankers' wives and ministers' mistresses,

37. He Yuzi. "On the International Peace Prize." *People's Daily* 18 December 1950, p. 4.

38. "Congratulating the World Peace Council, Picasso Contributes a New Dove Artwork." *People's Daily* 14 December 1952, p. 1.

39. Zhu Boxiong. "Picasso's Eccentricity and Legacy." People's Daily 23 June 1980, p. 7.

40. Ehrenburg, Ilya. "Picasso and Peace." *People's Daily* 21 June 1953, p. 3.

41. Penrose, Roland; Zhou Guozhen trans. *Picasso's Life and Work*. Beijing: People's Fine Arts Publishing House, 1986, p. 404.

42. Kubka, František, Shou Hua trans. "Picasso's Dove of Peace." *World Affairs* 1952 issue 12, pp. 21-22.

43. "Why the Dove Is a Symbol of Peace." *People's Daily* 8 July 1990, p. 8.

44. Text by Bizi, illustrations by Liu Zhigang. "Picasso and the Dove of Peace." *Art Panorama* 1998 issue 1, pp. 40-42.

has come around to the side of the common people."[40] Because the painter dedicated his dove to world peace, the Picasso favored by bankers' wives had become a member of "the people." This narrative implies a change in Picasso's class identity: he has gone from an artist who serves the bourgeoisie to an artist of the proletariat. This change could occur in large part because Picasso's dove had become a symbol of world peace.

Picasso's dove of peace circulated widely throughout China. People couldn't help but note the doves' origins, especially that of the first dove. Picasso's friend Roland Penrose published a biography of Picasso in 1958 in which he notes the dove looked just like one that Picasso kept in a cage in his studio.[41] In China, though, this dove had a more moving backstory. It was said that, one day, after Germany occupied Paris, the gatekeeper at Picasso's neighbor's house came to call. He told Picasso that he had lost an arm in the war with Germany in 1915, and his son, John, later sacrificed himself in World War II. He also said that, the day before, his grandson, Lucien, stood on the roof waving a red flag to call a dove to him, but he tumbled to his death when two German soldiers pushed him off the roof. Before the German soldiers left, they snapped the neck of one of the doves that had been called there, a bird named Xiaolaishi [ed. note: transliterated from the Chinese; original text inaccessible]. The old man said that he had a picture, and he begged Picasso to paint the dead dove as a memorial. So Picasso drew a white dove with "a crown of feathers on its head and beautiful blue eyes," yet this dove "had not died, but rather was vivid and lively. It is a symbol of life itself, a symbol of happiness, light, and peace." When the World Peace Council convened in 1949, Picasso thought of this old man, his son John, and his grandson Lucien, and, with them in mind, painted the same dove once more, and "dedicated this painting to those soldiers of peace [...] From their hearts, in this era of struggle for peace, millions of doves spread their wings and fly forth as Xiaolaishi once did."[42]

The origin of this story is the essay "Picasso's Dove of Peace" by František Kubka, which ran in a 1952 issue of the Chinese periodical *World Affairs*. This essay was originally published in the London-based magazine *The New Central European Observer* and was later discovered by *World Affairs* and translated into Chinese. This story was so moving, it was inevitable that it would be repeated, and it has been taken as the compelling reason that Picasso painted the dove of peace. For example, an article in the 8 July 1990 edition of *People's Daily* entitled "Why the Dove Is a Symbol of Peace" repeated this story.[43] The tale was also told in images, such as in the Chinese comic strip book *Picasso and the Dove of Peace*, published in 1998 by *Art Panorama*. In this comic, some details were changed to make the story even more sentimental. For example, the old man's son and daughter-in-law die in the war after joining an anti-fascist guerrilla army; the German soldiers kill the grandson by gunfire; and, most importantly, the pigeon was hurt but did not die immediately. Instead, on Picasso's drawing table, it "flapped its bloody wings and made the arduous effort to stand," only collapsing when Picasso finished the last brushstroke.[44] These stories burnished Picasso's image, because now he had not just painted a normal dove, but rather an innocent dove that was harmed and killed by fascism. As the dove died, fascism's victims and opponents died along with it. That Picasso painted this dove became evidence that the painter had fought against fascism. This is not just a "politically correct" story, but one that became even more "correct" over time.

Picasso's dove was later "quoted" by many 1950s and 60s painters who advocated peace and opposed war. It became one of the most common "meta-images" of the time. A relatively early example was *Make the Imperialists Shake in the Face of the World's People!*, a propaganda painting from 1951 that was a collaboration between Wu Zuoren, Zhang Guangyu, Jiang Zhaohe, Wei Qimei, Ye Qianyu, Luo Gongliu, Hu Yichuan, and other artists teaching at the Central Academy of Fine Arts. The painting featured the citizens of many nations holding aloft their countries' flags and

Wu Zuoren et al., *Make the Imperialists Shake in the Face of the World's People!*, 1951.

Zhang Huaijiang and Zhang Cizhong, *Unite to Protect Peace*, 1952, 76 x 53.5 cm.

marching in formation toward the imperialists. The flag leading the procession features Picasso's 1949 dove of peace.

The 1950 dove made an appearance in the propaganda painting *Unite to Protect Peace* by Zhang Huaijiang and Zhang Cizhong. In the painting, the citizens of many countries march forward arm-in-arm while raising an image of Picasso's dove. It even comes with its own explanatory note: "People from all countries in the Asia-Pacific region come together to strengthen and broaden the movement to safeguard peace!" This painting was published in September 1952 by People's Fine Arts Publishing House as a series of printed copies. This "quoting" of Picasso's dove in propaganda materials expanded his reputation across China in a lasting way.

In the 1950s, China was still relatively tolerant of Modernism. From 10 to 25 November 1956, the China Artists Association held the "French Modern Art Exhibition," in which they displayed replicas of works by Pablo Picasso, Maurice Utrillo, Raoul Dufy, Georges Rouault, Henri Matisse, Jean Lurçat, Pierre Bonnard, René Magritte, Fernand Léger, and others.[45] In 1961, *Meishu* magazine published an essay entitled "China Federation of Literary and Art Circles Chairman Guo Moruo's Letter of Congratulations to Picasso," which celebrated Picasso's eightieth birthday. In the letter, Guo writes, "I congratulate you for your heroic fight against Franco, Hitler, and Nazism, defending justice for the people. I congratulate you for your sacred work enthusiastically opposing wars of aggression and safeguarding world peace. I congratulate you for your glorious contributions to the world's artistic canon. May you live on forever."[46] The same issue of *Meishu* featured an essay by Ai Zhongxin entitled "Congratulating Picasso on his Eightieth Birthday." The article concisely introduced Picasso's artistic career, with a focus on *Guernica* from 1937 and his 1951 works *Massacre in Korea* and *Dove of Peace*.[47]

At the same time, China began to adopt a critical attitude toward modern art that was imported from the Soviet Union. In his essay "Art and Social Life," Georgi Plekhanov classified Cubism as a bourgeois Modernist art. He stated that Cubism rejects the view that art is a representation of real life, because Cubist painters believe that the "ego" is the "only reality." Outside of the "ego" nothing is real, such that "one may permit oneself anything one likes in painting and in everything else."[48] Plekhanov classified Modernist art for art's sake as "extreme individualism of the era of bourgeois decay," cutting off artists from all sources of true inspiration. "It makes them completely blind to what is going on in social life and condemns them to sterile preoccupation with personal emotional experiences that are entirely without significance and with the phantasies of a morbid imagination."[49] So in this sense, Picasso's paintings were just one facet of a degenerate bourgeoisie art.

45. Xinhua News Agency. "Modern French Art Exhibition." *People's Daily* 14 November 1956, p. 7.

46. Guo Moruo. "China Federation of Literary and Art Circles Chairman Guo Moruo's Letter of Congratulations to Picasso." *Meishu* 1961 issue 5, p. 45.

47. Ai Zhongxin. "Congratulating Picasso on his Eightieth Birthday." *Meishu* 1961 issue 5, pp. 45-46.

48. Plekhanov, Georgi; Cao Baohua trans. *The Collected Art Essays of Georgi Plekhanov*, pp. 877-78.

49. Ibid, p. 879.

50. For more on the relationship between Zhang Ding and Picasso, see Li Zhaozhong. "The Stones of Another Mountain: Zhang Ding and Picasso." *Masterpieces Review* 2016 issue 3, pp. 127-32.

51. Li Zhaozhong. "The Stones of Another Mountain: Zhang Ding and Picasso." *Masterpieces Review* 2016 issue 3, p. 130.

Pablo Picasso, *The Cock of Liberation*, 1944, oil on canvas, 100.33 x 80.65 cm, Milwaukee Art Museum.

Zhang Ding, *Rooster and Chick*, 1960s, colored ink on paper, 46 x 35 cm, private collection.

Zhang Ding, *Large Rooster*, 1960s, colored ink on paper, 69 x 46 cm, private collection.

In China during this period, Zhang Ding and his students were perhaps the only artists who openly modeled themselves after Picasso. At the time, Zhang was the vice president of the Central Academy of Arts & Design. He participated in the revolutionary movement in Yan'an, so there were relatively few restrictions on his personal work. Around 1960, Zhang painted copies of many Picasso works, such as *The Cock of Liberation* (1944). He also used Picasso's techniques in his own paintings, like the quite similar *Cock* (c. 1961). This series of works inspired renowned cartoonist Hua Junwu to call Zhang Ding "a combination of Picasso and *chenghuangmiao* [Chinese town deity temples]," an evaluation that circulated widely.

Zhang had a strong passion for Picasso ever since he was a student. In 1932, he was admitted to the School of Chinese Painting at the National Beiping Arts College. It was there that he first encountered Picasso's work in catalogues, and the Blue Period paintings deeply moved him.[50] In 1956, Zhang participated in an international fair in France as an exhibit designer, during which time he accompanied a Chinese cultural delegation visiting Picasso. Zhang was the only member of the group familiar with the artist's work, so he was chiefly responsible for communicating with Picasso. As Zhang later recalled:

It was afternoon when we arrived at Picasso's studio, which was a villa by the sea. Picasso had finished his midday nap, and he came downstairs to welcome us enthusiastically. He first gave us a tour of his studio... All the studio walls were completely covered with new works. One can imagine that all his attention, thoughts, feelings, inspirations, and even his life itself were invested in the world of art. His shocking artistic labor and exuberant energy were truly admirable.[51]

Zhang not only saw Picasso's newest works at this meeting, he also received a gift from the artist—the book *Picasso* by literary scholar and critic Jean Cassou. Picasso wrote Zhang's name in Chinese on the title page next to a drawing of his famous dove of peace.

In the decade following 1966, Picasso was taboo in the Chinese art world. In 1966, *People's Daily* published an essay entitled "Zhou Yang's 'Liberalization' Poisoned the Central Academy of Fine Arts." The article stated that Picasso was an indictment against Zhou Yang:

After Zhou Yang and his cronies raised this utterly revisionist literary and artistic program, a trend toward bourgeois liberalism appeared in cultural circles. Art academies were inundated with all manner of bourgeois and feudal art. Poisonous weeds that no one previously dared to bring forward were all worshiped as fresh flowers. In the studios of the Department of Printmaking, they were openly trafficking in Matisse, Picasso, and Fauvist art. A small salon was established outside the

Photograph of Zhang Ding and Picasso, 1956.

The dove of peace that Picasso drew for Zhang Ding, 1956.

Wang Xiangming and Jin Lili, *Yearning for Peace*, 1985, oil on canvas, 122 x 91.5 cm, National Art Museum of China.

Yu Xiaofu, *Children Comforting Picasso's Dove*, 1985, oil on canvas, 160 x 169 cm.

studio that took as its model the bourgeois, degenerate artists of the twentieth century. Under Zhou Yang's directive of a "stable educational order," not a single thing could be changed in the entire set of bourgeois pedagogical orientations, systems, content, and methods. They implemented a capitalist dictatorship within the Central Academy of Fine Arts.[52]

Even his membership in the Communist Party and his dove of peace could not save Picasso from being labeled a "bourgeois artist" and a "poisonous weed." It was not until 1980 that this situation changed dramatically.

52. The revolutionary professors and students of the Central Academy of Fine Arts Department of Printmaking. "Zhou Yang's 'Liberalization' Poisoned the Central Academy of Fine Arts." *People's Daily* 16 July 1966, p. 3

53. Li Xianting. "On the 'Stars' Exhibition." *Meishu* 1980 issue 3, p. 9.

54. Ibid.

04. The 1980s and Beyond

In November 1979, the "Stars" art exhibition was held outside the National Art Museum of China. The participating artists put forward two central appeals: first, artists must intervene in society, and second, artists must explore new artistic forms. They summarized these two points in a slogan: "Käthe Kollwitz is our banner; Pablo Picasso is our forerunner."[53] Their appeal was featured in the magazine *Meishu*, 1980 issue 3. In his essay, the critic Li Xianting stated that the artists "want to be like Picasso, exploring endless horizons."[54] And with that, Picasso once again entered the Chinese art discourse. His artistic spirit, though not his aesthetic forms, once again became a model that impelled Chinese artists forward.

Around 1980, Picasso's reputation in China began to formally recover. The 19 June 1980 edition of *People's Daily* featured Zou Difan's modern poem "Dove":

The dove of peace is a symbol of revisionism?
Is revisionism tantamount to peace?
To care only for your braised beef and potatoes
is truly detestable,
is there a need to exterminate the doves too?
Ah, the white-jade dove,
the silver-gray dove,
fly!
Under Picasso's brush,
you inhabit our fontanels
and fly forth from our skulls.

55. Zou Difan. "Dove." *People's Daily* 19 June 1980, p. 8.

56. Wu Bunai ed. *Picasso*. Beijing: People's Fine Arts Publishing House, 1982.

57. Penrose, Roland; Zhou Guozhen trans. *Picasso: His Life and Work*. Beijing: People's Fine Arts Publishing House, 1986. People's Fine Arts Publishing House republished this book in 1987. Guangxi Normal University Press also republished this book in 2002.

58. Huffington, Arianna; Hong Jian et al. trans. *Picasso: Creator and Destroyer*. Beijing: People's Fine Arts Publishing House, 1990. Retranslated in 1991 by Liu Jianjun, Jia Qi, Shanghai: Shanghai Literature and Art Publishing House. Retranslated in 2007 by Chen Zimu, Beijing: Gold Wall Press.

59. Wang Xiangming and Jin Lili. "*Yearning for Peace* and Us." *Meishu* 1985 issue 7, p. 45.

60. Zhang Qiang. "Brief Thoughts on Art: Viewing 'Young Art of Progressive China.'" Ibid, p. 25.

61. Richet, Michel ed. *Picasso: An Exhibition of Original Paintings*. Beijing: China Exhibition Company, 1983.

62. Xinhua News Agency. "An Exhibition of Original Picasso Paintings Opens in Beijing." *People's Daily* 7 May 1983, p. 3.

I know peace has a pair of wings:
with two stable and united wings,
it feeds the siren's power,
the crops's whey,
the rustling of schoolbooks…
Fly, fly dove
Peace, peace…[55]

It was also after 1980 that China began to publish monographs on Picasso. In 1982, Wu Bunai chose some of Picasso's works to be featured in his book *Picasso*, which was published by People's Fine Arts Publishing House.[56] Soon after, many catalogues of the artist's works were printed in large quantities by various publishing houses. Systematic introductions of Picasso's life and work, however, came to China through translation. In 1986, People's Fine Arts Publishing House produced a Chinese edition of English author Roland Penrose's *Picasso: His Life and Work* (1958). This book was later republished twice.[57] In 1990, People's Fine Arts Publishing House published a Chinese translation of American author Arianna Huffington's *Picasso: Creator and Destroyer*, which was also reprinted twice by two publishing houses.[58] These two books became the most common textual sources for Chinese art enthusiasts who wanted to learn about Picasso. Outside of the art itself, people also delighted in the artist's colorful personal life. As of 2018, there are over 300 monographs and catalogues about Picasso published in Chinese.

Among all Picasso's works, *Guernica* (1937) replaced the dove of peace to become his most popular. This work evinces a humanitarian impulse; it denounces war and yearns for peace. In China, the painting is seen as Picasso's greatest work, with *People's Daily* reporting on it several times. In 1985, the National Art Museum of China held an exhibition entitled "Young Art of Progressive China." One of the most popular works in this show was Wang Xiangming and Jin Lili's *Yearning for Peace*.[59] Floating in the center of the painting is a large, framed image, a collage of "many works by Western artists that oppose war and depict peace." The most eye-catching of these is Picasso's *Guernica*. Another work in the exhibition was *Children Comforting Picasso's Dove*. This painting gently pokes fun at the dove of peace. As one critical essay from the time put it, "Picasso's dove, created for the 1953 World Peace Council, once soared through the open skies, flying across all the world's oceans and continents. Yet now… the times have turned, and children perform music for it."[60] In this tender image, the dove of peace is no longer assertive–other aspects of Picasso's art and life have begun to emerge. He is at times a respected artistic master, and at times the object of satire.

Picasso's original paintings also began to enter China, presented to audiences through exhibitions. In May 1983, the National Art Museum of China held an exhibition of his work. The show's catalogue was published by the China Exhibition Company, and it included 33 of his artworks.[61] This was the first time China held a Picasso exhibition. Then French President François Mitterand, who was visiting China at the time, attended the show's opening ceremony.[62] Chinese Vice Minister of Culture Zhou Weizhi and French Minister of Culture Jack Lang spoke at the opening ceremony. While it's true that the exhibition was an opportunity for artistic exchange, it also represented closer political ties between China and France. In October 2011, the exhibition "Picasso: Masterpieces from the Musée national Picasso-Paris" was held at the China Pavilion in Shanghai as a key program of the 13th Shanghai China International Arts Festival. It featured 62 of Picasso's works. In March 2014, the Instituto de Crédito Oficial, the Embassy of Spain in China, the Spanish Agency for International Development Cooperation, and the National Museum of China organized "Picasso: Suite Vollard" at the National Museum of China. One of the events celebrating the forty-year anniversary of China and Spain reestablishing diplomatic relations, the show featured a hundred of Picasso's paintings from the 1930s. In January 2018, French President Emanuel Macron, during an official visit to China, expressed his hope that important French museums might organize exhibitions in China. In part a realization of this aspiration, UCCA organized the exhibition "Picasso – Birth of a Genius" in June 2019, presenting 103 artworks from the collection of the Musée national Picasso-Paris. Picasso's paintings are extremely valuable, and he is a household name in China, so lending his paintings to exhibitions in China naturally embodies the friendship between the two countries. In terms of the circulation of art, the more of these activities, the better. In this way, Chinese people have more and more opportunities to see Picasso's original works without leaving their home country.

In 1996, a Chinese museum finally obtained a collection of Picasso's work. That March, the German collectors Peter and Irene Ludwig donated 89 artworks from 82 European and American artists to the National Art Museum of China, including Picasso's *Figures* (1967), *Man Smoking a Pipe* (1969), *Man and Woman by a Flower Vase* (1971), and *The Infantry with a Bird* (1971). The same year, the National Art Museum of China organized an exhibition of works donated by the Ludwigs, bringing these pieces to a wider audience. In November 2011, the National Art Museum of China sent two of these to the Qi Baishi Memorial Hall in Hunan to be a part of the third China (Xiangtan) Qi Baishi International Culture & Art Festival's themed series of art exhibitions. They were placed alongside four works by Qi Baishi, allowing audiences to directly compare the Western and Chinese masters. In 2018, the National Art Museum of China once again exhibited these pieces as part of the show "International Art Collection of NAMOC." Peter and Irene Ludwig's donation opened the doors for China to collect Picasso's works. In the future, perhaps more of his art will enter China's museums through the world market.

Conclusion

Picasso became famous early in life and had a long artistic career. His introduction to and circulation throughout China seemed to progress in parallel with his own artistic growth. From 1917 on, Picasso was introduced to China as an important link in the development of Western art history. His newest works were quickly published in Chinese periodicals, and he became known as a living master. Of course, it was inevitable that he would also inspire criticism and controversy.

After Picasso joined the Communist Party in 1944, his political identity and leanings became a key metric by which his art was judged. After the founding of the PRC in 1949, Chinese approval of Picasso was due in large part to his political positions and his positive image as a defender of world peace. In their tendency toward abstract forms, however, his paintings became an icon for decadent, bourgeois art. These two visions of Picasso stood in constant opposition, but in this period the latter won out. From 1966 to 1980, Picasso became a taboo name.

After 1980, Picasso was restored to his place as one of the greatest artists in the world. His talent and achievements inspired countless young artists, and his works became a vehicle for cultural exchange between nations. His reputation not only spread throughout the Chinese art world, but was also well known to the general public. In today's China, Pablo Picasso is like Leonardo da Vinci and Vincent van Gogh, a foreign artist familiar to all Chinese people. However, although his name has become legend, China still wants for a deeper understanding of his art–in particular his works in the original.

展览作品　　Exhibited Works

序论 Introduction

“毕加索——一位天才的诞生”基于国立巴黎毕加索博物馆的馆藏，致力于回顾毕加索创作生涯的前30年，这是艺术家极为高产和富有创造力的一段时期。从1895年前后毕加索的求学时期，到1920年代初的“古典主义”黄金时期，展览贯穿了毕加索的蓝色和粉色时期，并且通过众多杰作，展现了他在原始主义和立体主义时期不同阶段的创作。

此次展出的一系列重要绘画、雕塑和纸本作品，大部分出自毕加索工作室的收藏，通过1979年和1990年的代税捐赠进入博物馆馆藏。通过这些作品，我们得以见证这位艺术奇才如何在极短时间内，吸收古代艺术的精华，掌握同时代艺术家的最新风格，同时发展出立体主义——这个全新的创作手法对传统的艺术表现形式提出了深刻质疑。

展览再现了这位非凡艺术家的创作历程，毕加索的作品让他成为古典与现代世界之间为数不多的调解者。与惯常将毕加索的艺术生涯简化为一系列严格定义和相互封闭的创作时期的策展方式有所不同，此次展览在不同时期之间保留了开放性和穿透性的视角，由此强调毕加索身上多种看似矛盾的艺术语言的共存。秉持同样的理念，展览的最后部分展示了艺术家1927年至1972年较为晚期的一系列杰出绘画和雕塑作品，勾勒出贯穿他创作生涯的主题与基本原则。他尤为关注对创作行为提出质疑和思考的自画像体裁、在不同的媒介间展开持续的对话、热衷于探索形体的变化。正是这些不同的方面构成了天才毕加索的整体创作。

Realized exclusively through the collection of the Musée national Picasso-Paris, the exhibition "Picasso – Birth of a Genius" is dedicated to the first thirty years of the artist's works, which are particularly intense and enriching in terms of productivity and creativity. Exploring the period that spans the artist's training circa 1895 to the golden age of Picasso's "classical" style in the early 1920s, the exhibition includes the Blue and Rose Periods and recounts, through numerous masterpieces, the African Period and the different phases of Cubism.

Through an important selection of paintings, sculptures, and graphic arts–most from the studio of Picasso himself, which entered the museum's collection through gifts-in-lieu in 1979 and 1990–the exhibition illustrates how the young prodigy succeeded, in record time, not only in assimilating the lessons of ancient art and absorbing the newest expressions of his contemporaries, but also and especially in how he managed to develop, with the invention of Cubism, a new approach that profoundly questioned the art of traditional representation.

The exhibition retraces the journey of an extraordinary man whose works constitute one of the rare intermediaries between the classical and modern worlds. By nuancing a vision that reduces his works into a succession of strictly defined and closed-off periods, the proposed path includes openings and points of view that traverse from one period to another, reaffirming the co-existence, in Picasso, of several seemingly contradictory languages. Following this idea, the exhibition concludes with an exceptional set of much later paintings and sculptures, made between 1927 and 1972, that reflect the continuity of subjects and founding principles implemented very early on in his work. Among these, notably, is the genre of self-portraiture, which questions and puts into perspective the creative act. Another is the constant dialogue between different mediums and a penchant for the metamorphosis of forms–facets of the Picassian genius that permeates all of his work.

早期毕加索：学习与影响

The First Picasso: Training and Influences

“……12 岁的时候，我就像拉斐尔一样画画。”

"…At age 12, I drew like Raphaël."

毕加索语，转引安东尼娜·瓦伦汀：《毕加索》，巴黎，阿尔班·米歇尔出版社 1957 年版。
Picasso quoted by Vallentin, Antonina. *Picasso*. Paris: Albin Michel, 1957.

巴勃罗·毕加索青年肖像，巴塞罗那，1895—1896 年
阿尔道夫·费尔南德兹·卡萨马约，国立巴黎毕加索博物馆，APPH15356
Portrait of young Picasso, Barcelona, 1895-96.
Adolfo Fernández Casamayor, Musée national Picasso-Paris. APPH15356.

毕加索父亲何塞·鲁伊兹·布拉斯科在巴塞罗那
出自《蓝色时期之前的毕加索（1881—1901）》，第 278 页
Photograph of Picasso's father, José Ruiz Blasco, in Barcelona.
From *Picasso Antes del azul (1881-1901)*, p. 278.

“奇怪的是，我从来没有像孩子那样画画。从来没有，即使在很小的时候。我记得我最早的一幅画，大概是 6 岁左右的时候，我父亲家的走廊上挂着一幅拿着大头棒的赫拉克勒斯。就是这样！我开始在走廊里画赫拉克勒斯。但这不是小孩子的涂鸦，而是一幅真正的画作，画的是赫拉克勒斯和他的大头棒。”[01]

毕加索 13 岁时创作的《古典雕塑石膏像写生习作》，见证了他聪颖的天资和娴熟的绘画技巧，当时他还用父亲的姓氏署名——P. 鲁伊斯。画中的赫拉克勒斯有着雕塑般的线条造型，运用木炭笔绘制出的巧妙阴影效果增加了一丝柔和感。这幅根据菲迪亚斯的石膏像所绘制的逼真习作，创作于毕加索在拉科鲁尼亚美术学院就读期间（1892—1894），展示出他扎实的学院训练和对古代传统的深刻了解。

1895 年，巴勃罗·毕加索还不到 14 岁时绘制的这幅《戴帽子的男人》，成为了他最早的重要油画作品之一。毕加索当时是拉科鲁尼亚美术学院的学生，他的父亲何塞·鲁伊斯·布拉斯科在该学院执教，本人也是画家、艺术品修复师，并偶尔在博物馆担任保管研究员。毕加索一生都保留着这幅作品，因为它见证了自己学习期间所受的西班牙艺术影响：其中既包括巴托洛梅·埃斯特巴·牟利罗、迭戈·委拉斯开兹和弗朗西斯科·戈雅这样的绘画大师，也包括一些装饰教堂和建筑的地区画派中小有名气的画师。不过才华早现的毕加索很快就超越了最初的古典影响。

进入世纪之交，年轻的毕加索抓住每一个主题、技术和材质，既创作风俗画（家庭场景、街景、斗牛），也创作肖像画（个人与集体）或讽刺画。他在巴塞罗那和马德里度过了学习时光，并在 1900 年 10 月第一次前往巴黎。这个时期的经历影响了他在创作中对自然主义的拒绝，以及对不同风格的尝试。保罗·高更、爱德华·蒙克、亚历山大·斯坦伦和亨利·德·图卢兹 - 罗特列克对他的影响尤为显著。他们的作品在巴塞罗那的前卫艺术圈子颇为知名，这个圈子经常在“四只猫”咖啡馆附近活动。毕加索沉浸在这个充满表现力的环境里，掌握了一系列的新造型方法：装饰性的线条、分散的笔触、鲜明的色彩对比。

A curious thing is that I never made any childhood drawings. Never. Even when I was very little. I remember one of my first drawings. I was perhaps six years old, or younger. In the hallway of my father's house, there was a Hercules and his club. Well! I put myself in the hallway, and I drew Hercules. But it wasn't a child's drawing. It was a true drawing, which represented Hercules and his club.[01]

Completed at the age of thirteen, *Academic Study of a Plaster After the Antique* is a testimony to the precocity and mastery of a boy who still signed his work with his father's name, P. Ruiz. This other Hercules, with sculptural modeling nuanced by a subtle play of light and shadow in charcoal, is a copying exercise after a Phidias cast. Undertaken while Picasso was still a student at the La Coruña School of Fine Arts, which he frequented between 1892 and 1894, the illusionistic study demonstrates his solid academic training and extensive knowledge of the grand ancient tradition.

In 1895, Picasso was only fourteen when he painted *Man with a Cap*, one of his first significant works of oil on canvas. He was then a student at the La Coruña School of Fine Arts, where his father, himself a painter, art restorer, and occasional museum conservator, was employed as a teacher. Picasso kept this painting throughout his life as testament to his years of apprenticeship marked by the influence of Spanish art: the grandmasters, such as Bartolomé Esteban Murillo, Diego Velázquez, and Francisco de Goya, but also the lesser known masters of regional schools who decorated churches and monuments. His precocious genius quickly extricated itself from these initial classical influences.

At the turn of the century, the young Picasso seized on all manner of subjects, techniques, and materials to produce genre images (familial scenes, street scenes, bullfights), portraits (of individuals and groups), and caricatures. His formative years, spent between Barcelona and Madrid, and including his first trip to Paris in October 1900, were marked by the rejection of naturalism and experimentation with different styles, influenced notably by the works of Paul Gauguin, Edvard Munch, Théophile Alexandre Steinlen, and Henri de Toulouse-Lautrec, whose works were known to the avant-garde in Barcelona who gravitated to the café Els Quatre Gats. Picasso immersed himself in this expressiveness and appropriated a range of new formal solutions: decorative lines, fragmented brushwork, and vibrant color contrasts.

01. 毕加索语，转引［法］伊莲·帕姆兰：《毕加索说……》，巴黎，龚梯耶尔出版社 1966 年版，第 86 页。

01. Parmelin, Hélène. *Picasso dit.* Paris: Gonthier, 1966, p.86.

古典雕塑石膏像写生习作
Academic Study of a Plaster After the Antique

拉科鲁尼亚，1893—1894 年
纸上炭笔和黑色铅笔画，49 x 31.5 cm
国立巴黎毕加索博物馆 / 毕加索代税捐赠 1979. MP405
La Coruña,1893-94
Fusain and black pencil on paper, 49 x 31.5 cm
Musée national Picasso-Paris / Pablo Picasso gift-in-lieu, 1979. MP405

93-94
P. Ruiz
Nº 11

斗牛

Corrida (Bullfight)

拉科鲁尼亚，1894 年 9 月 2 日
纸上石墨铅笔素描、羽管笔和墨水画，12.6 x 19.3 cm
国立巴黎毕加索博物馆 / 毕加索代税捐赠，1979. MP401 (r)
La Coruña, 2 September 1894
Pen and ink on graphite pencil sketch on paper, 12.6 x 19.3 cm
Musée national Picasso-Paris / Pablo Picasso gift-in-lieu, 1979. MP401 (r)

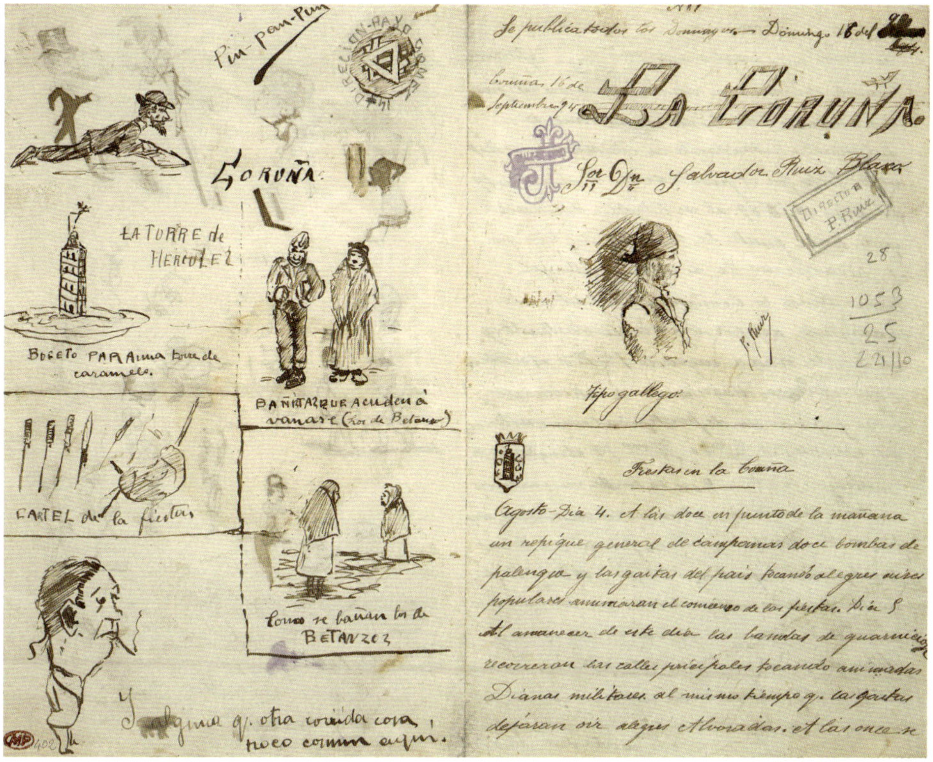

拉科鲁尼亚
La Coruña

拉科鲁尼亚，1894 年 9 月 16 日
纸上羽管笔、墨水和石墨铅笔画，21 x 26.8 cm
国立巴黎毕加索博物馆 / 毕加索代税捐赠，1979. MP402 (r)
La Coruña, 16 September 1894
Pen, ink, and graphite pencil on paper, 21 x 26.8 cm
Musée national Picasso-Paris / Pablo Picasso gift-in-lieu, 1979. MP402 (r)

约瑟法·塞巴斯蒂亚·孟布拉多的肖像
Portrait of Josefa Sabastia Membrado

埃布罗河岸的奥尔塔，1898 年 11 月
纸上硬蜡笔画，32 x 24.5 cm
国立巴黎毕加索博物馆 / 毕加索代税捐赠，1979.MP415 (r)
Horta de Ebro, November 1898
Conté crayon on paper, 32 x 24.5 cm
Musée national Picasso-Paris / Pablo Picasso gift-in-lieu, 1979. MP415 (r)

戴帽子的男人
Man with a Cap

拉科鲁尼亚，1895 年初
布面油画，72.5 x 50 cm
国立巴黎毕加索博物馆 / 毕加索代税捐赠，1979. MP1
La Coruña, beginning of 1895
Oil on canvas, 72.5 x 50 cm
Musée national Picasso-Paris / Pablo Picasso gift-in-lieu, 1979. MP1

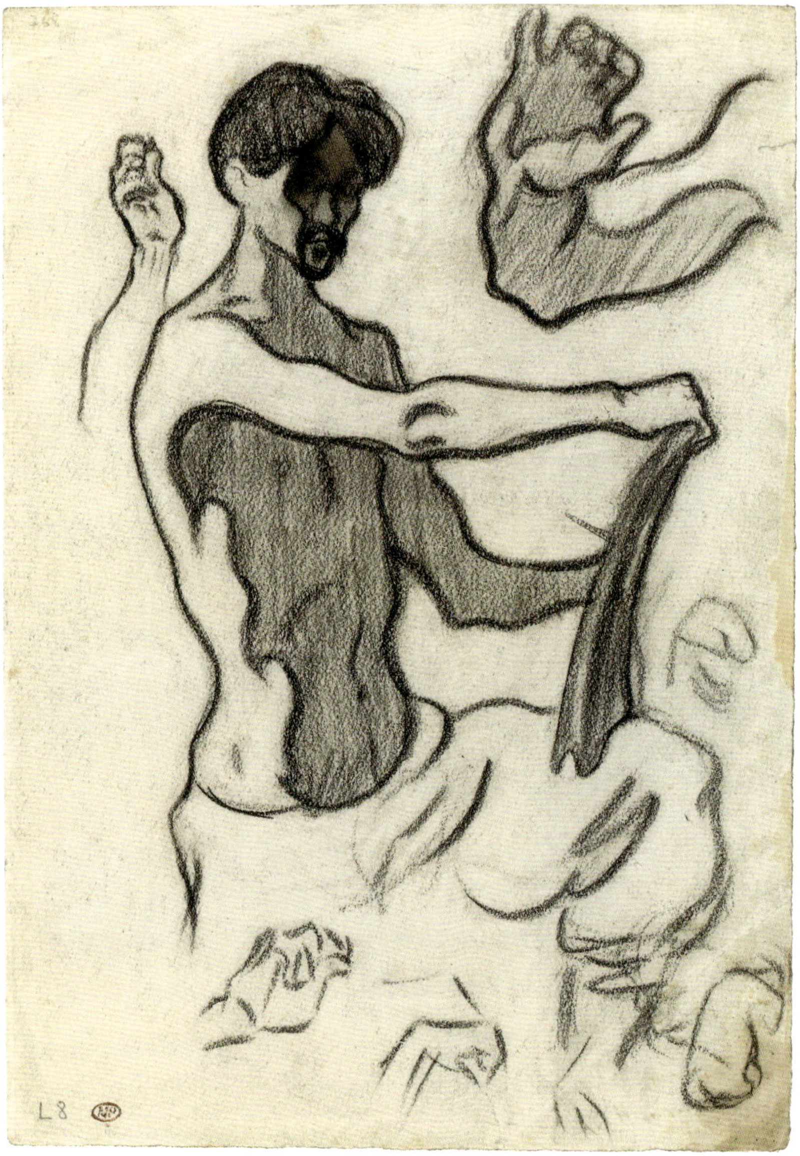

艺术家正在绘画和手的习作（正面）
The Artist Drawing and Studies of Hands (Recto)

1897—1899 年
纸上硬蜡笔画，33.2 x 23.4 cm
国立巴黎毕加索博物馆 / 毕加索代税捐赠，1979. MP410 (r)
1897-99
Conté crayon on paper, 33.2 x 23.4 cm
Musée national Picasso-Paris / Pablo Picasso gift-in-lieu, 1979. MP410 (r)

两幅自画像与形体（反面）
Two Self-portraits and Figures (Verso)

1897—1899 年
纸上硬蜡笔画，33.2 x 23.4 cm
国立巴黎毕加索博物馆 / 毕加索代税捐赠，1979. MP410 (v)
1897-99
Conté crayon on paper, 33.2 x 23.4 cm
Musée national Picasso-Paris / Pablo Picasso gift-in-lieu, 1979. MP410 (v)

寓言：年轻男人、女人和怪诞人物
Allegory: Young Man, Woman, and Grotesques

巴塞罗那，1899—1900 年
纸上炭笔、水彩和松节油稀释颜料画，34.6 x 31.1 cm
国立巴黎毕加索博物馆 / 毕加索代税捐赠，1979. MP419
Barcelona, 1899-1900
Fusain, watercolor, and oil paint diluted with turpentine on paper, 34.6 x 31.1 cm
Musée national Picasso-Paris / Pablo Picasso gift-in-lieu,1979. MP419

帕拉利罗咖啡音乐厅
El Paralelo Cafe-concert

巴塞罗那，约 1900 年
木板油画，36 x 48 cm
国立巴黎毕加索博物馆 / 法国政府购买，交付国立巴黎毕加索博物馆，2009. MP2008-2
Barcelona, c. 1900
Oil on wood, 36 x 48 cm
Musée national Picasso-Paris / Acquired by the French state, given to Musée national Picasso-Paris, 2009. MP2008-2

为“四只猫”咖啡馆设计的菜单
Design for a Menu for "Els Quatre Gats"

巴塞罗那，1899—1900 年
纸上羽管笔墨水画，32 x 22.5 cm
国立巴黎毕加索博物馆 / 毕加索代税捐赠 1979. MP416 (r)
Barcelona, 1899-1900
Pen and ink on paper, 32 x 22.5 cm
Musée national Picasso-Paris / Pablo Picasso gift-in-lieu, 1979. MP416 (r)

狂欢节海报设计
Design for a Carnival Poster

巴塞罗那，1899 年末
纸上硬蜡笔和油彩画，48.5 x 33 cm
国立巴黎毕加索博物馆 / 毕加索代税捐赠 1979. MP427 (r)
Barcelona, end of 1899
Conté crayon and oil on paper, 48.5 x 33 cm
Musée national Picasso-Paris / Pablo Picasso gift-in-lieu, 1979. MP427 (r)

习作：基督头像、年长女子坐像、女子侧面像和执画笔的手
Studies: Head of Christ, Seated Old Woman, Profile of Woman, and Hand

马拉加，1901 年初
纸上羽管笔、黑墨水和彩色铅笔画，23.5 x 15.4 cm
国立巴黎毕加索博物馆 / 毕加索代税捐赠，1979. MP428
Málaga, beginning of 1901
Pen, black ink, and colored pencil on paper, 23.5 x 15.4 cm
Musée national Picasso-Paris / Pablo Picasso gift-in-lieu, 1979. MP428

砍头者
The Cutter of Heads

巴塞罗那，1901 年春
纸上中国墨水、墨染和水粉画，50.2 x 32.5 cm
国立巴黎毕加索博物馆 / 毕加索代税捐赠，1979. MP431 (r)
Barcelona, spring 1901
Chinese ink, ink-wash, and gouache on paper, 50.2 x 32.5 cm
Musée national Picasso-Paris / Pablo Picasso gift-in-lieu, 1979. MP431 (r)

卡萨吉马斯之死
The Death of Casagemas

巴黎，1901 年夏
木板油画，27 x 35 cm
国立巴黎毕加索博物馆 / 毕加索代税捐赠，1979. MP3
Paris, summer 1901
Oil on wood, 27 x 35 cm
Musée national Picasso-Paris / Pablo Picasso gift-in-lieu, 1979. MP3

蓝色和粉色毕加索：最初的艺术身份

Picasso Blue and Rose:
A First Artistic Identity

“这位西班牙人和其他诗人、雕塑家和画家相比，
有着更为冷酷决绝的杀伤力。他的思考暴露在沉默之中。”

“More than any other poet, sculptor, or painter,
this Spaniard strikes us like a sudden chill.
His meditations are unveiled in silence.”

［法］纪尧姆・阿波利奈尔：《羽笔》1905 年 5 月 15 日刊。
Apollinaire, Guillaume. *La Plume* 15 May 1905.

毕加索在拉维尼昂广场上的肖像，蒙马特，1904 年
佚名，国立巴黎毕加索博物馆，APPH15301
Portrait of Picasso in Ravignon Square, Montmartre, 1904.
Anonymous, Musée national Picasso-Paris. APPH15301.

戈索尔概貌，戈索尔，1963 年
约瑟普・帕劳・I. 法布里，照片出自展览“帕劳眼中的毕加索”
马拉加，帕劳基金会，2017 年 10 月 19 日—2018 年 1 月 7 日
View of Gósol, Gósol, 1963.
Josep Palau i Fabre, photograph from the exhibition "Palau mira a Picasso,"
Málaga, Palau Foundation, 19 October 2017 – 7 January 2018.

“这幅作品很特别，这个年轻人的作品弥漫着一股荒芜的哀伤。……这就好像一位年轻的神灵想要重新塑造这个世界，但他是一位阴郁的神灵。”[01]

1901 年的夏天，毕加索放弃模仿前辈的后印象派绘画风格，转而塑造真正意义上最早的个人风格。自 1905 年起，人们参照诗人纪尧姆·阿波利奈尔的说法将这一风格命名为蓝色时期。这时期的特点是大量使用蓝色，选取感性的主题以及在形式中寻求表现力。根据毕加索本人的说法，这个时期的创作始于 1901 年 2 月他的好友卡洛斯·卡萨吉玛斯自杀之后，“我想念已经去世的卡萨吉玛斯，于是开始用蓝色来作画”。[02] 艺术家为卡萨吉玛斯创作了一系列绘画，画面从闪耀的色彩逐渐过渡到近乎单色调。虽然“蓝色时期”一词立刻会让人想到绘画，但毕加索的创作远不限于这一媒介。从绘画、雕塑、素描到雕版画，他其实一直围绕着男人与女人痛苦、消瘦、反抗的身体进行探索，通过僵硬而庄严的躯体寻求对痛苦的表达，直到 1904 年底，毕加索的世界都充斥着这样的人物。

同样的忧郁也渗透进粉色时期的作品中，该阶段发展于 1905 年间，紧接着蓝色时期之后。杂耍艺人是其中的重要主题，除了延续此前矫饰主义风格的身体变形扭曲之外，他还通过丑角阿尔列金的形象确立了艺术家的身份。1906 年初，一种新生的古典主义风格渗透到毕加索的作品中，与此同时，粉色逐渐变为赭色。1906 年 5 月至 8 月的戈索尔之旅，进一步明确了他这个时期的风格转向。戈索尔是一座似乎被时间所遗忘的村庄，坐落于加泰罗尼亚的比利牛斯山脉，毕加索的创作与这里的壮丽景色发生了一场独特的相遇。前一年冬天，毕加索在卢浮宫展览上看到了罗曼雕塑和伊比利亚艺术，与这些作品的接触让他开始回归本源，更激发了他对保罗·高更作品的兴趣。几个星期的旅途间，不论是在雕塑还是绘画作品中，我们都可以看到毕加索对形式和空间的粗砺简化，这预示着一场即将到来的造型革命。

It is extraordinary, the barren sorrow that weighs upon the entire work of this very young man. […] It seems like a young god who wants to remake the world. Yet it is a dark god.[01]

During the summer of 1901, Picasso abandoned the Post-Impressionist style that mimicked the paintings of his predecessors to forge what would eventually constitute his first personal mode. It would be named, in 1905 by the poet Guillaume Apollinaire, the Blue Period. Characterized by the dominant use of this color, sentimental themes, and the search for an expressivity in form, this Blue Period was, according to Picasso himself, triggered by the suicide of his friend Carles Casagemas in February 1901. "It was with the thought that Casegemas was dead that I started to paint in blue."[02] The artist devoted himself to a cycle of paintings in which he progressively moves from a brilliant palette to almost monochrome tonalities. If the term "Blue Period" immediately evokes painting, the art of Picasso is far from limited to this medium. Paintings, sculptures, drawings, and engravings proceed from the same investigations into the bodily suffering of men and women, emaciated, crying. These works search for an expression of pain, conveyed by the stiff and solemn bodies that populate the universe of the artist until the end of 1904.

The same melancholy suffuses the works of the Rose Period that followed and developed throughout 1905. Marked by the predominant theme of *saltimbanques*, itinerant circus performers, works of this period persist in the preceding mannerist distortions, all of which affirm the artist's identification with the character of Harlequin. In early 1906, a burgeoning classicism permeates Picasso's output, and the color pink gradually turns into ochre. These styles are reaffirmed by a residency in Gósol between May and August 1906, during which a singular encounter takes place, between his practice and the spectacular landscape of this timeless village in the Catalan Pyrenees. In contact with Romanesque sculpture and Iberian art–discovered the previous winter in an exhibition at the Louvre–Picasso began a return to the original source, which accentuated his interest in the works of Paul Gauguin. In the coming weeks, we see, in sculpture as in painting, rough simplifications in form and space that foreshadow and initiate coming formal revolutions.

01.［法］查尔斯·莫利斯：《MM. 毕加索，洛奈，皮绍特与吉里尔的展览》，载《法国信使》，1902 年 12 月 15 日，第 156 期，第 804—805 页。

02. 毕加索和［法］皮埃尔·戴克斯的对话，1965 年。

01. Morice, Charles. "Exhibition of Picasso, Launay, Pichot, and Girieud." *Mercure de France* issue 156 15 December 1902, pp. 804-05.

02. Picasso to Daix, Pierre, 1965.

自画像
Self-portrait

巴黎，1901 年末
布面油画，81 x 60 cm
国立巴黎毕加索博物馆 / 毕加索代税捐赠，1979. MP4
Paris, end of 1901
Oil on canvas, 81 x 60 cm
Musée national Picasso-Paris / Pablo Picasso gift-in-lieu, 1979. MP4

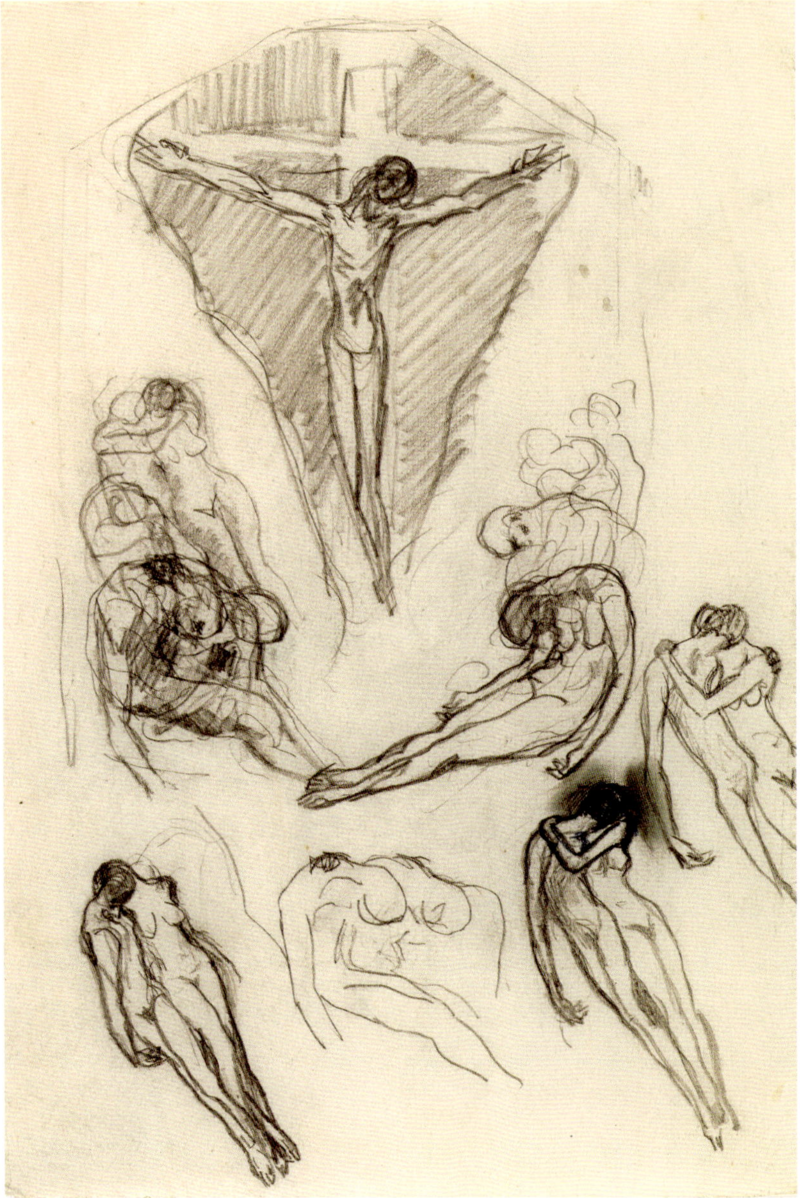

架上耶稣与拥抱
Crucifixion and Embraces

巴塞罗那，1901 年
纸上石墨铅笔画，以墨水擦抹、彩色铅笔修饰，31.8 x 21.7 cm
国立巴黎毕加索博物馆 / 毕加索代税捐赠，1979. MP477
Barcelona, 1901
Graphite pencil, rubbings of ink, and colored pencil highlights on paper, 31.8 x 21.7 cm
Musée national Picasso-Paris / Pablo Picasso gift-in-lieu, 1979. MP477

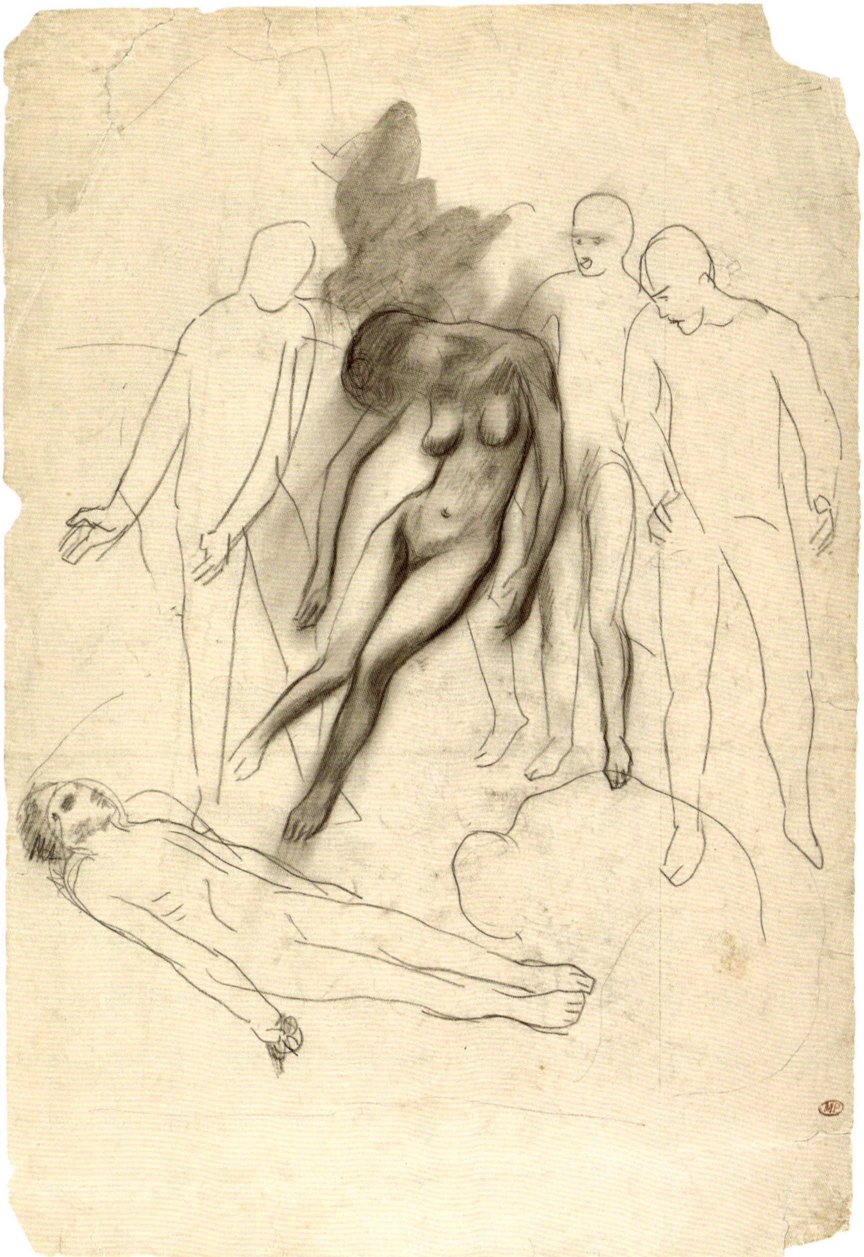

《招魂》习作
Study for *Evocation*

巴黎，1901 年春夏
纸上硬蜡笔画，41.8 x 29.1 cm
国立巴黎毕加索博物馆 / 毕加索代税捐赠，1979. MP442
Paris, spring - summer 1901
Conté crayon on paper, 41.8 x 29.1 cm
Musée national Picasso-Paris / Pablo Picasso gift-in-lieu, 1979. MP442

照镜子的女人
Woman with a Mirror

巴塞罗那，1903 年
纸上石墨铅笔画，21.9 x 23.2 cm
国立巴黎毕加索博物馆 / 毕加索代税捐赠，1979. MP476
Barcelona, 1903
Graphite pencil on paper, 21.9 x 23.2 cm
Musée national Picasso-Paris / Pablo Picasso gift-in-lieu, 1979. MP476

俯在床边女子和女子头像
Woman Prostrate at the Edge of a Bed and Woman's Head

巴黎，1901 年秋
纸上中国墨水、水彩和水粉画，25.5 x 37.3 cm
国立巴黎毕加索博物馆 / 毕加索代税捐赠，1979. MP438 (v)
Paris, autumn 1901
Chinese ink, watercolor, and pastel on paper, 25.5 x 37.3 cm
Musée national Picasso-Paris / Pablo Picasso gift-in-lieu, 1979. MP438 (v)

坐着的女人
Seated Woman

巴塞罗那，1902 年
生土雕塑， 14.5 x 8.5 x 11.5 cm
国立巴黎毕加索博物馆 / 毕加索代税捐赠，1979. MP230
Barcelona, 1902
Raw earth, 14.5 x 8.5 x 11.5 cm
Musée national Picasso-Paris / Pablo Picasso gift-in-lieu, 1979. MP230

两位女子，一位支撑着另一位
Two Women, One Supporting the Other

巴塞罗那，1903 年
贴纸纸板、石墨铅笔和炭笔素描、羽管笔和黑墨水画，27.5 x 20.4 cm
国立巴黎毕加索博物馆 / 毕加索代税捐赠，1979. MP461
Barcelona, 1903
Pen and black ink on charcoal and graphite pencil sketch on cardboard glued paper, 27.5 x 20.4 cm
Musée national Picasso-Paris / Pablo Picasso gift-in-lieu, 1979. MP461

男子群像
Group of Men

巴黎—巴塞罗那，1902 年 1 月
纸上石墨铅笔素描、羽管笔和棕色墨水画，28.4 x 19.7 cm
国立巴黎毕加索博物馆 / 毕加索代税捐赠，1979. MP459
Paris – Barcelona, January 1902
Pen and brown ink on graphite pencil sketches on paper, 28.4 x 19.7 cm
Musée national Picasso-Paris / Pablo Picasso gift-in-lieu, 1979. MP459

赛乐丝汀娜（患眼翳症的妇人）
Celestina (Woman with a Cloudy Eye)

巴塞罗那，1904 年 3 月
布面油画，74.5 x 58.5 cm
国立巴黎毕加索博物馆 / 弗莱德里克・罗斯捐赠，1989. MP1989-5
Barcelona, March 1904
Oil on canvas, 74.5 x 58.5 cm
Musée national Picasso-Paris / Donated by Fredrik Roos, 1989. MP1989-5

朴素的一餐
The Frugal Repast

巴黎，1904 年 9 月
蚀刻与刮刀加工锌版画，德拉特印制，61.6 x 44.3 cm
国立巴黎毕加索博物馆 / 毕加索代税捐赠，1979. MP1889
Paris, September 1904
Etching and scraping on zinc, printed by Delâtre, 61.6 x 44.3 cm
Musée national Picasso-Paris / Pablo Picasso gift-in-lieu, 1979. MP1889

《熨衣服的女人》习作
Study for *The Ironing Woman*

巴黎，1904 年春
纸上黑色墨水晕染素描，羽管笔和棕色墨水画，37.2 x 26.7 cm
国立巴黎毕加索博物馆 / 毕加索代税捐赠，1979. MP480
Paris, spring 1904
Pen and brown ink on sketch with black ink faded on paper, 37.2 x 26.7 cm
Musée national Picasso-Paris / Pablo Picasso gift-in-lieu, 1979. MP480

莫里哀剧院的《圣罗莱特》
Molière Theater *Sainte Roulette*

巴黎，1904 年
纸上水粉和水彩画，118.2 x 87.6 cm
国立巴黎毕加索博物馆 / 购买于贝雷斯画廊与威登斯坦画廊，2012. MP2012-3
Paris, 1904
Gouache and watercolor on paper, 118.2 x 87.6 cm
Musée national Picasso-Paris / Purchased from Galerie Berès and Wildenstein & Company, 2012. MP2012-3

Théâtre Moliere
ex-Bouffes-du-Nord
SAINTE
-Picasso-
PIECE EN 4 ACTES D MM.
JEAN LORRAIN ET GUSTAVE

在马戏团
At the Circus

巴黎，1906 年春
干点直刻圆角铜版画，德拉特印制，30.5 x 22.4 cm
国立巴黎毕加索博物馆 / 毕加索代税捐赠，1979. MP1898
Paris, spring 1906
Drypoint on copper with rounded corners, printed by Delâtre, 30.5 x 22.4 cm
Musée national Picasso-Paris / Pablo Picasso gift-in-lieu, 1979. MP1898

杂耍艺人一家
Family of Saltimbanques

巴黎，1905 年
纸上硬铅笔和石墨铅笔画，带有铅笔高光，37.2 x 26.6 cm
国立巴黎毕加索博物馆 / 毕加索代税捐赠，1979. MP500
Paris, 1905
Conté crayon, graphite pencil, and pencil highlights on paper, 37.2 x 26.6 cm
Musée national Picasso-Paris / Pablo Picasso gift-in-lieu, 1979. MP500

习作：丑角阿尔列金，纪尧姆·阿波利奈尔和亨利·德洛梅的夸张肖像
Studies: Harlequins and Caricatures of Guillaume Apollinaire and Henri Delormel

巴黎，1905 年 12 月 24 日
纸上羽管笔、墨水、渲染和擦痕画，25.5 x 17.6 cm
国立巴黎毕加索博物馆 / 毕加索代税捐赠，1979. MP509
Paris, 24 December 1905
Pen, ink, washes, and scrapes on paper, 25.5 x 17.6 cm
Musée national Picasso-Paris / Pablo Picasso gift-in-lieu, 1979. MP509

年轻杂耍女演员跪在戴皇冠的男演员面前
Young Female Saltimbanque Kneeling in Front of a Crowned Saltimbanque

巴黎，1905 年
纸上羽管笔和黑墨水画，24 x 16.2 cm
国立巴黎毕加索博物馆 / 毕加索代税捐赠，1979. MP501
Paris, 1905
Pen and black ink on paper, 24 x 16.2 cm
Musée national Picasso-Paris / Pablo Picasso gift-in-lieu, 1979. MP501

疯子
The Jester

巴黎，1905 年
青铜雕塑，为艺术品商人安伯斯·佛拉铸造的版本，41.5 x 37 x 22.8 cm
国立巴黎毕加索博物馆 / 毕加索代税捐赠，1979. MP231
Paris, 1905
Bronze, edition for the merchant Ambroise Vollard, 41.5 x 37 x 22.8 cm
Musée national Picasso-Paris / Pablo Picasso gift-in-lieu, 1979. MP231

杂耍艺人群像
Group of Saltimbanques

巴黎，1905 年
纸上羽管笔、黑墨水、水粉渲染和炭笔线条画，20.2 x 31.2 cm
国立巴黎毕加索博物馆 / 毕加索代税捐赠，1979. MP503
Paris, 1905
Pen, black ink, and ink-wash of gouache on features drawn in fusain on paper, 20.2 x 31.2 cm
Musée national Picasso-Paris / Pablo Picasso gift-in-lieu, 1979. MP503

杂耍艺人：交谈、梳妆和马的表演排练
Saltimbanques: Conversation, Toilette, and Horse Performance Rehearsal

巴黎，1905 年
纸上石墨铅笔素描、羽管笔和深褐色墨水画，17.7 x 25.4 cm
国立巴黎毕加索博物馆 / 毕加索代税捐赠，1979. MP505
Paris, 1905
Pen and ink on graphite pencil sketches on paper, 17.7 x 25.4 cm
Musée national Picasso-Paris / Pablo Picasso gift-in-lieu, 1979. MP505

杂耍艺人
The Saltimbanques

巴黎，1905 年春夏
干点直刻铜版画，德拉特印制，43.9 x 61.3 cm
国立巴黎毕加索博物馆 / 毕加索代税捐赠，1979. MP1896
Paris, spring - summer 1905
Drypoint on copper, printed by Delâtre, 43.9 x 61.3 cm
Musée national Picasso-Paris / Pablo Picasso gift-in-lieu, 1979. MP1896

饮水处（洗澡的马群）
The Watering Place (Horses Bathing)

1906 年春
干点直刻斜面铜版画，德拉特印制，22.1 x 30.5 cm
国立巴黎毕加索博物馆 / 毕加索代税捐赠，1979. MP1897
Paris, spring 1906
Drypoint on beveled copper, printed by Delâtre, 22.1 x 30.5 cm
Musée national Picasso-Paris / Pablo Picasso gift-in-lieu, 1979. MP1897

兄弟俩
The Two Brothers

戈索尔，1906 年夏
纸板水粉画，80 x 59 cm
国立巴黎毕加索博物馆 / 毕加索代税捐赠，1979. MP7
Gósol, summer 1906
Gouache on cardboard, 80 x 59 cm
Musée national Picasso-Paris / Pablo Picasso gift-in-lieu, 1979. MP7

戴白头巾的费尔南德
Fernande with a White Mantilla

戈索尔，1906 年春夏
纸上炭笔与晕色画，63.1 x 47.4 cm
国立巴黎毕加索博物馆 / 毕加索代税捐赠，1979. MP510
Gósol, spring - summer 1906
Fusain and shading on paper, 63.1 x 47.4 cm
Musée national Picasso-Paris / Pablo Picasso gift-in-lieu, 1979. MP510

女子半身像（费尔南德）
Bust of a Woman (Fernande)

戈索尔，1906 年夏
黄杨木雕，带有红色颜料痕迹和黑色颜料线条，77 x 17 x 16 cm
国立巴黎毕加索博物馆 / 毕加索代税捐赠，1979. MP233
Gósol, summer 1906
Boxwood sculpture with traces of red paint and features in black paint, 77 x 17 x 16 cm
Musée national Picasso-Paris / Pablo Picasso gift-in-lieu, 1979. MP233

《后宫》习作：梳妆女子
Study for *The Harem*: Woman at Her Toilette

戈索尔，1906 年春夏
纸上羽管笔、墨水和水彩画，画于“西蒙乳霜”广告标签背面，7 x 5 cm
国立巴黎毕加索博物馆 / 毕加索代税捐赠，1979. MP514
Gosol, spring – summer 1906
Pen, ink, and watercolor on paper, on the back of an advertising label for “Simon Cream,” 7 x 5 cm
Musée national Picasso-Paris / Pablo Picasso gift-in-lieu, 1979. MP514

梳头女子
Woman Styling Her Hair

巴黎，1906 年
青铜雕塑，42.2 x 26 x 31.8 cm
国立巴黎毕加索博物馆 / 乔治・贝乐柯和可拉捐赠，1980. MP1981-3
Paris, 1906
Bronze, 42.2 x 26 x 31.8 cm
Musée national Picasso-Paris / Donated by Georges Pellequer and Colas, 1980. MP1981-3

驱魔人毕加索：《阿维尼翁的少女》的革命

Picasso the Exorcist: The Revolution of *Les Demoiselles d'Avignon*

“那个时候，对于大多数人来说，非洲面具不过是一个民族学物品……我强迫自己留下来研究这些面具。人们为了神圣与魔法的目的制作这些物品，让它们在人类与不可知的敌对力量之间斡旋，通过这个方式，赋予其颜色与形状，从而克服自身的恐惧感。这时我才意识到这就是绘画的意义。绘画不是一个美学过程；而是介于这些力量与我们之间的一种魔法，一种获取权力的方式，它凌驾于我们的恐惧与欲望之上。当我理解这一点的时候 ，我知道自己找到了前进的方向。”

“For most people at that time, an African mask was an ethnographic object. [...] I forced myself to remain, to examine those masks, all those objects that men had made for a sacred purpose, a magic purpose, to serve as intermediaries between themselves and the unknown, the hostile forces that surrounded them, in order to overcome their fears by giving them form and color. And then I realized that this was the very meaning of painting. It is not an aesthetic process; it is a form of magic that interposes between us and the hostile universe, a way of seizing power by imposing a form on our terrors and our desires. The day I understood that, I knew I had found my way.”

[法] 弗朗索瓦丝·吉洛：《与毕加索一起生活》，巴黎，加尔曼-勒维出版社 1965 年版，第 248—259 页
Gilot, Françoise. *Vivre avec Picasso*. Paris: Calmann-Lévy, 1965, pp. 248-49.

巴勃罗・毕加索在"洗衣船"工作室，1908 年
出自吉利特・伯吉斯的文章插图《巴黎狂野之人》（《建筑记录》，1910 年 5 月 5 日），
弗兰克・吉利特・伯吉斯（1866—1951），国立巴黎毕加索博物馆，ARCREC1910
Pablo Picasso in his Bateau-Lavoir Studio, 1908
Illustration from Burgess, Gelett Frank. "The Wild Men of Paris." *Architectural Record* 5 May 1910
Burgess Gelett Frank, Musée national Picasso-Paris. ARCREC1910.

巴勃罗・毕加索的"洗衣船"工作室，位于巴黎蒙马特拉维尼昂街 13 号，1956 年
翻底片，时间不详，原版底片上有毕加索的批注，国立巴黎毕加索博物馆，FPPH225
Picasso's Studio at Bateau-Lavoir, 13 Rue Ravignan, Montmartre, Paris, 1956.
Lee Miller, internegative without date, annotation by Picasso on the reverse of the original, Musée national Picasso-Paris. FPPH225.

Fenêtres de
mon atelier
13 R:
Ravigna

“所有巫术崇拜物的功能都一样。它们是帮助人们不再服从于鬼神的武器，让人们变得独立。它们是工具。如果我们赋予鬼神以形状，我们就可以获得独立。鬼神、无意识（人们过去很少讨论到这一点）和感情，都是一样的东西。我明白为什么我是画家了。”[01]

1906 年秋天回到巴黎后，毕加索继续他简化形式和空间的探索，并且不知不觉地走上了一条即将彻底改变 20 世纪艺术的全新道路。1907 年，他创作了立体主义的源起之作《阿维尼翁的少女》（纽约现代艺术博物馆），灵感来自巴塞罗那的一家妓院。从那时起，艺术家几乎只对女性人体感兴趣。他为此创作了许多作品和习作，摈弃模仿现实的手法，采用全新的表现语言：组合连接基本形状，运用紧密影线，将色彩搭配限制在赭色调之内。

粗野主义，即将身体部位简化为符号，这个原初的艺术语言的出现很大程度上和毕加索对原始文化、非洲和大洋洲艺术的兴趣有关，他自 1907 年起，经常前往特罗卡德罗人类博物馆参观这类作品。这也是毕加索对于塞尚艺术的遗产——将物体的体积几何化——的实践运用：“以圆柱体、球体、锥体来处理大自然，用透视法展现一切。”在这个毕加索的创作实验场里，他在绘画、雕塑和雕版画之间建立的实验关系，开始发挥决定性的作用。

1908 年伊始，毕加索的创作进入了一个极富实验性的关键阶段，他对塞尚式立体主义的探索体现在对形状的多元化呈现上：中断的曲线破坏了平面的连续性，彩色的影线定义了空间的碎片化纹理，带有棱角和立体的结构再次凸显出物体的体积感。非西方艺术和民间传统的影响也在其间显露，例如影线的使用让人想起非洲面具的彩色条纹，以及反古典的人物身体比例。

Yet all fetish objects served the same thing. They were weapons to help people to no longer obey spirits, to become independent. They were tools. If we give a shape to spirits, we become independent. The spirits, the unconscious (it is still not spoken of much), emotion, it is all the same thing. I understood why I was a painter.[01]

Returning to Paris in autumn 1906, Picasso continued his work in simplifying form and space. He engaged, still unknowingly, a new direction that would revolutionize the art of the twentieth century and result in a 1907 proto-Cubist masterpiece inspired by a brothel in Barcelona, *Les Demoiselles d'Avignon* (The Museum of Modern Art, New York). From then on, the artist was almost exclusively interested in the female form. He dedicated himself to many works and studies characterized by the abandonment of illusionistic methods in favor of a new expressive language: construction through the articulation of essential forms, the use of tight hatching, and limiting his palette to ochres.

The emergence of this first brutalist vocabulary, which reduced parts of the body to signs, interested Picasso largely due to the indigenous cultures and African and Oceanic arts then on view in the Trocadero Ethnography Museum, which he visited from 1907 onwards. It also corresponded to Paul Cézanne's lesson in geometric volumes: "Treat nature in terms of the cylinder, the sphere, and the cone, all in perspective." In the laboratory of Picasso's work, the experimental relationship between painting, sculpture, and engraving played a decisive role.

From 1908 on, the experimental profusion that characterizes this fundamental period of Cézannian Cubism manifested itself in the diversity of forms considered: interrupted curves that introduce a discontinuity of planes, colored hatchings that define a fragmented texture of space, and angular, cubic constructions that reaffirm volume. This reflected the influence non-Western art and folk traditions, in the adoption of hatching that recalled the striped colorations of African masks as well as in the anti-classical proportions of the body.

01. 毕加索语，转引［法］安德烈·马尔罗：《黑曜岩之头》，巴黎，伽利玛出社 1974 年版。

01. Picasso quoted in Malraux, André. *La Tête d'obsidienne.* Paris: Gallimard, 1974.

习作：自画像（正面）
Studies for Self-portraits (Recto)

巴黎，1906 年秋
纸上石墨铅笔画，31.5 x 47.5 cm
国立巴黎毕加索博物馆 / 毕加索代税捐赠，1979. MP524 (r)
Paris, autumn 1906
Graphite pencil on paper, 31.5 x 47.5 cm
Musée national Picasso-Paris / Pablo Picasso gift-in-lieu, 1979. MP524(r)

习作：自画像（反面）
Studies for Self-portraits (Verso)

巴黎，1906 年秋
纸上石墨铅笔画，31.5 x 47.5 cm
国立巴黎毕加索博物馆 / 毕加索代税捐赠，1979. MP524 (v)
Paris, autumn 1906
Graphite pencil on paper, 31.5 x 47.5 cm
Musée national Picasso-Paris / Pablo Picasso gift-in-lieu, 1979. MP524(v)

自画像
Self-portrait

巴黎，1906 年秋
布面油画，65x 54 cm
国立巴黎毕加索博物馆 / 毕加索代税捐赠，1979. MP8
Paris, autumn 1906
Oil on canvas, 65 x 54 cm
Musée national Picasso-Paris / Pablo Picasso gift-in-lieu, 1979. MP8

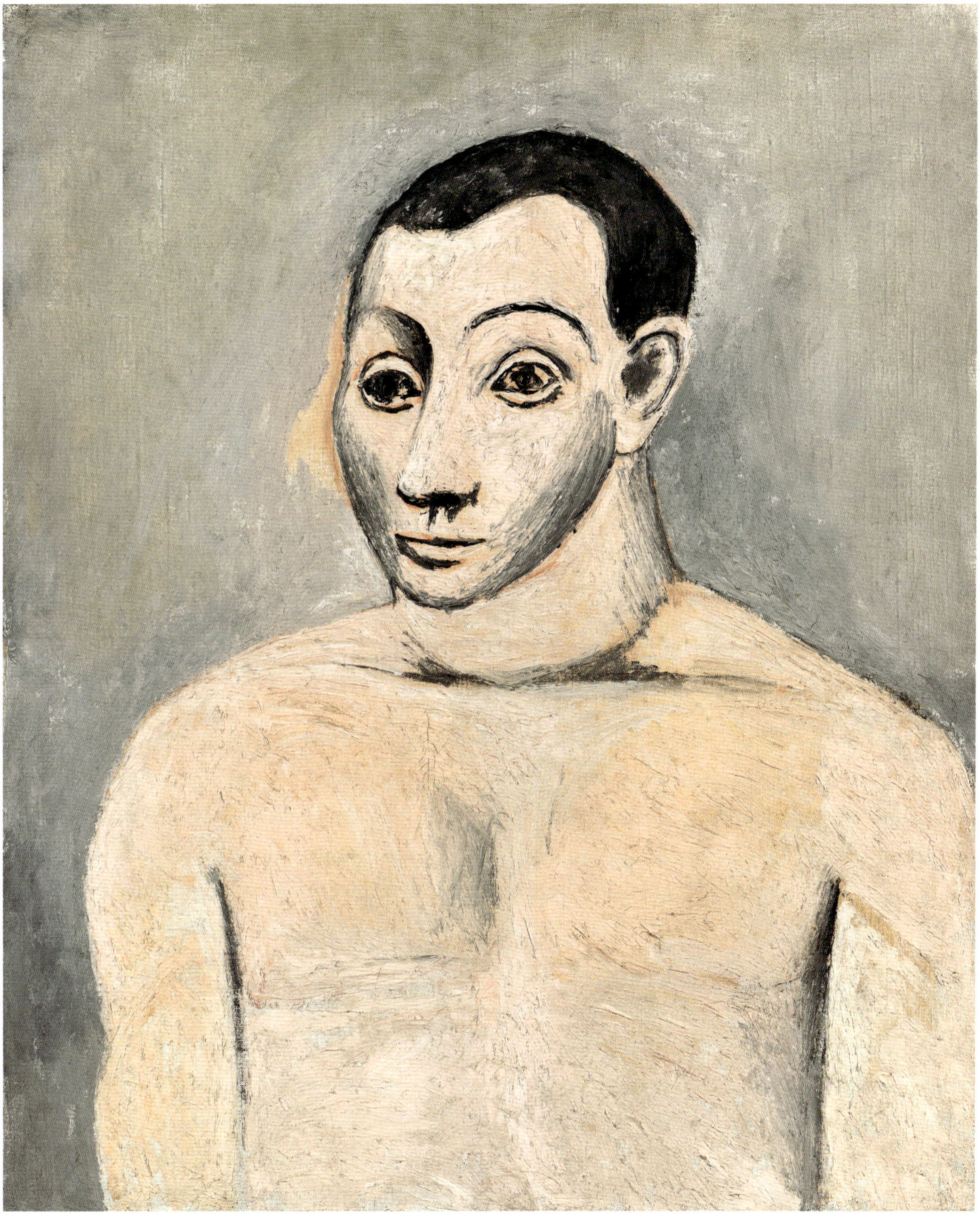

裸体男孩
Nude Boy

巴黎，1906 年秋
布面油画，67 x 43 cm
国立巴黎毕加索博物馆 / 毕加索代税捐赠，1979. MP6
Paris, autumn 1906
Oil on canvas, 67 x 43 cm
Musée national Picasso-Paris / Pablo Picasso gift-in-lieu, 1979. MP6

双手合握的女人（《阿维尼翁的少女》习作）
Woman with Clasped Hands (Study for *Les Demoiselles d'Avignon*)

巴黎，1907 年春
布面油画，90.5 x 71.5 cm
国立巴黎毕加索博物馆 / 毕加索代税捐赠，1979. MP16
Paris, spring 1907
Oil on canvas, 90.5 x 71.5 cm
Musée national Picasso-Paris / Pablo Picasso gift-in-lieu, 1979. MP16

男子半身像（《阿维尼翁的少女》习作）
Bust of a Man (Study for *Les Demoiselles d'Avignon*)

巴黎，1907 年春
布面油画，56 x 46.5 cm
国立巴黎毕加索博物馆 / 毕加索代税捐赠，1979. MP14
Paris, spring 1907
Oil on canvas, 56 x 46.5 cm
Musée national Picasso-Paris / Pablo Picasso gift-in-lieu, 1979. MP14

《阿维尼翁的少女》习作：拉窗帘的裸体女人
Study for *Les Demoiselles d'Avignon*: Nude Woman Pulling Back a Curtain

巴黎，1907 年 5 月—6 月
纸上炭笔和阴影画，63 x 48 cm
国立巴黎毕加索博物馆 / 毕加索代税捐赠，1979. MP541
Paris, May – June 1907
Fusain and shading on paper, 63 x 48 cm
Musée national Picasso-Paris / Pablo Picasso gift-in-lieu, 1979. MP541

《阿维尼翁的少女》习作：蹲下的女子头像
Study for *Les Demoiselles d'Avignon*: Head of the Young Woman Squatting

巴黎，1907 年 6 月—7 月
纸上水粉画，63 x 48 cm
国立巴黎毕加索博物馆 / 毕加索代税捐赠，1979. MP539
Paris, June – July 1907
Gouache on paper, 63 x 48 cm
Musée national Picasso-Paris / Pablo Picasso gift-in-lieu, 1979. MP539

《三个女人》习作：左边女人的半身像
Study for *Three Women*: Bust of the Woman on the Left

巴黎，1908 年春
纸上石墨铅笔和炭笔素描、水粉和中国墨水画，62.5 x 48 cm
国立巴黎毕加索博物馆 / 毕加索代税捐赠，1979. MP577
Paris, spring 1908
Gouache and Chinese ink on graphite pencil and fusain sketch on paper, 62.5 x 48 cm
Musée national Picasso-Paris / Pablo Picasso gift-in-lieu, 1979. MP577

小幅裸女坐像
Small Seated Nude

巴黎，1907 年夏
木板油画，17.6 x 15 cm
国立巴黎毕加索博物馆 / 毕加索代税捐赠，1979. MP20
Paris, summer 1907
Oil on wood, 17.6 x 15 cm
Musée national Picasso-Paris / Pablo Picasso gift-in-lieu, 1979. MP20

裸女坐像（《阿维尼翁的少女》习作）
Seated Nude (Study for *Les Demoiselles d'Avignon*)

巴黎，1906—1907 年冬
布面油画，121 x 93.5 cm
国立巴黎毕加索博物馆 / 毕加索代税捐赠，1979. MP10
Paris, winter 1906-07
Oil on canvas, 121 x 93.5 cm
Musée national Picasso-Paris / Pablo Picasso gift-in-lieu, 1979. MP10

站立的形体
Standing Figure

巴黎，1907 年
彩绘冷杉木雕，31.5 x 6 x 6 cm
国立巴黎毕加索博物馆，毕加索代税捐赠，1979. MP239
Paris, 1907
Painted fir sculpture, 31.5 x 6 x 6 cm
Musée national Picasso-Paris / Pablo Picasso gift-in-lieu, 1979. MP239

树下三人
Three Figures Beneath a Tree

巴黎，1907 年冬至 1908 年
布面油画，99 x 99 cm
国立巴黎毕加索博物馆 / 威廉・麦克凯西・库伯捐赠，1986. MP1986-2
Paris, winter 1907-08
Oil on canvas, 99 x 99 cm
Musée national Picasso-Paris / Donated by William McCarthy Cooper, 1986. MP1986-2

Picasso

形体
Figure

巴黎，1907 年春
黄杨木雕，带有铅笔和颜料痕迹，35.2 x 12.2 x 12 cm
国立巴黎毕加索博物馆 / 毕加索代税捐赠，1979. MP237
Paris, spring 1907
Boxwood sculpture with traces of pencil and paint, 35.2 x 12.2 x 12 cm
Musée national Picasso-Paris / Pablo Picasso gift-in-lieu, 1979. MP237

形体
Figure

巴黎，1908 年
橡木雕塑，带有颜料修饰，80.5 x 24 x 20.8 cm
国立巴黎毕加索博物馆 / 毕加索代税捐赠，1979. MP238
Paris, 1908
Oak sculpture with painted highlights, 80.5 x 24 x 20.8 cm
Musée national Picasso-Paris / Pablo Picasso gift-in-lieu, 1979. MP238

母与子
Mother and Child

巴黎，1907 年夏
布面油画，81 x 60 cm
国立巴黎毕加索博物馆 / 毕加索代税捐赠，1979. MP19
Paris, summer 1907
Oil on canvas, 81 x 60 cm
Musée national Picasso-Paris / Pablo Picasso gift-in-lieu, 1979. MP19

站着的裸体女人
Nude Woman Standing

巴黎，1908 年冬至 1909 年
纸上炭笔和黑铅笔画，62.5 x 48.2 cm
国立巴黎毕加索博物馆 / 毕加索代税捐赠，1979. MP631
Paris, winter 1908-09
Fusain and black pencil on paper, 62.5 x 48.2 cm
Musée national Picasso-Paris / Pablo Picasso gift-in-lieu, 1979. MP631

《农妇》习作
Study for *The Farmer*

拉鲁德布瓦，1908 年夏
纸上硬蜡笔画，48.2 x 62.8 cm
国立巴黎毕加索博物馆 / 毕加索代税捐赠，1979. MP606 (r)
La Rue-des-Bois, summer 1908
Conté crayon on paper, 48.2 x 62.8 cm
Musée national Picasso-Paris / Pablo Picasso gift-in-lieu, 1979. MP606 (r)

女子头像
Head of Woman

巴黎，1906—1907 年
青铜雕塑，11.5 x 8 x 9 cm
国立巴黎毕加索博物馆 / 毕加索代税捐赠，1979. MP235
Paris, 1906-07
Bronze, 11.5 x 8 x 9 cm
Musée national Picasso-Paris / Pablo Picasso gift-in-lieu, 1979. MP235

《友情》习作
Study for *Friendship*

巴黎，1907 年冬至 1908 年
纸上水粉和炭笔素描画，62.6 x 48.3 cm
国立巴黎毕加索博物馆 / 毕加索代税捐赠，1979. MP559
Paris, winter 1907-08
Gouache on fusain sketch on paper, 62.6 x 48.3 cm
Musée national Picasso-Paris / Pablo Picasso gift-in-lieu, 1979. MP559

立体主义者毕加索：符号的胜利

Picasso the Cubist: The Triumph of the Sign

“《组合—吉他》的发明，可以说催化了纸上拼贴的诞生……纸上拼贴是这场名副其实的革命里最具标志性的材料，它彻底改变了架上绘画的意义。自此之后，拼贴变成了造型表达上的一个独特案例，与绘画和木板一样，变得不可或缺。”

"The creation of *Guitar* emerged as a catalyst for papiers collés [...] Papiers collés were the most distinctive medium of a genuine revolution that completely changed the meaning of easel painting, which became a particular case of plastic expression in which painting, no more than the block, is now indispensable."

[法] 皮埃尔·戴克思：《新毕加索词典》，罗贝尔·拉封出版社 2012 年版，第 427 页。
Daix, Pierre. *Le nouveau dictionnaire Picasso*. Robert Laffont, 2012, p. 427.

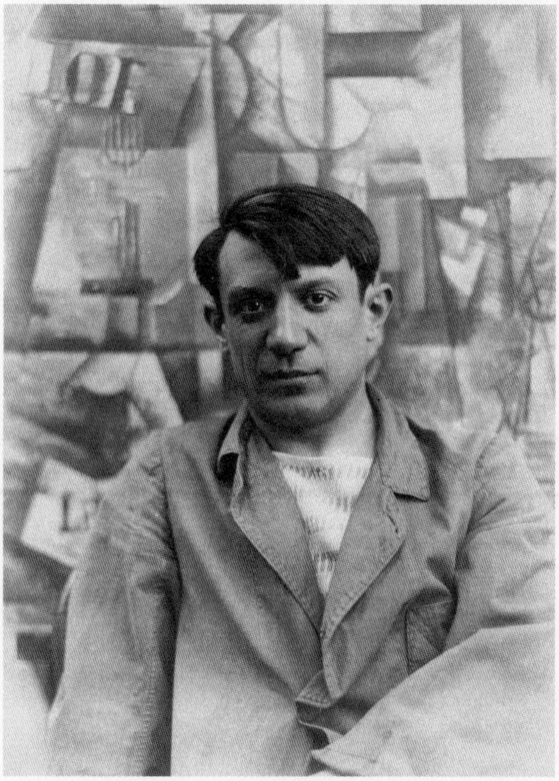

巴勃罗·毕加索在画作《斗牛爱好者》前，铃铛别墅，索尔格，1912 年夏
佚名，国立巴黎毕加索博物馆，APPH2861
Pablo Picasso in front of the painting *The Aficionado* at the Villa les Clochettes, Sorgues, summer 1912.
Anonymous, Musée national Picasso-Paris. APPH2861.

毕加索坐在克里希大街 11 号的工作室的沙发上，手里抱着一只猫（局部），1910 年 12 月，巴黎
佚名，翻底片，国立巴黎毕加索博物馆，MPPH15301
Picasso sitting on a couch holding a cat in his studio on 11 Boulevard de Clichy (detail), December 1910, Paris.
Anonymous, print internegative, Musée national Picasso-Paris. MPPH15301.

“我们试图摆脱视觉陷阱，却掉入了‘精神陷阱’。”[01]

毕加索与乔治·布拉克自 1908 年共同创立的立体主义可以说为 20 世纪的艺术奠定了基础。立体主义的第一阶段是塞尚阶段（1908—1909 年），其特征是继承了保罗·塞尚作品中几何化和开放性的形体。随后是被称为“分析立体主义”的第二阶段（1910—1911 年），该阶段最基本的要素是将主体分裂为多个平面，然后将其铺展于以直线表格重新布局的空间里。第三阶段被称为“综合立体主义”，自 1912 年拼贴画出现之后，其美学性几乎立刻就被转用到画布上，由此带来了这一阶段立体主义的发展。无论是作为物品本身，还是纯粹考虑造型质量，拼贴画都拥有自身的价值，它使得人们可以同时面对现实世界和对其的认知。正如毕加索曾在一本素描本中写道，这是“在自然与想象之间寻找平衡”。[02] 换言之，无论是绘画还是雕塑，立体主义的意义都在于“重现”，不仅要（从单一视角）呈现出事物在人们眼中的形象，还要传达出它们在脑海中的模样（包括内部和外部体积感所有的复杂性）。

《弹曼陀林的男子》是解析式立体主义的代表作，这一时期的作品通常有些晦涩难懂。画面由一系列灰棕色调的小平面组成，如果缺少其中几个解读“信号”，我们完全可以将这幅作品视为抽象画。这些被毕加索称为“标志物”的元素是能够帮助人们破译构图的指示。其中乐器音孔是一个在立体主义阶段明确反复出现的重要元素。这一符号不仅直接指向具体的现实，保证了主题的连贯性，也成为整个立体主义运动的象征。音乐的主题也常常以音谱的形式出现，再次确立了绘画不仅是一种视觉语言，同时也具有思想上的维度。艺术家之所以偏爱这些物品，也可能是对他的祖国西班牙的影射。除此之外，曼陀林和吉他造型上既饱满又具有凹陷和开口，因此成为分析空间平面连接最受欢迎的载体。

We have tried to rid ourselves of tricks of the eye to find “tricks of the mind.” [01]

The Cubism that Picasso invented in tandem with Georges Braque in early 1908 most likely founded the art of the twentieth century. After an initial Cézannian phase (1908-09), marked by the geometrizing and opening of forms inherited from the paintings of Paul Cézanne, the second phase, termed Analytical Cubism (1910-11), rested on a splintering of the subject into a multitude of planes deployed in a space reconfigured into linear grids. The third phase, called Synthetic Cubism, began in 1912 with the appearance of glued paper cut-outs, or papiers collés, the aesthetic qualities of which are almost immediately transposed onto the canvas. With value unto themselves, both as objects and for their purely formal qualities, the papiers collés allow for a simultaneous encounter with the real world and one's knowledge of it. This, as described by Picasso in one of his notebooks, consists of “finding the balance between nature and our imagination.”[02] In other words, in painting as in sculpture, the Cubist project consists of re-presenting things not only as they are presented to the eye (from a single angle) but as they appear to the mind (in all the complexity of their volume, inside and out).

Characteristic of the hermetic phase of Analytical Cubism, *Man with a Mandolin*, with its faceting in shades of grey and brown, could pass for abstract if not for certain signs that provide interpretive evidence. These elements, which Picasso calls “attributes,” are all indices that enable the deciphering of the composition. Among them, the sound hole of a stringed instrument is a formal leitmotif that one finds throughout the Cubist years. This motif is not only a direct reference to a concrete reality that assures the permanence of the subject; it is also an emblem for the Cubist project as a whole. Through the music that he evokes, often also presented in the form of a musical score, Picasso reaffirms the cerebral, and not exclusively visual, dimension of painting. As fetish objects that could also be an allusion to the artist's native Spain, the mandolin and the guitar are, by their at once full, hollow, and open shape, preferred media in analyzing the articulation of planes in space.

01. 毕加索语，转引［法］弗朗索瓦丝·吉洛与［法］卡尔顿·莱克：《与毕加索一起生活》，巴黎，加尔曼 - 勒维出版社 1965 年版，第 69—70 页。

02.《索尔格素描本》，羽管笔，黑墨水，棕墨水，石墨铅笔，1912 年 6 月至 9 月，藏于国立巴黎毕加索博物馆，MP1864，第 16 页背面。

01. Picasso quoted by Gilot, Françoise and Lake, Carlton. *Vivre avec Picasso*. Paris: Calmann-Lévy, 1965, pp. 69-70.

02. Notebook entitled *Sorgues*, pen, black ink, brown ink, and graphite pencil, June – September 1912, Musée national Picasso-Paris. MP1864, folio 16, recto.

静物：磨剃刀的皮革
Still Life with Shaving Strop

巴黎，1909 年
布面油画，55 x 40.5 cm
国立巴黎毕加索博物馆 / 路易斯・雷利画廊遗赠，1977. MP1980-1
Paris, 1909
Oil on canvas, 55 x 40.5 cm
Musée national Picasso-Paris / Donated by Galerie Louise Leiris, 1977. MP1980-1

圣心大教堂
Sacré-Coeur

巴黎，1909 年冬—1910 年
布面油画，92.5 x 65 cm
国立巴黎毕加索博物馆 / 毕加索代税捐赠，1979. MP30
Paris, winter 1909-10
Oil on canvas, 92.5 x 65 cm
Musée national Picasso-Paris / Pablo Picasso gift-in-lieu, 1979. MP30

弹曼陀林的男子
Man with a Mandolin

巴黎，1911 年秋
布面油画，162 x 71 cm
国立巴黎毕加索博物馆 / 毕加索代税捐赠，1979. MP35
Paris, autumn 1911
Oil on canvas, 162 x 71 cm
Musée national Picasso-Paris / Pablo Picasso gift-in-lieu, 1979. MP35

丑角阿尔列金的头像
Head of Harlequin

赛雷，1913 年
纸上剪纸、拼贴、图钉固定、硬蜡笔与炭笔画，62.7 x 47 cm
国立巴黎毕加索博物馆 / 毕加索代税捐赠，1979. MP377
Céret, 1913
Cut out, glued, and pinned paper, Conté crayon, and charcoal pencil on paper, 62.7 x 47 cm
Musée national Picasso-Paris / Pablo Picasso gift-in-lieu, 1979. MP377

持烟斗的男子
Man with a Pipe

巴黎，1914 年春
布面油彩与印花布料拼贴画，138 x 66.5 cm
国立巴黎毕加索博物馆 / 毕加索代税捐赠，1979. MP39
Paris, spring 1914
Oil and printed fabric glued on canvas, 138 x 66.5 cm
Musée national Picasso Paris / Pablo Picasso gift-in-lieu, 1979. MP39

壁炉旁的男人
Man Beside Fireplace

巴黎，1916 年
布面油画，130 x 81 cm
国立巴黎毕加索博物馆 / 毕加索代税捐赠，1979. MP54
Paris, 1916
Oil on canvas, 130 x 81 cm
Musée national Picasso-Paris / Pablo Picasso gift-in-lieu, 1979. MP54

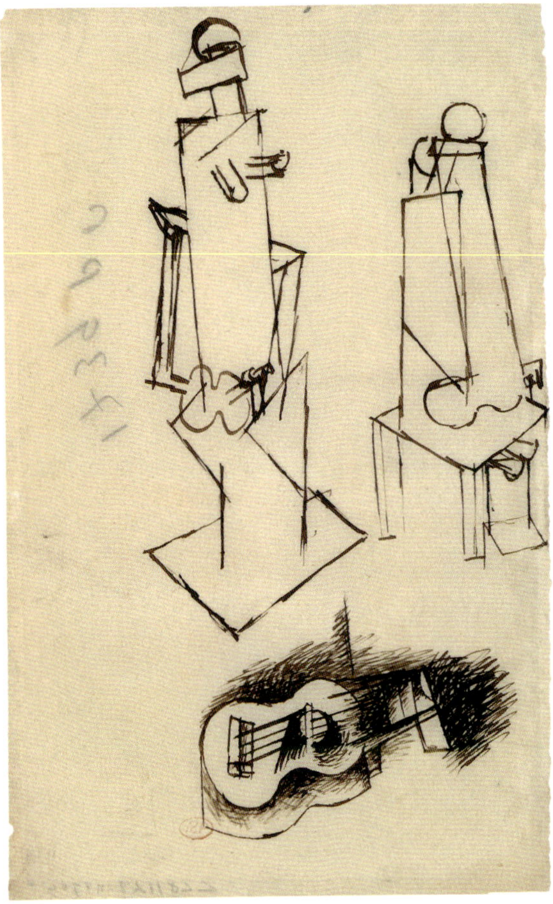

习作：吉他手与吉他（构图想法？）
Studies: Guitarist and Guitar (Idea for a Composition?)

1912—1913 年
纸上羽管笔和深褐色墨水画，21.2 x 13.3 cm
国立巴黎毕加索博物馆 / 毕加索代税捐赠，1979. MP702
1912-13
Pen and sepia ink on paper, 21.2 x 13.3 cm
Musée national Picasso-Paris / Pablo Picasso gift-in-lieu, 1979. MP702

习作：吉他手（构图想法？）
Studies: Guitarist (Idea for a Composition?)

1912—1913 年
纸上羽管笔和深褐色墨水画，21.2 x 13.2 cm
国立巴黎毕加索博物馆 / 毕加索代税捐赠，1979. MP703
1912-13
Pen and sepia ink on paper, 21.2 x 13.2 cm
Musée national Picasso-Paris / Pablo Picasso gift-in-lieu, 1979. MP703

吉他“我爱伊娃”
“I Love Eva” Guitar

索尔格，1912 年夏
布面油画，35 x 27 cm
国立巴黎毕加索博物馆 / 毕加索代税捐赠，1979. MP37
Sorgues, summer 1912
Oil on canvas, 35 x 27 cm
Musée national Picasso-Paris / Pablo Picasso gift-in-lieu, 1979. MP37

小提琴与乐谱
Violin and Music Sheet

巴黎，1912 年秋
纸板剪纸拼贴画，78 x 63.5 cm
国立巴黎毕加索博物馆 / 毕加索代税捐赠，1979. MP368
Paris, autumn 1912
Papers cut and glued on cardboard, 78 x 63.5 cm
Musée national Picasso-Paris / Pablo Picasso gift-in-lieu, 1979. MP368

小提琴
Violin

巴黎，1915 年
经切割和弯曲的彩绘金属板、铁丝，100 x 63.7 x 18 cm
国立巴黎毕加索博物馆 / 毕加索代税捐赠，1979. MP255
Paris, 1915
Painted, crushed, and cut-out metal sheets and iron wires, 100 x 63.7 x 18 cm
Musée national Picasso-Paris / Pablo Picasso gift-in-lieu, 1979. MP255

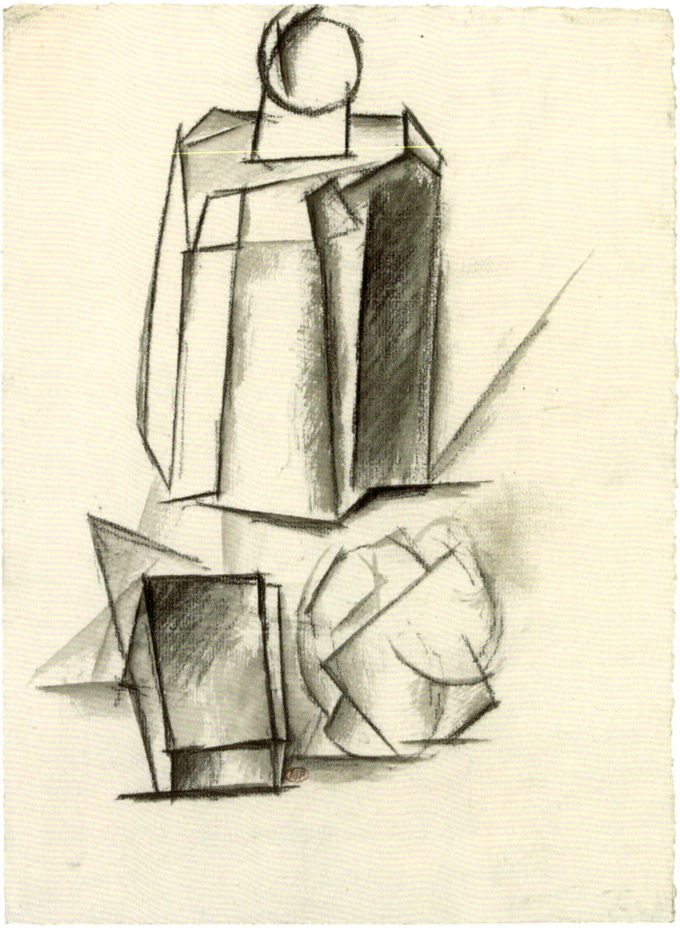

习作：小瓶、盒子和苹果
Studies: Bottle, Box, and Apple

巴黎，1909 年秋
纸上硬蜡笔和中国水墨画，31.4 x 23.9 cm
国立巴黎毕加索博物馆 / 毕加索代税捐赠，1979. MP640
Paris, autumn 1909
Conté crayon and Chinese ink-wash on paper, 31.4 x 23.9 cm
Musée national Picasso-Paris / Pablo Picasso gift-in-lieu, 1979. MP640

苹果
Apple

巴黎，1909 年秋冬
石膏雕塑，10.5 x 10 x 7.5 cm
国立巴黎毕加索博物馆 / 毕加索代税捐赠，1979. MP242
Paris, autumn – winter 1909
Plaster, 10.5 x 10 x 7.5 cm
Musée national Picasso-Paris / Pablo Picasso gift-in-lieu, 1979. MP242

静物：瓶与杯
Still Life: Bottle and Glass

巴黎，1911 年春
纸上中国水墨画，44.5 x 48.7 cm
国立巴黎毕加索博物馆 / 毕加索代税捐赠，1979. MP652
Paris, spring 1911
Chinese ink-wash on paper, 44.5 x 48.7 cm
Musée national Picasso-Paris / Pablo Picasso gift-in-lieu, 1979. MP652

杯子、烟盒与梅花 A
Glass, Tobacco Pack, and Ace of Clubs

阿维尼翁，1914 年夏
木板油彩、铅笔和沙画，15 x 17.7 cm
国立巴黎毕加索博物馆 / 毕加索代税捐赠，1979. MP50
Avignon, summer 1914
Oil, pencil, and sand on wood, 15 x 17.7 cm
Musée national Picasso-Paris / Pablo Picasso gift-in-lieu, 1979. MP50

杯子和骰子
Glass and Dice

巴黎，1914 年春
彩绘松木结构组件，17 x 16.2 x 5.5 cm
国立巴黎毕加索博物馆 / 毕加索代税捐赠，1979. MP252
Paris, spring 1914
Construction: painted pieces of pine wood, 17 x 16.2 x 5.5 cm
Musée national Picasso-Paris / Pablo Picasso gift-in-lieu, 1979. MP252

杯子、烟斗、报纸和扑克牌
Glass, Pipe, Newspaper, and Playing Card

巴黎，1914 年
纸上石墨铅笔画，32.5 x 23 cm
国立巴黎毕加索博物馆 / 毕加索代税捐赠，1979. MP765
Paris, 1914
Graphite pencil on paper, 32.5 x 23 cm
Musée national Picasso-Paris / Pablo Picasso gift-in-lieu, 1979. MP765

三组静物
Three Still Lifes

阿维尼翁，1914 年秋
纸上羽管笔和棕色墨水画，38 x 49.5 cm
国立巴黎毕加索博物馆 / 毕加索代税捐赠，1979. MP743
Avignon, autumn 1914
Pen and brown ink on paper, 38 x 49.5 cm
Musée national Picasso Paris / Pablo Picasso gift-in-lieu, 1979. MP743

多变毕加索：致敬、引用与古典革新

Picasso the Chameleon: Tributes, Citations, and Classical Revival

“从根本上看，我也许是一个没有风格的画家。风格这种东西，通常将艺术家年复一年，有时甚至是一辈子，限定在同一个视角、技术与程式里……当然也有一些伟大的风格画家。我变化与移动得太快。你看到的是此刻的我，而这个我已经改变了，去到了别的地方。我从不停留在一个地方，这也就是为什么我没有风格。”

“At the root of it, I am perhaps a painter without style. Style is often something that locks the painter into the same vision, the same technique, the same formula for years and years, sometimes for a whole lifetime. […] There are, nevertheless, great painters of style. I myself stir too much, move too much. You see me here, and yet I've already changed; I'm already somewhere else. I'm never fixed, and that's why I have no style.”

[法] 安德烈・韦尔代，《访谈，关于绘画的摘要与写作，布拉克、莱热、马蒂斯与毕加索》，
巴黎，加利利出版社 1978 年版（节选自《说话》杂志集册，格勒诺布尔，1960 年）。
Verdet, André. *Entretiens, notes et écrits sur la peinture, Braque, Léger, Matisse et Picasso.*
Paris: Éditions Galilée, 1978 (excerpts published in the collected volumes of the magazine *Parler*, 1960).

寄给雅克琳与纪尧姆·阿波利奈尔的明信片，照片上是毕加索与奥尔加
1918 年在比亚里茨，奥尔加·毕加索，国立巴黎毕加索博物馆，MP2001-2
Postcard to Jacqueline and Guillaume Apollinaire showing Picasso and Olga in Biarritz in 1918.
Olga Picasso, Musée national Picasso-Paris. MP2001-2.

弗拉迪米尔·波卢宁送给巴勃罗·毕加索的相册，1919 年
弗拉迪米尔·波卢宁和维奥莱特·波卢宁寄来的相册，记录了关于 1919 年夏天在伦敦考文特花园的工作室制作芭蕾舞剧《三角帽》幕布的过程
佚名，国立巴黎毕加索博物馆，APPH15451
Photographic album given to Picasso by Vladimir Polunin, 1919.
Photographic album of Vladimir and Violette Polunin, documenting Picasso producing the curtain for the ballet *Tricorne* in his Covent Garden studio in London.
Anonymous, Musée national Picasso-Paris. APPH15451.

“当我听到人们谈论一位艺术家的演变时，我仿佛看到一个人站在两个面对面的镜子之间，镜子将他的形象无限再现。人们注视着其中一面镜子中的形象，仿佛这代表了他的过去，而另一面镜子则代表了他的未来，同时他自己真正的形象被视为他的现在。人们并没有意识到这些其实都是同一个形象，只不过视角不同而已。”[01]

在立体主义的伟大时代结束之后，1917 年至 1923 年通常被视作毕加索的“古典主义”时期，见证了他对安格尔作品的欣赏和对画布平面性的肯定，这让人联想到他的拼贴画，体现出一种持续的美学追求。前超现实主义风格的作品《恋人》展现出毕加索身上激进的现代性探索，尽管他也同时宣称自己对另一位画坛领袖爱德华・马奈的认同。拒绝被限定于“回归秩序”这种一概而论的说法之中，他挑战所有的分类：不仅如饥似渴地从自己的作品中吸取经验，继续综合立体主义的实践，同时也创作一些更具写实倾向的作品。

《习作》恰好体现了这个独特的创作方式，毕加索在这幅画中聚集并浓缩了自己在 1920 年代早期的一系列艺术探索。新古典主义的灵感（古代样式的女性侧脸）、奥古斯特・雷诺阿的绘画主题（一对舞者）和水晶立体主义（静物）都出现在同一幅画面上，不仅将毕加索受到的各种影响拼贴在一起，也将他同时期充满矛盾性的关注和思考以惊人的方式浓缩呈现。这种多变的新风格出现在毕加索私人生活发生剧烈变化的时期：1918 年，他与一年前在罗马相识的俄罗斯舞蹈家奥尔加・科克洛瓦结婚，随后他们搬到巴黎波艾蒂路上一片美丽的住宅区定居，随着 1921 年 2 月保罗的出生，毕加索初为人父。

1917 年，毕加索为俄罗斯芭蕾舞剧《游行》进行创作，由此开启了他的跨界冒险。1919 年，他接受谢尔盖・佳吉列夫的邀请，热情地为芭蕾舞剧《三角帽》（曼努埃尔・德・法拉作曲，莱奥尼德・马赛因编舞）设计幕布、舞台装饰和服装。在妻子奥尔加的陪伴下，他在伦敦度过了两个多月的时间，创作出这件既具有经典现代性，同时又浸润着典型西班牙影响的代表作。

When I hear talk of the development of an artist, it feels to me like we see him standing between two mirrors face to face, which reproduce his image infinitely. We contemplate the successive images in one of the mirrors as if they represent his past, and those reflected in the other as his future, while his true image is considered his present. We do not perceive that these are the same images, only viewed on different planes.[01]

After the grand years of Cubism, the period between 1917-23, often characterized as “classical,” testifies as much to the artist’s strong admiration for the works of Jean-Auguste-Dominique Ingres as to the permanence of an aesthetic that asserts the flatness of the canvas, which recalls that of his papiers collés. In *The Lovers*, a pre-Surrealist work, Picasso evinces a radical modernity while proclaiming his attachment to another leading figure in painting: Édouard Manet. His work, in rejecting the trappings of a generalized “return to order,” defies categorization: he draws at will on his own work by continuing to practice a Synthetic Cubism, while also realizing pieces with a more illusionistic bent.

A clear illustration of this singular approach, *Studies* concentrates, in one canvas, the research that animated Picasso at the beginning of the 1920s. The work combines Neoclassical inspirations (the atavistic female profile), the iconography of Auguste Renoir (his *Dancing Couple*), and Crystal Cubism (still lifes) into a collage of influences and a striking condensation of the artist’s conflicting, concurrent concerns. This new, chameleon-like style flourished at a time when Picasso’s personal life was marked by major upheavals: marriage, in 1918, to the Russian dancer Olga Khokhlova, whom he met in Rome in 1917; their relocation to the beautiful neighborhood of Rue la Boétie; and the birth of his first child, Paul, in February 1921.

In 1919, following his multi-disciplinary adventure *Parade* with the Ballets Russes in 1917, Picasso accepted an invitation from Sergei Diaghilev and began to work passionately on the curtain, sets, and costumes for the ballet *Tricorne* (music by Manuel de Falla, choreography by Léonide Massine). Accompanied by his wife Olga, he spent over two months in London, where he realized an emblematic work of classic Modernism enriched by distinctively Spanish influences.

01. 毕加索语，转引［墨］马里尤斯・德・扎亚斯：《毕加索说：艺术家的陈述》，载《艺术》1923 年 5 月 19 日。

01. Picasso quoted by de Zayas, Marius. “Picasso Speaks. A Statement by the Artist.” *The Arts* 19 May 1923.

习作
Studies

1920 年
布面油画，100 x 81 cm
国立巴黎毕加索博物馆 / 毕加索代税捐赠，1979. MP65
1920
Oil on canvas, 100 x 81 cm
Musée national Picasso-Paris / Pablo Picasso gift-in-lieu, 1979. MP65

恋人
The Lovers

巴黎，1919 年
布面油画，185 x 140 cm
国立巴黎毕加索博物馆 / 毕加索代税捐赠，1979. MP62
Paris, 1919
Oil on canvas, 185 x 140 cm
Musée national Picasso-Paris / Pablo Picasso gift-in-lieu, 1979. MP62

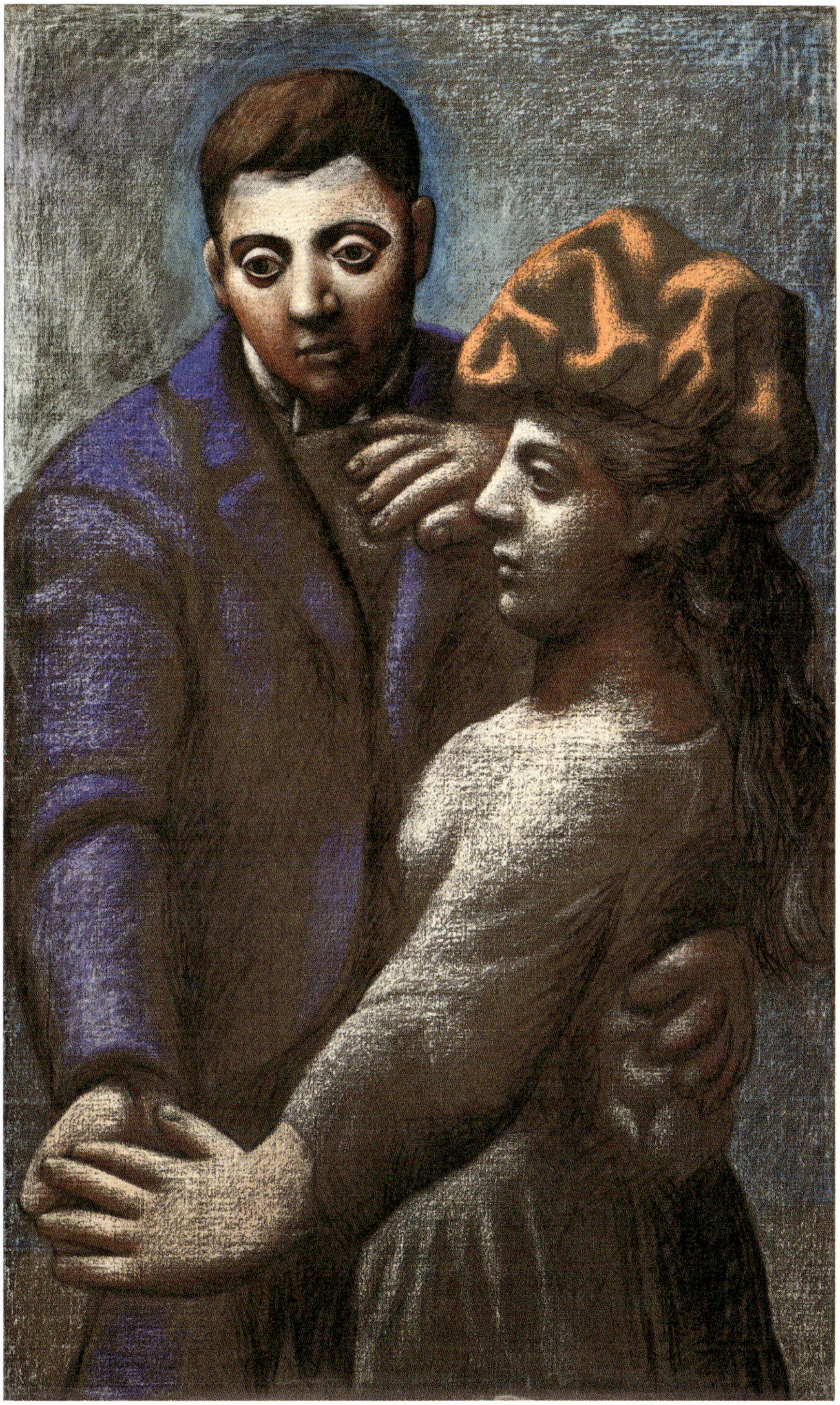

乡村舞蹈
The Village Dance

巴黎，1922 年
布面固定色粉与油彩画，139.5 x 85.5 cm
国立巴黎毕加索博物馆 / 毕加索代税捐赠，1979. MP73
Paris, 1922
Fixed pastel and oil on canvas, 139.5 x 85.5 cm
Musée national Picasso-Paris / Pablo Picasso gift-in-lieu, 1979. MP73

初领圣餐者
The First Communion

1919 年
布面油画，100 x 81 cm
国立巴黎毕加索博物馆 / 雅克琳・毕加索代税捐赠，1990. MP1990-6
1919
Oil on canvas, 100 x 81 cm
Musée national Picasso-Paris / Jacqueline Picasso gift-in-lieu, 1990. MP1990-6

烟斗、杯子和扑克牌
Pipe, Glass, and Playing Card

1918 年
布面油画，38 x 46 cm
国立巴黎毕加索博物馆 / 毕加索代税捐赠，1979. MP58
1918
Oil on canvas, 38 x 46 cm
Musée national Picasso-Paris / Pablo Picasso gift-in-lieu, 1979. MP58

静物：罐子与苹果
Still Life with Pitcher and Apples

1919 年
布面油画，65 x 43 cm
国立巴黎毕加索博物馆 / 毕加索代税捐赠，1979. MP64
1919
Oil on canvas, 65 x 43 cm
Musée national Picasso-Paris / Pablo Picasso gift-in-lieu, 1979. MP64

杯子和烟盒
Glass and Packet of Tobacco

巴黎，1921 年
经切割和弯曲的彩绘金属板与铁丝，14.7 x 48.5 x 17.5 cm
国立巴黎毕加索博物馆 / 毕加索代税捐赠，1979. MP259
Paris, 1921
Painted, crushed, and cut-out metal sheets and iron wires, 14.7 x 48.5 x 17.5 cm
Musée national Picasso-Paris / Pablo Picasso gift-in-lieu, 1979. MP259

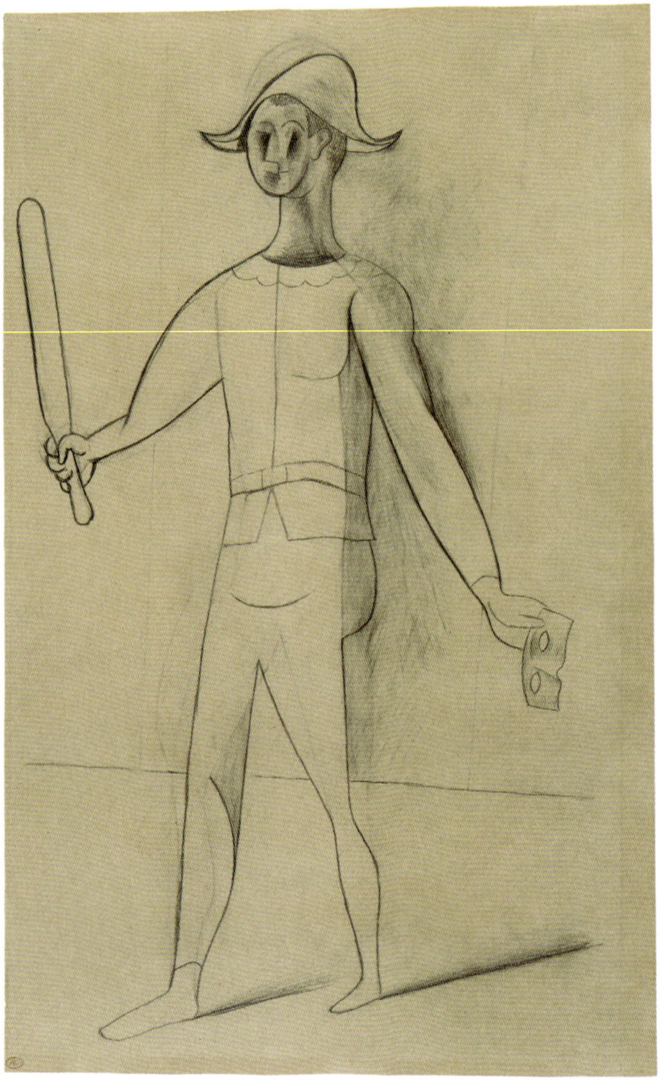

拿着棍子和半截面具的丑角阿尔列金
Harlequin with Bat and Loup

1916 年
纸上石墨铅笔和黑色铅笔画，笔记本册页，48.9 x 30.8 cm
国立巴黎毕加索博物馆 / 毕加索代税捐赠，1979. MP781
1916
Graphite pencil and black pencil on paper, journal page, 48.9 x 30.8 cm
Musée national Picasso-Paris / Pablo Picasso gift-in-lieu, 1979. MP781

小丑皮埃罗与丑角阿尔列金
Pierrot and Harlequin

巴黎，约 1920 年
犊皮纸水粉印模画，保罗·罗森伯格画廊版本，根据毕加索 1920 年夏创作的水粉画复制，30.8 x 24 cm
国立巴黎毕加索博物馆 / 毕加索代税捐赠，1979. MP3507
Paris, c. 1920
Gouache applied with stencil on vellum paper, Galerie Paul Rosenberg edition, based on the original summer 1920 gouache by Picasso, 30.8 x 24 cm
Musée national Picasso-Paris / Pablo Picasso gift-in-lieu, 1979. MP3507

《三角帽》的幕布习作
Study for *Tricorne* Curtain

1920 年
纸上印模画，根据毕加索 1919 年绘制的装饰与服饰设计稿复制，26.1 x 18.3 cm
国立巴黎毕加索博物馆 / 毕加索代税捐赠，1979. MP3576 (2)
1920
Stencil on paper, based on the original 1919 set and costume design by Picasso, 26.1 x 18.3 cm
Musée national Picasso-Paris / Pablo Picasso gift-in-lieu, 1979. MP3576 (2)

《三角帽》装饰习作：最终版装饰模型
Study for *Tricorne* Set: Model for the Final Set

1920 年
纸上印模画，根据毕加索 1919 年绘制的装饰与服饰设计稿复制，20.5 x 27 cm
国立巴黎毕加索博物馆 / 毕加索代税捐赠，1979. MP3576 (1)
1920
Stencil on paper, based on the original 1919 set and costume design by Picasso, 20.5 x 27 cm
Musée national Picasso-Paris / Pablo Picasso gift-in-lieu, 1979. MP3576 (1)

《三角帽》装饰习作：风景
Study for *Tricorne* Set: Landscape

伦敦，1919 年
木板油画，10 x 15 cm
国立巴黎毕加索博物馆 / 毕加索代税捐赠，1979. MP60
London, 1919
Oil on wood, 10 x 15 cm
Musée national Picasso-Paris / Pablo Picasso gift-in-lieu, 1979. MP60

《三角帽》服饰习作：男磨坊主
Study for *Tricorne* Costume: The Miller

1920 年
纸上印模画，根据毕加索 1919 年绘制的装饰与服饰设计稿复制，26.1 x 18.3 cm
国立巴黎毕加索博物馆 / 毕加索代税捐赠，1979. MP3576 (17)
1920
Stencil on paper, based on the original 1919 set and costume design by Picasso, 26.1 x 18.3 cm
Musée national Picasso-Paris / Pablo Picasso gift-in-lieu, 1979. MP3576 (17)

《三角帽》服饰习作：乡村法官
Study for *Tricorne* Costume: The Corregidor

1920 年
纸上印模画，根据毕加索 1919 年绘制的装饰与服饰设计稿复制，26.1 x 18.3 cm
国立巴黎毕加索博物馆 / 毕加索代税捐赠，1979. MP3576 (3)
1920
Stencil on paper, based on the original 1919 set and costume design by Picasso, 26.1 x 18.3 cm
Musée national Picasso-Paris / Pablo Picasso gift-in-lieu, 1979. MP3576 (3)

《三角帽》服饰习作：赛维利亚舞者
Study for *Tricorne* Costume: The Sevillanas Dancer

1920 年
纸上印模画，根据毕加索 1919 年绘制的装饰与服饰设计稿复制，26.2 x 18.8 cm
国立巴黎毕加索博物馆 / 毕加索代税捐赠，1979. MP3576 (8)
1920
Stencil on paper, based on the original 1919 set and costume design by Picasso, 26.2 x 18.8 cm
Musée national Picasso-Paris / Pablo Picasso gift-in-lieu, 1979. MP3576 (8)

《三角帽》服饰习作：斗牛士
Study for *Tricorne* Costume: The Matador

1920 年
纸上印模画，根据毕加索 1919 年绘制的装饰与服饰设计稿复制，26 x 19.2 cm
国立巴黎毕加索博物馆 / 毕加索代税捐赠，1979. MP3576 (11)
1920
Stencil on paper, based on the original 1919 set and costume design by Picasso, 26 x 19.2 cm
Musée national Picasso-Paris / Pablo Picasso gift-in-lieu, 1979. MP3576 (11)

《三角帽》服饰习作：女磨坊主
Study for *Tricorne* Costume: The Miller

1920 年
纸上印模画，根据毕加索 1919 年绘制的装饰与服饰设计稿复制，25.5 x 19.2 cm
国立巴黎毕加索博物馆 / 毕加索代税捐赠，1979. MP3576 (14)
1920
Stencil on paper, based on the original 1919 set and costume design by Picasso, 25.5 x 19.2 cm
Musée national Picasso-Paris / Pablo Picasso gift-in-lieu, 1979. MP3576 (14)

《三角帽》服饰习作：乡村法官的妻子
Study for *Tricorne* Costume: The Corregidor's Wife

1920 年
纸上印模画，根据毕加索 1919 年绘制的装饰与服饰设计稿复制，25.9 x 19 cm
国立巴黎毕加索博物馆 / 毕加索代税捐赠，1979. MP3576 (10)
1920
Stencil on paper, based on the original 1919 set and costume design by Picasso, 25.9 x 19 cm
Musée national Picasso-Paris / Pablo Picasso gift-in-lieu, 1979. MP3576 (10)

“我本想成为一个画家，然而我却成为了毕加索。”

“I wanted to be a painter, and so I became Picasso.”

[法] 皮埃尔・戴克思：《新毕加索词典》，罗贝尔・拉封出版社 2012 年版，第 124 页。
Daix, Pierre. *Le nouveau dictionnaire Picasso*. Robert Laffont, 2012, p. 124.

毕加索右手扶头肖像，位于富尔纳的工作室，瓦洛里斯，1954 年 6 月 2 日
纽曼·阿布纳·阿尔诺，（又称）阿尔诺·纽曼
国立巴黎毕加索博物馆，APPH2505
Portrait of Picasso with his head in his right hand in his studio at Le Fournas, Vallauris, 2 June 1954.
Arnold Abner Newman, also known as Arnold Newman,
Musée national Picasso-Paris. APPH2505.

毕加索在位于戛纳的“加利福尼亚”工作室里绘画，1957 年
2013 年冲印，大卫·邓肯·道格拉斯，国立巴黎毕加索博物馆，DunDav097
Pablo Picasso drawing in his studio La Californie in Cannes in 1957.
David Douglas Duncan, reprinted in 2013, Musée national Picasso-Paris. DunDav097.

阅读
Reading

波格鲁，1932 年 1 月 2 日
布面油画，130 x 97.5 cm
国立巴黎毕加索博物馆 / 毕加索代税捐赠，1979. MP137
Boisgeloup, 2 January 1932
Oil on canvas, 130 x 97.5 cm
Musée national Picasso-Paris / Pablo Picasso gift-in-lieu, 1979. MP137

玛丽 - 特瑞斯肖像
Portrait of Marie-Thérèse

巴黎，1937 年 1 月 6 日
布面油画，100 x 81 cm
国立巴黎毕加索博物馆 / 毕加索代税捐赠，1979. MP159
Paris, 6 January 1937
Oil on canvas, 100 x 81 cm
Musée national Picasso-Paris / Pablo Picasso gift-in-lieu, 1979. MP159

扔石头的女人
Woman Throwing a Stone

巴黎，1931 年 3 月 8 日
布面油画，130.5 x 195.5 cm
国立巴黎毕加索博物馆 / 毕加索代税捐赠，1979. MP133
Paris, 8 March 1931
Oil on canvas, 130.5 x 195.5 cm
Musée national Picasso-Paris / Pablo Picasso gift-in-lieu, 1979. MP133

白色背景上的裸体
Nude on White Background

巴黎，1927 年
布面油画，130 x 97 cm
国立巴黎毕加索博物馆 / 毕加索代税捐赠，1979. MP102
Paris, 1927
Oil on canvas, 130 x 97 cm
Musée national Picasso-Paris / Pablo Picasso gift-in-lieu, 1979. MP102

头顶瓮罐的女人
Woman Carrying a Jar

1935 年
水泥与木质底座、彩绘木料、现成品、钉子，60 x 14 x 18.4 cm
国立巴黎毕加索博物馆 / 毕加索代税捐赠，1979. MP315
1935
Pieces of painted wood, objects, nails on base made of cement and wood, 60 x 14 x 18.4 cm
Musée national Picasso-Paris / Pablo Picasso gift-in-lieu, 1979. MP315

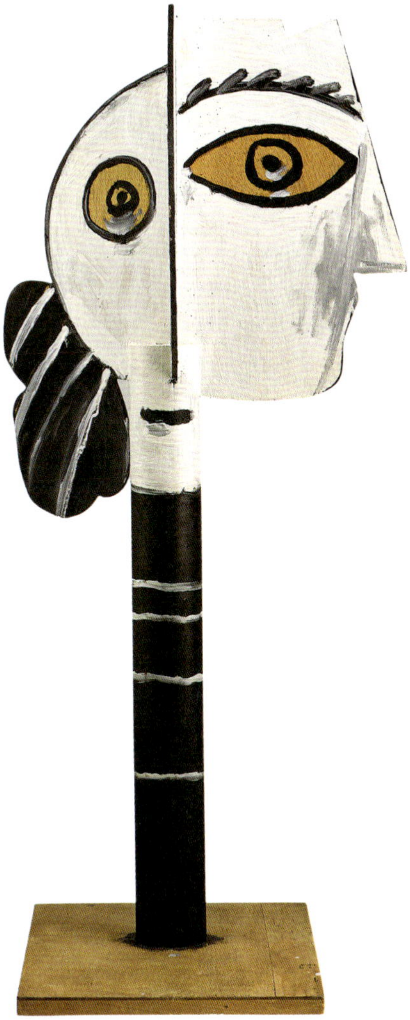

女子头像
Head of Woman

戛纳，1957 年
彩绘切割木料，78.5 x 34 x 36 cm
国立巴黎毕加索博物馆 / 毕加索代税捐赠，1979. MP350
Cannes, 1957
Painted and cut wood, 78.5 x 34 x 36 cm
Musée national Picasso-Paris / Pablo Picasso gift-in-lieu, 1979. MP350

年轻的画家
The Young Painter

穆然，1972 年 4 月 14 日
布面油画，91 x 72.5 cm
国立巴黎毕加索博物馆 / 毕加索代税捐赠，1979. MP228
Mougins, 14 April 1972
Oil on canvas, 91 x 72.5 cm
Musée national Picasso-Paris / Pablo Picasso gift-in-lieu, 1979. MP228

画布前的艺术家
Artist in Front of His Canvas

巴黎，1938 年 3 月 22 日
布面炭笔画，130 x 94 cm
国立巴黎毕加索博物馆 / 毕加索代税捐赠，1979. MP172
Paris, 22 March 1938
Fusain on canvas, 130 x 94 cm
Musée national Picasso-Paris / Pablo Picasso gift-in-lieu, 1979. MP172

吻
The Kiss

穆然，1969 年 10 月 26 日
布面油画，97 x 130 cm
国立巴黎毕加索博物馆 / 毕加索代税捐赠，1979. MP220
Mougins, 26 October 1969
Oil on canvas, 97 x 130 cm
Musée national Picasso-Paris / Pablo Picasso gift-in-lieu, 1979. MP220

附录　　Appendix

年 表

1881
10 月 25 日，巴勃罗・毕加索在马拉加出生，其父亲何塞・鲁伊兹・布拉斯科 (1838—1913) 是一位画家与绘画老师，其母亲是玛利亚・毕加索・洛佩兹 (1855—1939)。

1888
毕加索在他父亲的鼓励之下开始绘画。

1891
毕加索一家搬到拉科鲁尼亚。1892 年至 1895 年，毕加索在他父亲任教的美术学院学习装饰课。

1895
毕加索的父亲被任命为巴塞罗那美术学院（又称为“隆哈美院”）的老师。毕加索首次参观位于马德里的普拉多美术馆。回到巴塞罗那之后，他创作了多幅自然主义风格的作品，包括《光脚的女人》（藏于国立巴黎毕加索博物馆）。

1897
毕加索被马德里圣费尔南多学院录取，学习风景画与古典素描。他在这里创作了艺术生涯中的第一幅大尺寸油画《科学与仁爱》（藏于巴塞罗那毕加索博物馆）。这幅作品在马德里获得荣誉提名，然后在“马拉加综合艺术展览”获得金奖。

1899
毕加索回到巴塞罗那之后，与当地的先锋艺术家往来密切，他们经常在“四只猫”咖啡馆聚会。他在这里遇到了艺术家朱尼尔 - 维达勒、尚耶尔、卡萨吉马斯、马诺洛・胡古埃（人称马诺洛）。

1900
毕加索因为作品《最后的时刻》（1903 年，他在这幅作品之上绘制了另一幅作品《生命》，藏于克利夫兰博物馆），而入选 4 月 14 日在巴黎开幕的世界博览会。当年 10 月中旬，他第一次来到法国首都，并且在蒙马特居住了一段时间。他经常前往西班牙艺术家在巴黎的聚集地，与陶瓷艺术家帕克・杜里奥，以及雕塑家马诺洛往来尤为密切。年底，毕加索回到了马德里。

1901
毕加索在马德里得知好友卡萨吉马斯在巴黎的一家咖啡店自杀身亡。他创立发行了自己的第一本杂志《年轻艺术》（*Arte Joven*）。20 岁的毕加索回到巴黎，筹备他将于 6 月在佛拉画廊开幕的首次个展。毕加索在这一年找到了新的艺术方向，开启了蓝色时期，其特点是以忧郁的形象展现当时的社会苦难，色调以蓝色为主。

1902
毕加索往返于巴黎与巴塞罗那之间，在这个时期的绘画中，可以清晰地感受到巴黎蓝色的夜晚与西班牙光线的相遇。毕加索开始创作雕塑。他在巴黎因生活拮据，不得不与诗人马克斯・雅各布在一间狭小的酒店房间内合住。画廊主贝尔特・威仪为毕加索举办了他在巴黎的第二次展览。

1903
毕加索在巴塞罗那的这一年创作力旺盛，创作了包括《生命》在内的杰作，这是一件关于生命周而复始的寓言，隐喻神圣与世俗之爱。

1904
4 月回到巴黎之后，毕加索搬到了蒙马特山丘上的“洗衣船”工作室。他的调色盘逐渐丰富起来，蓝色时期进入尾声。毕加索结识了他的模特同时也是邻居费尔南德・奥利维耶，两个人一起生活至 1912 年。

1905
毕加索重新将色彩引入他的作品之中，马戏主题大量出现，成为了粉色时期的标志性特点。他在这一年认识的诗人朋友纪尧姆・阿波利奈尔也将这个时期称为“杂耍艺人”时期。毕加索在瑟鲁利耶画廊举办展览之后，2 月与美国收藏家雷欧与格特鲁德・斯泰因相识。这两位藏家购买毕加索的作品，从资金上支持毕加索的创作。毕加索在秋季参观了安格尔的回顾展，他在展览上看到了《土耳其浴室》（藏于巴黎卢浮宫博物馆）。

1906
这一年毕加索 25 岁，他在卢浮宫参观了来自奥苏纳和赛罗德罗斯桑托斯（西班牙）的出土文物展，由此发现了古代伊比利亚的雕塑艺术。

毕加索在加泰罗尼亚一个名叫戈索尔的偏僻村庄度过了夏天，他第一次运用直刻雕塑的创作手法，并且绘制了一系列的绘画。当年秋天，他参观了秋季沙龙的保罗・高更回顾展，备受震动。

1907
毕加索购买了两尊伊比利亚的雕刻头像。在阿波利奈尔的介绍下，他在巴黎的独立艺术家沙龙上认识了乔治・布拉克，并且参观了特罗卡德罗艺术和人类博物馆。夏天的时候，他完成了《阿维尼翁的少女》（藏于纽约现代艺术博物馆），他仅向周围亲近的朋友展示了这件作品。《阿维尼翁的少女》如今被认为是立体主义的奠基之作与现代艺术的革新之作。

1908
毕加索在亨利・马蒂斯的介绍下，结识了俄罗斯收藏家谢尔盖・休金。为了表达对画家“海关关税员卢梭”的敬意，毕加索在 11 月组织了一场晚餐聚会，参加者包括阿波利奈尔、安德烈・萨尔蒙、乔治・布拉克和格特鲁德・斯泰因。从这年冬天开始，毕加索和布拉克每天都讨论图像创作的议题。

1909
毕加索在巴塞罗那居住了一段时间，随后前往埃布罗河岸的奥尔塔（西班牙）绘制了一系列原始主义与塞尚主义风格结合的几何风景。回到巴黎之后，他与费尔南德・奥利维耶一起搬到克里希大街 11 号的工作室居住，他在那里创作了几件《女子头像》石膏作品。毕加索以多个刻面呈现女子的脸庞，将自己对立体主义的探索转移到雕塑之中。

巴勃罗・毕加索青年肖像
阿尔道夫・费尔南德兹・卡萨马约
巴塞罗那，1895—1896 年
国立巴黎毕加索博物馆，APPH15356

素描本 1，27 页背面，1899 年至 1900 年冬
纸上彩色铅笔、炭笔、油彩素描，31.5 x 22cm
国立巴黎毕加索博物馆，MP1990-93

毕加索父亲何塞・鲁伊兹・布拉斯科在巴塞罗那
出自《蓝色时期之前的毕加索（1881—1901）》，第 278

光脚的小女孩
拉科鲁尼亚，1895 年
布面油画，75 x 50 cm
国立巴黎毕加索博物馆，MP2

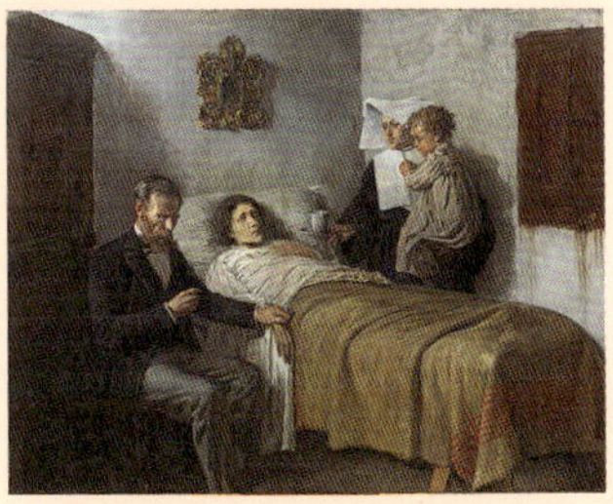

科学与仁爱
巴塞罗那，1897 年 1—4 月
布面油画，197.5 x 250 cm
巴塞罗那毕加索美术馆，毕加索捐赠，1970 年
MPB 110.046

“四只猫”咖啡馆的菜单
1899 年，巴塞罗毕加索美术馆

毕加索，安吉尔·迪索多和卡洛斯·卡萨吉玛斯在梅尔塞德街 3 号
帕拉列斯·I. 格鲁·曼努尔
巴塞罗那，约 1900 年
1950 年，翻底片，18.2 x 24 cm
国立巴黎毕加索博物馆，APPH15324.

男子肖像
巴塞罗那，1902 年冬至 1903 年
布面油画，93 x 78 cm
国立巴黎毕加索博物馆，MP5

生命
巴塞罗那，1903 年
布面油画，196.5 x 129.2 cm
克利夫兰艺术博物馆

巴勃罗·毕加索肖像，拍摄于里卡多·卡纳尔斯
在“洗衣船”的工作室，里卡多·卡纳尔斯
巴黎，1904 年，翻底片
冲印时间未知，明胶银盐相纸，16 x 11.2 cm
国立巴黎毕加索博物馆，FPPH130

疯子
巴黎，1905 年
青铜雕塑，为艺术品商人安伯斯·佛拉铸造
的版本，41.5 x 37 x 22.8 cm
国立巴黎毕加索博物馆，毕加索代税捐赠
1979. MP231

杂耍艺人之家
巴黎，1905 年
布面油画，212.8 x 229.6 cm
华盛顿国家艺术馆

1910

毕加索的创作朝着“分析立体主义”的风格发展。他开始创作一系列的肖像。丹尼尔 - 亨利·康维勒成为他的代理商。

1911

毕加索的作品在德国（1 月和 2 月在卡希尔画廊，5 月在分离派）和美国（3 月和 4 月在纽约 291 画廊）展出。巴黎秋季沙龙的立体主义展厅里，布拉克与毕加索的作品均缺席其中，因为他们的立体主义风格作品已经日益变得隐晦费解。

毕加索和马诺洛、布拉克、胡安·格里斯一起在塞雷度过了夏天。11 月，他遇到了伊娃·谷维，她是路易斯·马库锡的前任情人。他与伊娃的关系将一直持续到 1915 年末。

1912

1 月份的时候，毕加索的作品在莫斯科“金羊毛”展出。他和阿波利奈尔一起创立了《巴黎之夜》杂志。

2 月份，与“蓝骑士”团体一起在慕尼黑和柏林分离派展出。与布拉克在勒阿弗尔短住。

5 月份，毕加索在他的绘画中引入镂空字母版与沙子，该年春天，他创作出第一件拼贴作品《藤椅上的静物》（藏于国立巴黎毕加索博物馆）。

夏天，他与伊娃在塞雷和索戈尔短住。他在这期间与康维勒通信密切。

回到巴黎之后，他搬到拉斯帕伊大道的工作室，在那里制作了第一批拼贴画和构建作品《吉他》（纽约现代艺术博物馆）。这件由日常材料组装而成（纸板、报纸、线）的三维作品为雕塑界带来了一场革命。

1913

参加纽约军械库的“国际现代艺术展”，随后在慕尼黑的唐豪瑟画廊参展。在塞雷居住期间，他开始创作一系列全新的拼贴作品。毕加索的父亲 5 月 3 日去世。从巴塞罗那回到巴黎之后，毕加索搬到了舍尔歇街副 5 号的新工作室，埃米勒·德勒唐在这个工作室里为康维勒拍摄了多幅组合装置的照片。

1914

弗拉基米尔·塔特林参观了毕加索的工作室。毕加索和伊娃一起前往阿维尼翁，与布拉克、安德烈·德兰汇合。

8 月 3 日，德国向法国宣战：布拉克与德兰被征召入伍，阿波利奈尔也加入军队。毕加索没有被征调。他与伊娃·谷维一直在塞雷居住到 11 月。

1915

2 月 18 日，毕加索成为了马克斯·雅各布的孩子的教父。布拉克受伤严重。伊娃·谷维生重病于 12 月去世。毕加索创作了一系列“安格尔式”风格的作品。

1916

阿波利奈尔受伤并进行了穿颅手术。在安德烈·德兰的组织下，《阿维尼翁的少女》首次在巴黎的安廷沙龙展示。康维勒前往瑞士避难。经让·科克托介绍，毕加索结识了俄罗斯芭蕾舞团团长谢尔盖·佳吉列夫。毕加索搬至蒙鲁日的维克多·雨果街 22 号。

1917

毕加索与俄罗斯芭蕾舞团一道前往意大利，一路从罗马旅行至庞贝，结识了芭蕾舞者奥尔加·科克洛娃以及伊戈尔·斯特拉文斯基。5 月 18 日，芭蕾舞剧《游行》在巴黎的夏特莱剧院首演（让·科克托编写剧情大纲，埃里克·萨蒂配乐，莱奥尼德·马赛因编舞，毕加索设计幕布、装饰与服饰，纪尧姆·阿波利奈尔撰写剧目介绍）。

1918

展览“马蒂斯—毕加索”在保罗·纪尧姆画廊开幕。7 月 12 日，毕加索与奥尔加·科克洛娃在巴黎的俄罗斯教堂结婚。马克斯·雅各布、阿波利奈尔、科克托是证婚人。保罗·罗森伯格成为毕加索的经纪人 。与安德烈·布勒东相识。 11 月 9 日，阿波利奈尔因为感染西班牙流感去世。两天之后，签署了第一次世界大战停战协议。前往比亚里茨蜜月旅行之后，这对新婚夫妇搬到波艾蒂路 23 号居住。

1919

毕加索与胡安·米罗相识。他与佳吉列夫合作，在伦敦与弗拉迪米尔·波卢宁一起为芭蕾舞剧《三角帽》设计舞台装饰与服饰。该剧在 7 月 22 日在阿罕布拉剧院首演即大获成功（佩德罗·德·阿拉康编写剧情大纲，曼努埃尔·德·法利亚配乐，毕加索设计幕布与服饰）。毕加索与佳吉列夫再次合作，为佩尔戈莱西的舞剧《普钦奈拉》（巴黎歌剧院，直至 1920 年）设计立体主义的布景，服饰则从意大利即兴喜剧（Commedia dell'Arte）中汲取灵感。毕加索首次前往昂蒂布海角短住。

1920

康维勒回到巴黎，创立西蒙画廊。毕加索为妻子绘制了多幅油画与素描，奥尔加当时正怀着他们的第一个孩子。

1921

2 月 4 日，他的第一个儿子保罗出生。毕加索一家在枫丹白露度过了夏天，这次假期给了他灵感绘制诸如《喷泉边的三女子》（藏于国立巴黎毕加索博物馆）等多幅作品。安德烈·布勒东写信给雅克·杜塞，劝他购买《阿维尼翁的少女》“这幅标志着立体主义诞生的作品”。

1924

杜塞购买了《阿维尼翁的少女》。

1925

毕加索在皮埃尔画廊参加超现实主义群展。

1926

克里斯汀·泽尔沃斯创办的《艺术手册》首刊发行。

素描册 10，18 页背面：第 12 幅习作，5 位女子与 1 位海员的 6 人群像
《阿维尼翁少女》的素描本，1907 年 5 月—6 月
羽笔和中国墨水素描，10.5 x 13.5cm
国立巴黎毕加索博物馆，MP1862folio18recto

阿维尼翁的少女
巴黎，1907 年 6—7 月
布面油画， 243.9 x 233.7 cm
纽约现代艺术博物馆，莉莉·P. 布里斯遗赠：333.1939

藤椅上的静物
1912 年春
绳框蜡布面油彩，29 x 37cm
国立巴黎毕加索博物馆，MP36

巴勃罗·毕加索在雕塑家伊格纳西奥·皮纳佐·马蒂内兹位于“洗衣船”的工作室
佚名，巴黎，1908 年
明胶银盐相纸，17.1 x 12.3cm
国立巴黎毕加索博物馆，APPH2810

习作《站立的裸体像》，位于“洗衣船”工作室
巴黎，1908 年春
明胶溴化银玻璃负片，12 x 9cm
国立巴黎毕加索博物馆，APPH17404

毕加索在最终版本的《把臂肘支在桌子上的男子》前，他于 1916 年巴黎在舍尔歇街的工作室重新改动了这幅作品，朵拉·玛尔
巴黎，1916 年
佚名照片复制，约 1937—1940 年
明胶银盐相纸，23.7 x 17.2 cm
国立巴黎毕加索博物馆，MP1998-138

弹曼陀林的男子
巴黎，1911 年秋
布面油画，162 x 71 cm
国立巴黎毕加索博物馆，巴勃罗·毕加索代税捐赠，1979.MP35

吉他
巴黎，1912 年 12 月
纸板、细绳和布料组合，22 x 14.5 x 0.7cm
国立巴黎毕加索博物馆，MP245

吉他
巴黎，1912 年 10—12 月
纸板、纸、线、绳、麻绳和带涂层电线
65.4 x 33 x 19 cm
纽约现代艺术博物馆，艺术家捐赠，640.1973

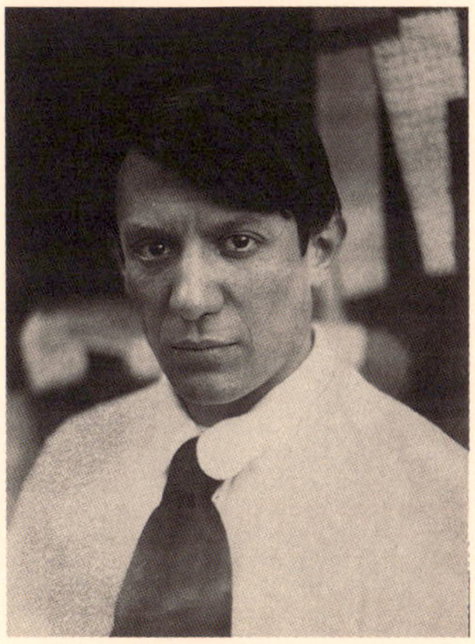

毕加索肖像，拍摄于舍尔歇街的工作室
佚名，巴黎，1915—1916 年
明胶银盐相纸，18 x 12.9 cm
国立巴黎毕加索博物馆，APPH2829

为《游行》设计的幕布
1917 年，布面油画，1050 x 1640cm
巴黎蓬皮杜国家艺术文化中心，1955 年购买AM3365P

《游行》的幕布设计方案
1916—1917 年
纸上水彩与铅颜料
国立巴黎毕加索博物馆，MP1557

1927

毕加索开始与玛丽 - 黛莱丝・瓦尔代尔秘密交往。

1928

这年夏天，毕加索全家前往迪纳尔度假，他开始以“女浴者”为主题创作，画中女子形象的灵感来自他秘密相见的年轻情人。

同年，他的作品中开始出现“米诺牛”的主题，这也是毕加索与妻子的关系不断恶化的迹象。

1930

毕加索买下布瓦吉鲁城堡（诺曼底），从此拥有了一间宽敞的工作室，这里不仅为放置雕塑提供了空间，也方便集中创作雕版画。

1932

这是毕加索艺术生涯具有关键性的一年。泽尔沃出版了第一卷毕加索作品集（1896—1906），该系列作品集到毕加索去世时一共出版了 33 卷。同年，乔治・佩蒂特画廊为毕加索举办了首次回顾展，这个展览随后巡展至苏黎世美术馆。

毕加索创作了大量以玛丽 - 黛莱丝・瓦尔代尔为灵感的女性形象。

1935

与奥尔加和保罗在西班牙短住之后，这对夫妻正式分别。9 月 5 日，玛丽 - 黛莱丝・瓦尔代尔生下了玛莉亚・狄・拉・康塞普西翁，小名玛雅。

毕加索遇到了摄影师朵拉・玛尔，两人发展成情人关系，这期间他中断了绘画创作并开始写作诗歌。

1937

毕加索搬到大奥古斯丁街 7 号。应西班牙共和国政府的邀请，毕加索为在巴黎举行的“国际现代生活艺术与技术博览会”的西班牙馆创作一件作品——巨幅作品《格尔尼卡》（藏于索菲亚王后艺术中心，马德里），控诉与弗朗哥将军联盟的纳粹军队对西班牙巴斯克地区的村庄的空袭。

1939–1945

第二次世界大战期间（1939—1945），毕加索在巴黎与法国南部居住。

1943

5 月，与弗朗索瓦丝・吉洛相识，她将成为毕加索 1944 年到 1953 年间的伴侣，并为他生下两个孩子: 1947 年 5 月 15 日出生的克劳德，1949 年 4 月 19 日出生的帕洛玛。1944 年 10 月，毕加索在《人道报》宣布自己加入法国共产党。

1946

罗姆奥德・多尔・德・拉苏切尔邀请毕加索来到自己位于昂蒂布的格里马尔迪城堡，并允许毕加索将城堡的一部分作为工作室使用。毕加索在这里创作了一系列的作品，并将一部分作品寄存在昂蒂布。这些作品将构成 20 年之后开幕的世界上第一座毕加索博物馆的藏品。

同年在美国，阿尔弗雷德・巴尔在纽约现代艺术博物馆出版了《毕加索：50 年的艺术创作》。

1950 年代

世界多地都在举行他的作品展：先后在大阪和东京举行的大型回顾展，同时也包括欧洲（尤其是米兰）或拉丁美洲，毕加索在第二届圣保罗双年展展出了他的《格尔尼卡》。一个大型的回顾展在科隆、慕尼黑和汉堡巡回举办。

1950

毕加索来到法国南部定居，继续他的创作实验，尤其在陶瓷、组合雕塑方面。该年，他获得国际列宁和平奖。

1955

2 月 11 日，奥尔加在戛纳去世。该年夏天，亨利・乔治・克鲁佐拍摄了《毕加索的秘密》，该片获得了戛纳电影节评委会特别奖。

1957

毕加索围绕委拉斯凯兹的《宫娥》这一主题进行研究与创作。

1958

联合国教科文组织在巴黎设立总部，毕加索为此创作了装饰壁画《伊卡洛斯的坠落》。

1960 年代

这十年间的创作重点是“画家与模特”系列，以及一系列情色主题的雕版画作品。

1960

伦敦泰特美术馆举行了大型毕加索回顾展。

1962

与杰奎琳・洛克结婚。同年第 2 次获得国际列宁和平奖。

1963

巴塞罗那毕加索博物馆成立。1966 年，巴黎小皇宫、大皇宫与法国国家图书馆举办大型回顾展“致敬毕加索”。

1970 年代

毕加索向巴塞罗那毕加索博物馆捐赠了一批极为重要的作品，极大丰富了该美术馆的馆藏，使其成为世界上毕加索年轻时期作品馆藏最丰富的美术馆。毕加索从 1969 年到 1970 年的作品，也就是他最后一段高产创作时期的作品在阿维尼翁教皇宫展出。

毕加索在卢浮宫的大画廊展示了 8 幅画作。巴黎市政府授予其荣誉市民称号。

1973

4 月 8 日，巴勃罗・毕加索在位于穆然的住所“生命圣母院”去世，享年 91 岁。毕加索死后葬于沃维纳尔格城堡。

阿维尼翁教皇宫举行了包含两百幅毕加索遗作的展览“巴勃罗・毕加索 1970—1972”。

毕加索和奥尔加・科克洛娃在米涅尔娃酒店的屋顶花园
佚名，罗马，1917
明胶银盐相纸，7 x 11.42cm
国立巴黎毕加索博物馆，APPH3627(11)

毕加索 1920 年代的肖像
佚名，约 1920 年
国立巴黎毕加索博物馆，APPH6738

毕加索和奥尔加抱着保罗，美丽玫瑰别墅的花园
佚名，胡安莱潘，1925 年夏
明胶银盐相纸，7.6 x 12cm
国立巴黎毕加索博物馆，APPH6464

红扶手椅上的裸体
巴黎，1929 年 5 月 5 日
布面油画，195 x 129cm
国立巴黎毕加索博物馆，MP113

女子头像
1931 年
木头与石膏，128.5 x 54.5 x 62.5 cm
国立巴黎毕加索博物馆，MP301

山洞前的米诺牛与死去的母马，面对带着面纱的女孩
胡安莱潘，1936 年 5 月 6 日
中国墨水水粉画，50 x 65cm
国立巴黎毕加索博物馆，MP1163

格尔尼卡
1937 年
布面油画，350 x 782cm
马德里索菲亚王后国家艺术中心博物馆

鸽子
1949 年 1 月 9 日
锌版上水墨，56.7 x 76.2 cm
国立巴黎毕加索博物馆，MP3414

毕加索右手扶头肖像，位于富尔纳的工作室
阿尔诺・纽曼，瓦洛里斯
1954 年 6 月 2 日
明胶银盐相纸，24.5 x 19.6cm
国立巴黎毕加索博物馆，APPH2505

音乐家
穆然，1972 年 5 月 26 日
布面油画，194.5 x 129.5cm
国立巴黎毕加索博物馆，MP229

Chronology

1881

25 October
Pablo Picasso is born in Málaga. He is the son of José Ruiz y Blasco (1838-1913), painter and drawing instructor, and María Picasso y López (1855-1939).

1888

Encouraged by his father, Picasso paints his first works.

1891

The Picasso family moves to La Coruña. From 1892 to 1895, Picasso attends his father's art school, where he takes classes in the decorative arts.

1895

Don José becomes a professor at the School of Fine Arts in Barcelona, La Llotja. Picasso makes his first visit to the Prado Museum in Madrid. On his return to Barcelona, he produces several works in a naturalist vein, including *The Barefoot Girl* (Musée national Picasso-Paris).

1897

Picasso is admitted to the Real Academia de Bellas Artes de San Fernando in Madrid, where he attends classes in landscape painting and classical drawing. He produces his first great work, *Science and Charity* (Museu Picasso, Barcelona). The work receives an honorable mention at the General Exhibition of Fine Arts in Madrid, and later wins the Gold Medal at the Provincial Exhibition of Málaga.

1899

Picasso returns to Barcelona and becomes a member of the avant-garde there, who hold meetings at the café Els Quatre Gats. He makes the acquaintances of artists Sebastià Junyer i Vidal, Joaquim Sunyer, Carles Casagemas, and Manolo Hugué (known as Manolo).

1900

With the work *Last Moments* (painted over in 1903 with *La Vie*, Cleveland Museum of Art), Picasso is selected for display at the Exposition Universelle, which opens in Paris on 14 April. He arrives in the French capital for the first time in the middle of October and stays in Montmartre for a period. He frequents the community of Spanish artists there and becomes close with ceramicist Paco Durio and sculptor Manolo. He returns to Madrid at the end of the year.

1901

Picasso is staying in Madrid when he learns that his friend Casagemas has committed suicide in a Parisian café. He publishes his first magazine, *Arte Joven*. At twenty years old, Picasso returns to the French capital to prepare for his first exhibition at Galerie Vollard, set to open in June. This is the year when Picasso's art takes a new direction, marking the beginning of his Blue Period: a style characterized by melancholic depictions of the era's social destitution and a palette dominated by blue.

1902

Picasso is living between Paris and Barcelona. This is echoed in his works, where the blue of the Parisian night meets Spanish sunlight. He also creates his first sculptures. Amid financial difficulties, Picasso moves into a small hotel room in Paris, which he shares with the poet Max Jacob. Gallery owner Berthe Weill exhibits Picasso for the second time in Paris.

1903

Picasso has a prolific year living in Barcelona, where he realizes his masterpiece *La Vie*, an allegory for the cycle of life and a metaphor for love both sacred and profane.

1904

In April, upon his return to Paris, Picasso moves into a studio in Bateau-Lavoir, Montmartre. His color palette gradually expands at the end of the year. It is the end of his Blue Period. He meets Fernande Olivier, a model and neighbor, with whom he lives until 1912.

1905

The reintroduction of color and the predominance of circus themes that characterize works from this year come to constitute the Rose Period. This style is also called the Saltimbanques Period by Guillaume Apollinaire, a poet whom Picasso befriends at this time. Following his exhibition at Serrurier Gallery in February, Picasso meets American collectors Leo and Gertrude Stein, who desire to support him financially through the purchase of his works. In autumn, he visits a retrospective of Jean-Auguste-Dominique Ingres, where he discovers the painting *The Turkish Bath* (Louvre Museum, Paris).

1906

Now 25, Picasso visits an exhibition at the Louvre of objects discovered in archeological digs in Osuna and Cerro de los Santos, Spain. Here, he discovers classical Iberian sculpture for the first time.

While spending the summer in Gósol, a remote village in Catalonia, Picasso works on his first sculpture that employs direct carving, and he produces an important cycle of paintings. In autumn, he is moved by a retrospective of Paul Gauguin's works, part of the Salon d'Automne.

1907

Picasso purchases two Iberian head sculptures. Through Apollinaire, he meets Georges Braque at the Salon des Indépendants in Paris, and he also visits the Trocadéro Ethnography Museum. During the summer, he completes *Les Demoiselles d'Avignon* (Museum of Modern Art, New York), which he shows only to his close friends. Today, this work is considered the foundation of Cubism and a revolution in modern art.

1908

Picasso meets the Russian art collector Sergei Shchukin through fellow painter Henri Matisse. In homage to the painter Henri Rousseau, Picasso organizes a dinner in November, attended by Apollinaire, André Salmon, Georges Braque, and Gertrude Stein. By winter, Picasso is engaging in daily discussions on art with Braque.

1909

Picasso stays in Barcelona for a while, then spends the summer in Horta de Ebro in Spain, where he paints a series of geometric landscapes. With these works, he achieves a synthesis of Primitivism and a Cézanne-like style. He returns to Paris and moves into a workshop at 11 Boulevard de Clichy with Fernande Olivier, where he creates the plaster mold for *Head of a Woman*. By representing the face through various planes, Picasso transposes his Cubist research onto the field of sculpture.

Portrait of young Picasso
Adolfo Fernández Casamayor
Barcelona, 1895-96
Musée national Picasso-Paris. APPH15356

Sketchbook 1, Folio 27 Recto, Goyaesque Scene
Barcelona, winter 1899-1900
Charcoal, colored pencil, and oil on paper 31.5 x 22cm
Musée national Picasso-Paris
Gift-in-lieu Jacqueline Picasso, 1990. MP1990-93

Photograph of Picasso's father, José Ruiz Blasco, in Barcelona
From Picasso *Antes del azul (1881-1901)*, p. 278

The Barefoot Girl
La Coruña, 1895
Oil on canvas, 75 x 50 cm
Musée national Picasso-Paris. MP2

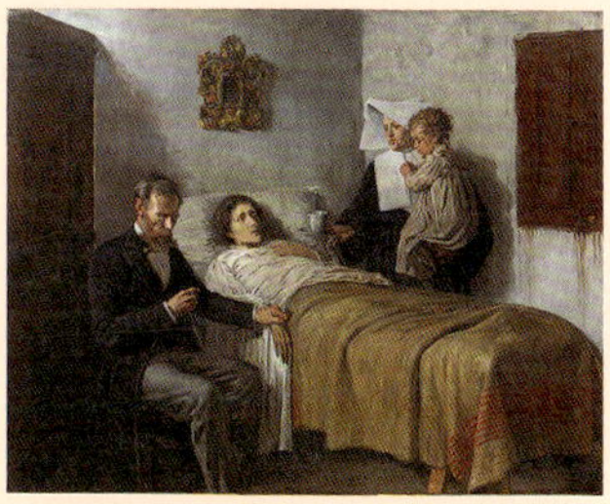

Science and Charity
Barcelona, January – April 1897
Oil on canvas, 197.5 x 250 cm
Museu Picasso, Barcelona, gift of Pablo Picasso, 1970. MPB 110.046

Menu from 'Els Quatre Gats'
1899
Museu Picasso, Barcelona

Pablo Picasso, Angel de Soto, and Carles Casagemas on the roof of 3 Rue de la Merced
Pallarès i Grau Manuel
Barcelona, around 1900, 18.2 x 24 cm
Internegative produced c. 1950
Musée national Picasso-Paris. APPH15324

Portrait of a Man
Barcelona, winter 1902-03
Oil on canvas, 93 x 78 cm
Musée national Picasso-Paris. MP5

La Vie
Barcelona, May 1903
Oil on canvas, 196.5 x 129.2 cm
The Cleveland Museum of Art

Portrait of Picasso in the studio of Ricard Canals in Bateau-Lavoir
Ricard Canals
Paris, 1904
Printing date unknown, silver gelatin print, 16 x 11.2 cm
Musée national Picasso-Paris. FPPH130

The Jester
Paris, 1905
Bronze, edition for art dealer Ambrose Voillard, 41.5 x 37 x 22.8 cm
Musée national Picasso-Paris
Pablo Picasso gift-in-lieu, 1979. MP231

Family of Saltimbanques
Paris, 1905
Oil on canvas, 212.8 x 229.6 cm
Washington D.C., National Gallery of Art
1963.10.190

1910

Picasso's style evolves toward Analytical Cubism, and he begins a series of portraits. Daniel-Henry Kahnweiler becomes Picasso's dealer.

1911

Picasso exhibits his work both in Germany, at the gallery of Paul Cassirer from January to February and at the Berlin Secession in May, and in the United States, at the gallery 291 in New York from March to April. Back in Paris, the Cubist room of the Salon d'Automne features no work by Braque or Picasso as their Cubism becomes more and more abstruse.

Picasso spends the summer in Céret in the company of Manolo, Braque, and Juan Gris. In November, he meets Eva Gouel (also known as Marcelle Humbert), the former mistress of artist Louis Marcoussis. Picasso begins an affair with her, which lasts until the end of 1915.

1912

In January, Picasso's works are exhibited at the Golden Fleece in Moscow. Apollinaire founds the publication *Les Soirées de Paris*.

In February, Picasso exhibits in collaboration with the artist group Der Blaue Reiter in Munich and in the Berlin Secession. Picasso stays in Le Havre with Braque.

In May, Picasso introduces stenciled characters and sand into his repertoire. He completes his first collage in spring: *Still Life with Chair Caning* (Musée national Picasso-Paris).

During the summer, Picasso resides with Gouel in Céret, followed by a sojourn in Sorgues. He also begins a lengthy correspondence with Kahnweiler.

On his return to Paris, he moves into a studio at 242 Boulevard Raspail, where he produces his first papiers collés and his first construction: *Guitar* (The Museum of Modern Art, New York). This three-dimensional object is an assemblage of humble materials (cardboard, newspaper, string), which ultimately revolutionizes the field of sculpture.

1913

Picasso participates in the "International Exhibition of Modern Art," also known as the Armory Show, in New York, and in a show at Heinrich Thannhauser's Modern Gallery in Munich. He stays in Céret, where he begins a new series of papiers collés. His father passes away on 3 May. He returns to Barcelona, and later he moves into a new studio at 5 Bis Rue Schoelcher in Paris, where Émile Delétang photographs several of his assemblages for Kahnweiler.

1914

Vladimir Tatlin visits Picasso in his studio. Picasso leaves for Avignon with Gouel, where he meets with Braque and André Derain.

On 3 August, Germany declares war on France. Braque and Derain are drafted into the military, and Apollinaire enlists. Picasso avoids conscription. Accompanied by Gouel, he resides in Céret until November.

1915

On 18 February, Picasso becomes the godfather of Max Jacob at the latter's baptism. Braque is seriously injured. Gouel falls gravely ill and passes away in December. Picasso produces a small series of works in a style called "Ingresque."

1916

Apollinaire is injured in a conflict and undergoes cranial trepanation. André Salmon organizes the first public showing of *Les Demoiselles d'Avignon* at the Salon d'Antin in Paris. Jean Cocteau introduces Picasso to Sergei Diaghilev, a Russian ballet director. Kahnweiler takes refuge from the war in Switzerland. Picasso moves to 22 Rue Victor Hugo in Montrouge.

1917

Picasso travels to Italy with the Ballets Russes, visiting Rome and Pompei. He meets the ballerina Olga Khokhlova and the composer Igor Stravinsky. The premiere of the ballet *Parade* (story by Jean Cocteau; score by Erik Satie; choreography by Léonide Massine; curtain, set, and costumes by Picasso; program by Guillaume Apollinaire) takes place at the Théâtre du Châtelet in Paris on 18 May.

1918

The exhibition "Matisse-Picasso" is held at Galerie Paul Guillaume. Picasso marries Olga Khokhlova on 12 July at the Russian church in Paris. Jacob, Apollinaire, and Cocteau are witnesses. Paul Rosenburg becomes Picasso's dealer. Picasso meets André Breton. Apollinaire dies from Spanish flu on 9 November, two days before the armistice that ends the First World War. After a summer honeymoon in Biarritz, the couple move into 23 Rue La Boétie.

1919

Picasso meets Joan Miró. He works alongside Diaghilev on the design and costumes for the ballet *Tricorne* in London with Vladimir Polunin. The premiere, on 22 July at the Alhambra Theater, is well-received (story by Pedro de Alarcón; choreography by Léonide Massine; score by Manuel de Falla; curtain, set, and costumes by Picasso). As part of a new collaboration with Diaghilev on Pergolesi's *Pulcinella* for the Paris Opera (1920), Picasso creates a Cubist stage design and costumes inspired by Commedia dell'Arte. Picasso makes his first sojourn to the Cape of Antibes.

1920

Kahnweiler returns to Paris and opens Galerie Simon. Picasso devotes several paintings and drawings to his wife Khokhlova, who is pregnant with their first child.

1921

Picasso's first son Paul is born on 4 February. Picasso spends the summer with his family in Fontainebleau, where he is inspired to paint such works as *Three Women at the Spring* (Musée national Picasso-Paris). André Breton writes to Jacques Doucet to convince him to purchase *Les Demoiselles d'Avignon*, saying, "These women mark the birth of Cubism."

1924

Doucet purchases *Les Demoiselles d'Avignon*.

1925

Picasso participates in a Surrealist group exhibition at Galerie Pierre.

1926

The first issue of the magazine *Cahiers d'Art*, founded by Christian Zervos, is published.

Sketchbook 10, Folio 18 Recto
Study 12 for an Ensemble of Six People, Five Women, and a Marine
Sketchbook for *Les Demoiselles d'Avignon*
May – June 1907
Pen and Chinese ink, 10.5 x 13.5 cm
Musée national Picasso-Paris. MP1862folio18recto

Les Demoiselles d'Avignon
Paris, June – July 1907
Oil on canvas, 243.9 x 233.7 cm
New York, The Museum of Modern Art (MoMA)
Acquired through the Lillie P. Bliss Bequest
333.1939

Still Life with Chair Caning
Spring 1912
Oil on canvas, 29 x 37 cm
Musée national Picasso-Paris. MP36

Portrait of Picasso in the studio of sculptor Ignacio Inazo Martinez in Bateau-Lavoir
Anonymous
Paris, 1908
Silver gelatin print, 17.1 x 12.3 cm
Succession Picasso. APPH2810

Study of a Standing Nude in the Studio at Bateau-Lavoir
Paris, spring 1908
Silver gelatin dry glass plate negative, 12 x 9 cm
Musée national Picasso-Paris. APPH17404

Picasso in front of the finished work *Man Leaning on a Table*, reworked in 1916 in his studio on Rue Schoelcher in Paris
Paris, 1916
Reproduction of an anonymous photograph c. 1937-40, Dora Maar
Silver gelatin print, 23.7 x 17.2 cm
Musée national Picasso-Paris. MP1998-138

Man with a Mandolin
Paris, autumn 1911
Oil on canvas, 162 x 71 cm
Musée national Picasso-Paris
Pablo Picasso gift-in-lieu, 1979. MP35

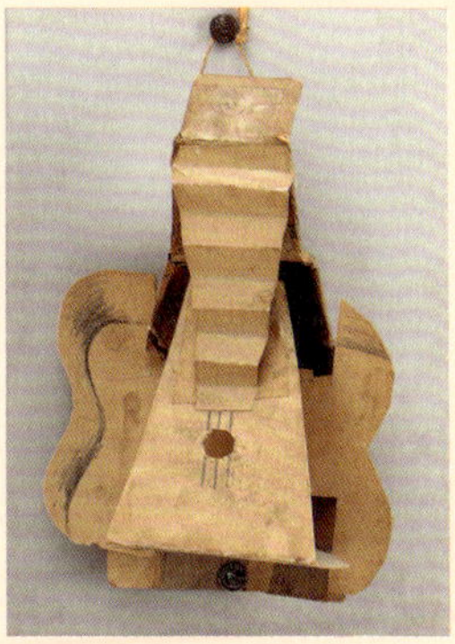

Guitar
Paris, December 1912
Cardboard, string, and canvas 22 x 14.5 x .7cm
Musée national Picasso-Paris. MP245

Guitar
Paris, October – December 1912
Paperboard, paper, thread, string, twine, and coated wire, 65.4 x 33 x 19 cm
New York, The Museum of Modern Art (MoMA)
Gift of the artist. Acc. no.: 640.1973

Portrait of Picasso in his studio on Rue Schoelcher
Anonymous
Paris, 1915-16
Silver gelatin print, 18 x 12.9 cm
Musée national Picasso-Paris. APPH2829

Curtain for the Ballet Parade
1917
Oil on canvas, 1050 x 1640 cm
Centre Pompidou, 1955. AM3365P

Draft for the Curtain Design of Parade
1916-17
Blacklead, watercolor, 27.3 x 39.5 cm
Musée national Picasso-Paris. MP1557

1927

Picasso begins a secret affair with Marie-Thérèse Walter.

The following summer, Picasso stays with his family in Dinard, where bathers become a major theme in his paintings. This is a reference to his young lover, with whom he meets in secret. Picasso's relationship with his wife continues to deteriorate, resulting in the theme of the Minotaur in his works starting in 1928.

1930

Picasso purchases a chateau in Boisgeloup, Normandy, allowing the artist to install a large sculpture studio and work intensively on engravings.

1932

This year is crucial in the life of Picasso, as it is the year in which the first volume of the artist's catalogue raisonné (1896-1906) is published by Zervos, an undertaking that will result in 33 volumes during Picasso's lifetime. It is also the year of his first retrospective at the Galeries Georges Petit in Paris, followed by a presentation in Switzerland at the Kunsthaus Zürich.

1935

Picasso's works depict several female figures inspired by Walter.

Following a stay in Spain with Olga and his son Paul, the couple separate. Walter gives birth to Maria de la Concepción, known as Maya, on 5 September. Picasso meets the photographer Dora Maar, with whom he begins an affair. He takes a break from painting to write poetry.

1937

In 1937, Picasso moves to 7 Rue des Grands-Augustins. He is invited by the Republican government of Spain to produce a work for the Spanish pavilion of the Exposition Internationale des Arts et Techniques dans la Vie Moderne, Paris. In response, he produces a monumental painting, *Guernica* (Museo Nacional Centro de Arte Reina Sofía, Madrid), which he painted following the bombing of the civilian population of a Basque village by the Nazi air force, allied with General Franco.

1940s

During the Second World War (1939-45), Picasso lives between Paris, Royan, and the south of France.

1943

In May, he meets Françoise Gilot, who is his companion from 1944 to 1953, and with whom he will have two children: Claude, born on 15 May 1947, and Paloma, born on 19 April 1949.

1944

In October, Picasso declares his loyalty to the French Communist Party (PCF) in the newspaper *L'Humanité*.

1946

Romuald Dor de la Souchère suggests to Picasso that he convert part of the Château Grimaldi at Antibes into a studio. There, Picasso produces numerous artworks, several of which he leaves as a deposit to the town. These works will go on to constitute the collection of the very first museum dedicated to Picasso, which will open twenty years later.

In summer, The Museum of Modern Art, New York, publishes *Picasso: Fifty Years of His Art*, by Alfred H. Barr, Jr.

1950s

Living in the south of France, Picasso continues experimenting, now in the fields of ceramics and sculpture, especially with his assemblages. In 1950, he receives the Lenin Peace Prize.

Numerous exhibitions dedicated to his work take place around the world: major retrospectives are held not only in Osaka and Tokyo, but also in Europe (notably Milan) and in South America, where *Guernica* is presented at the second Bienal de São Paulo. A major traveling retrospective is shown in Cologne, Munich, and Hamburg.

1955

On 11 February, Khokhlova dies in Cannes. During the summer, shooting takes place for the film *The Mystery of Picasso*, directed by Henri-Georges Clouzot, which receives the Special Jury Prize at the Cannes Film Festival.

1957

Picasso produces several works inspired by the painting *Las Meninas* by Vélazquez.

1958

This year marks the inauguration of UNESCO's permanent headquarters, which features a mural by Picasso entitled *The Fall of Icarus*.

1960s

The decade is marked by an important series entitled "Painter and His Model" and suites of engravings that frequently depict erotic subjects.

1960

A major retrospective of Picasso's work is held at the Tate Gallery in London.

1962

Picasso marries Jacqueline Roque. He receives the Lenin Peace Prize for the second time.

1963

The Museu Picasso in Barcelona opens its doors.

1966

The major retrospective "Tribute to Picasso" takes place at the Petit Palais, the Grand Palais, and the National Library of France in Paris.

1970s

Picasso makes a significant donation of important works to the Museu Picasso in Barcelona, expanding its collection considerably and making the museum the leading steward of the artist's early works.

Following Picasso's last period of intensive productivity from 1969-70, an exhibition is held at the Palais des Papes in Avignon.

Picasso exhibits eight works in the Grand Galerie of the Louvre. The city of Paris names him an honorary citizen.

1973

On 8 April, Picasso passes away in his house Notre-Dame-de-Vie in Mougins at the age of 91. He is interred in the Château of Vauvenargues.

A posthumous exhibition of 200 works entitled "Pablo Picasso, 1970-1972" is held at the Palais des Papes in Avignon.

Pablo Picasso with Olga Khokhlova on the rooftop garden of the Hotel Minerva
Anonymous
Rome, 1917
Silver gelatin print, 7 x 11.42 cm
Musée national Picasso-Paris. APPH3627(11)

Portrait of Picasso in the 1920s
Anonymous
C. 1920
Musée national Picasso-Paris. APPH6738

Picasso and Olga holding Paulo in their arms in the garden of the Ville Belle Rose
Anonymous
Juan-les-Pins, summer 1925
Silver gelatin print, 7.6 x 12 cm
Musée national Picasso-Paris. APPH6464

Large Nude in a Red Armchair
Paris, 5 May 1929
Oil on canvas, 195 x 129 cm
Musée national Picasso-Paris. MP113

Head of a Woman
1931
Wood and plaster, 128.5 x 54.5 x 62.5 cm
Musée national Picasso-Paris. MP301

Minotaur with Dead Horse in Front of a Cave Facing a Girl in Veil
Juan-les-Pins, 6 May 1936
Chinese ink and gouache, 50 x 65 cm
Musée national Picasso-Paris. MP1163

Guernica
1937
Oil on canvas, 350 x 782 cm
Museo Nacional Centro de Arte Reina Sofia

Dove
9 January 1949
Ink on zinc, artist's proof for Mourlot, 56.7 x 76.2 cm
Musée national Picasso-Paris. MP3414

Portrait of Picasso with his head in his right hand, in the studio at Fournas
Arnold Newman
Vallauris, 2 June 1954
Silver gelatin print, 24.5 x 19.6 cm
Musée national Picasso-Paris. APPH2505

Musician
Mougins, 26 May 1972
Oil on canvas, 194.5 x 129.5 cm
Musée national Picasso-Paris. MP229

部分参考书目

参考资料

01. 作品图录

巴尔 1986—1989
布丽吉特·巴尔：《画家 - 雕版师毕加索：雕版画与单刷版画编制图录，1899—1972》，8 卷，伯尔尼，科恩菲尔德 1986—1996 年版。

布洛奇 1968—1979
乔治·布洛奇：《巴勃罗·毕加索：雕版画与石版画图录》，4 卷，伯尔尼，科恩菲尔德与克利普施泰因 1968—1979 年版。

博佐 1985
多米尼克·博佐（主编）：《毕加索美术馆，馆藏概要，卷 1：绘画，拼贴，绘画 - 浮雕，雕塑，陶瓷》，巴黎，法国国家博物馆联盟 1985 年版。

戴克思，布达耶，罗斯雷 1988
皮埃尔·戴克思，乔治·布达耶，乔安·罗斯雷：《绘画作品编制图录，毕加索，1900—1906：求学时期，前野兽派，蓝色时期，粉色时期，粉色古典时期，前立体主义》，纳沙泰尔，伊德和加兰德 1988 年版。（第一版：纳沙泰尔，伊德和加兰德 1966 年版）

皮埃尔·戴克思，乔安·罗斯雷：《毕加索的立体主义，绘画作品、纸本拼贴和组合装置，1907—1916》，纳沙泰尔，伊德和加兰德 1979 年版。

莱亚尔 1996
布丽吉特·莱亚尔（主编）：《素描本：毕加索美术馆素描图录》，2 卷，巴黎，法国国家博物馆联盟 1996 年版。

欧卡纳 1984
玛利亚·特蕾莎·欧卡纳（主编）：《毕加索美术馆：绘画与素描图录》，巴塞罗那市政府 1984 年版。

帕洛·I. 法布雷 1998
约瑟夫·帕洛·I. 法布雷：《生动的毕加索，1881—1907》，巴黎，柯尼曼 1998 年版。
约瑟夫·帕洛·I. 法布雷：《毕加索立体主义，1907—1917》，巴黎，柯尼曼 1998 年版。
约瑟夫·帕洛·I. 法布雷：《毕加索，戏剧芭蕾，1917—1926》，巴黎，柯尼曼 1999 年版。

里歇 1988
米谢勒·里歇（主编）：《毕加索美术馆，馆藏图录，卷 2：素描，水彩画，树胶水彩画，色粉画》，巴黎，法国国家博物馆联盟 1988 年版。

施皮斯 1971
施皮斯·韦尔纳：《毕加索的雕塑》，洛桑，克莱尔枫丹 1971 年版。

泽尔沃斯 1932—1970
克里斯蒂安·泽尔沃斯：《巴勃罗·毕加索编制图录》，卷 1—22，巴黎，艺术手册 1932—1970 年版。

02. 专著，见证与回忆录

贝尔纳达克，米卡耶尔 1998
玛丽 - 劳尔·贝尔纳达克，安德鲁拉·米卡耶尔（编）：《艺术谈话：毕加索》，巴黎，伽利玛 1998 年版。

布拉萨伊 1964
布拉萨伊：《与毕加索的谈话》，巴黎，伽利玛 1964 年版。

卡巴纳 1979
皮埃尔·卡巴纳：《毕加索的世纪：1. 立体主义的诞生，1881—1912》，巴黎，德诺埃勒 1979 年版。

凯泽尔格，塞克尔 1992
皮埃尔·凯泽尔格，埃莱娜·塞克尔（编）：《通信集：毕加索与阿波利奈尔》，巴黎，伽利玛与法国国家博物馆联盟 1992 年版。

西尔洛特 1972
胡安·埃杜阿尔多·西尔洛特：《巴勃罗·毕加索，一位天才的诞生》，巴黎，阿尔班·米歇尔 1972 年版。

达根 2008
菲利普·达根：《毕加索》，巴黎，哈赞 2008 年版。

戴克斯 1977
皮埃尔·戴克斯：《巴勃罗·毕加索的画家生涯》，巴黎，瑟伊出版社 1977 年版。

戴克斯 1995
皮埃尔·戴克斯：《毕加索词典》，巴黎，罗伯特·拉封 1995 年版。

戴克斯 2012
皮埃尔·戴克斯：《新毕加索词典》，巴黎，罗伯特·拉封 2012 年版。

吉洛，拉克 1973
弗朗索瓦丝·吉洛，卡尔顿·拉克：《与毕加索一起生活》，巴黎，口袋书 1973 年版。

韦林·鲁伊兹 - 布拉斯科 1975
里卡尔多·韦林·鲁伊兹 - 布拉斯科：《巴勃罗·鲁伊兹·毕加索》，马德里，西方杂志图书馆 1975 年版。

雅各布 1927
马克斯·雅各布：《马克斯·雅各布回忆毕加索》，《艺术手册》第 6 期，1927 年，第 199—203 页。

雅各布 1953
马克斯·雅各布：《通信集，卷一》，巴黎，卡尔尼尔 1953 年版。

雅各布 1956
马克斯·雅各布：《英雄时代专栏》，巴黎，路易·布罗德 1956 年版。

奥利维耶 2001
费尔南德·奥利维耶：《毕加索与他的朋友》，此版本由埃莱娜·克兰介绍与注疏，巴黎，斯多克 2001 年版。

奥利维耶 1988
费尔南德·奥利维耶：《私密回忆，写给毕加索》，巴黎，加尔曼 - 勒维，1988。

麦卡利 1981
玛丽莲·麦卡利：《毕加索选集：文献，批评与回忆录》，伦敦，大不列颠艺术委员会与泰晤士与哈德逊出版社 1981 年版。

麦卡利 2015
玛丽莲·麦卡利（编）：《毕加索与雷文朵：友人通信集》，巴塞罗那，毕加索博物馆基金会 2015 年版。

帕洛·I. 法布雷 1971
约瑟夫·帕洛·I. 法布雷：《毕加索和他的加泰罗尼亚朋友》，巴塞罗那，阿埃多斯出版社 1971 年版。

帕默林 2013
埃莱娜·帕默林：《毕加索说》，巴黎，美文出版社 2013 年版。

彭罗斯 1958
彭罗斯·罗兰：《毕加索：他的生活和创作》，伦敦，V. 戈兰茨 1958 年版。

勒韦迪 1999
皮埃尔·勒韦迪：《毕加索》，法国水星出版社 1999 年版。

理查森 1992
强尼·理查森，与玛丽莲·麦卡利合作：《毕加索的生活，卷 1，1881—1906》，法文版由威廉·O. 德斯蒙德翻译，巴黎，橡树出版社 1992 年版。

强尼·理查森，与玛丽莲·麦卡利合作：《毕加索的生活，卷 2，1907—1917》，伦敦，乔纳森·凯普 1996 年版。

强尼·理查森，与玛丽莲·麦卡利合作：《毕加索的生活，卷 3，1917—1932》，纽约，阿尔弗雷德·A. 克诺普夫 2007 年版。

萨瓦特斯 1996
海梅·萨瓦特斯：《毕加索：肖像与回忆》，巴黎，休闲学校出版社 1996 年版。

早先版本来自 1902 年的日记：萨瓦特斯·海梅，《毕加索：肖像与回忆》，巴黎，休闲学校出版社 1996 年版。

萨瓦特斯 1954
海梅·萨瓦特斯：《毕加索：图像志文献》，日内瓦，皮埃尔·卡耶 1954 年版。

萨勒蒙 1955
安德烈·萨勒蒙：《无尽的回忆，卷一，1903—1908》，巴黎，伽利玛 1955 年版。

斯泰因 1973
格特鲁德·斯泰因：《艾丽斯·托克拉斯自传》，贝尔纳·法依（译），巴黎，伽利玛 1973 年版。

斯泰因 1984
格特鲁德·斯泰因：《毕加索》，纽约，多佛出版社 1984 年版。

斯泰因 1985
格特鲁德·斯泰因：《毕加索：文字全集》，波士顿，比肯出版社 1985 年版。

佛拉 1948
安伯斯·佛拉：《一位画商的回忆录》，巴黎，阿尔班·米歇尔 1948 年版。

03. 研究与论文

阿波利奈尔 1960
纪尧姆·阿波利奈尔：《艺术专栏（1902—1918）》，巴黎，伽利玛 1960 年版。

阿波利奈尔 1965
纪尧姆·阿波利奈尔：《立体主义画家：美学冥想》，巴黎，埃尔芒 1965 年版。

巴尔 1946
阿尔弗雷德·巴尔：《毕加索：50 年的艺术创作》，纽约现代艺术博物馆 1946 年版。

贝尔纳达克，皮奥 1964
玛丽 - 劳尔·贝尔纳达克和克里斯丁·皮奥（编）：《毕加索：文字》，巴黎，伽利玛 1964 年版。

布朗特，普尔 1962
安东尼·布朗特和菲比·普尔：《毕加索：风格形成时期》，伦敦，工作室书籍出版社 1962 年版。

波孔特·科勒，2016
康塞普西奥·波孔特·科勒（主编）：《毕加索：从〈安道尔的农民〉到〈阿维尼翁的少女〉：罗马之旅》，安道尔，安道尔政府 2016 年版。

克雷斯佩勒 1991
让 - 保罗·克雷斯佩勒：《毕加索时代的蒙马特日常生活，1900—1910》，巴黎，阿歇特 1991 年版。

戴克斯 1987
皮埃尔·戴克斯：《创造者毕加索：私人生活与艺术创作》，巴黎，瑟伊 1987 年版。

戴克斯 1994
皮埃尔·戴克斯，《毕加索在“洗衣船”》：巴黎，弗拉马里翁 1994 年版。

戴克斯，伊思拉埃尔 2003
皮埃尔·戴克斯和阿尔芒·伊思拉埃尔：《毕加索：警察局卷宗，1901—1940》，巴黎，编制图录出版与穆东 / 阿卡托斯 2003 年版。

戴克斯，莫拉维亚，里卡勒丹诺 1980
皮埃尔·戴克斯，阿尔贝托·莫拉维亚，保罗·里卡勒丹诺：《毕加索绘画作品全集，卷一：蓝色与粉色时期》，巴黎，弗拉马里翁 1980 年版。

伊轮法特 2011
菲利普·J. 伊轮法特（主编）：《毕加索与马戏团，19 世纪末的巴黎与杂耍艺人》，卡莱勒，鳟鱼画廊与狄金森学院 2011 年版。

雅克·皮 2007
杰西卡·雅克·皮：《毕加索在戈索尔，1906：一个夏天的现代性》，马德里，A·马查杜书籍 2007 年版。

卡普兰 1992
特玛·卡普兰：《红色城市，蓝色时期：毕加索在巴塞罗那的社会运动》，伯克利，加州大学出版社 1992 年版。

勒莫尔旺 2011
玛丽安娜·勒莫尔旺：《贝尔特·韦尔（1865—1951），大艺术家们的小画廊商》，奥尔良，勒卡尔拉特 2011 年版。

利伯曼 1955
威廉·S. 利伯曼：《毕加索：蓝色与粉色时期》，纽约，艾布拉姆斯 1954 年版（法语版 1955 年）。

马德琳 2006
劳伦斯·马德琳：《梵高 - 毕加索》，巴黎，拉马蒂尼埃 2006 年版。

麦卡利 1978
玛丽莲·麦卡利（编）：《四只猫咖啡馆：1900 年前后的巴塞罗那艺术》，普林斯顿，艺术廊 1978 年版。

鲁比 1972
威廉·鲁比：《现代艺术博物馆藏毕加索作品》，纽约现代艺术博物馆 1972 年版。

萨瓦特斯 1963
海梅·萨瓦特斯（编）：《毕加索：蓝色巴塞罗那》，巴黎，阿尔勒之风出版 1963 年版。

斯塔罗宾斯基 2014
让·斯塔罗宾斯基：《艺术家的杂耍艺人肖像》，巴黎，伽利玛 2014 年版（日内瓦，史基拉 1970 年首版）。

德德 1928
威廉·德德，《毕加索与法国传统》，巴黎，四条道路出版社 1928 年版。

瓦莱斯 2015
爱德华·瓦莱斯，2015，《毕加索和加泰罗尼亚文学界：1897—1904》，巴塞罗那，加泰罗尼亚百科全书 2015 年版。

展览图录

纽约 1980
《巴勃罗·毕加索：回顾展》（纽约，现代艺术博物馆，1980 年 5 月 22 日—9 月 16 日），威廉·鲁比（编），纽约 / 伦敦，现代艺术博物馆 / 泰晤士与哈德逊出版社 1980 年版。

华盛顿 1980
《毕加索：杂耍艺人》（华盛顿，国家艺术博物馆，1980 年 12 月 14 日—1981 年 3 月 15 日），E·A. 卡米安（主编），华盛顿，国家艺术博物馆 1980 年版。

伯尔尼 1984
《青年毕加索：蓝色时期的萌芽》（伯尔尼美术馆，1984 年 12 月 6 日—1985 年 1 月 17 日），于尔根·格拉斯莫（主编），伯尔尼，伯尔尼美术馆 1984 年版。

巴塞罗那，伯尔尼，1992
《毕加索，1905—1906：粉色时期》（巴塞罗那，毕加索美术馆，1992 年 2 月 5 日—4 月 19 日；伯尔尼，美术馆，1992 年 5 月 8 日—7 月 26 日），玛利亚·特蕾莎·奥卡纳（主编），巴塞罗那，西班牙埃莱克塔 1992 年版。

巴黎，南特 1992
《毕加索：青春与创造：1893—1905 的素描》（巴黎，毕加索美术馆，1991 年 9 月 17 日—11 月 25 日；南特，南特美术馆，1991 年 12 月 6 日—1992 年 2 月 16 日），布丽吉特·莱亚尔（主编），巴黎，法国国家博物馆联盟 1992 年版。

坎佩尔，巴黎 1994
《马克斯·雅各布与毕加索》（坎佩尔，坎佩尔美术馆，1994 年 6 月 21 日—9 月 4 日；巴黎，毕加索美术馆，1994年10月4日—12月12日），埃莱娜·塞克尔（主编），巴黎，法国国家博物馆联盟1994年版。

巴塞罗那 1995
《毕加索和四只猫咖啡馆：现代性的关键（巴塞罗那，毕加索美术馆，1995年11月—1996年2月）》，玛利亚·特蕾莎·奥卡纳（主编），巴塞罗那，毕加索美术馆/朗沃格1995年版。

纽约、巴黎 1996
《毕加索与肖像》（纽约，现代艺术博物馆，1996年4月28日—9月17日；巴黎，大皇宫国家美术馆，1996年10月15日—1997年1月20日），威廉·鲁比，巴黎，法国国家博物馆联盟/弗拉马里翁1996年版。

巴塞罗那 1997
《毕加索：天才的形成，1890—1904：巴塞罗那毕加索美术馆藏素描》（巴塞罗那，毕加索美术馆，1997），玛利亚·特蕾莎·奥卡纳（主编），巴塞罗那，朗沃格1997年版。

巴黎 1997
《黑镜：毕加索，照片之源，1900—1928》（巴黎，毕加索美术馆，1997年3月12日—6月9日），安妮·巴尔达萨里（主编），巴黎，法国国家博物馆联盟1997年版。

华盛顿，波士顿 1997
《毕加索：早年创作，1892—1906》（华盛顿，国家艺术博物馆，1997年3月30日—7月27日；波士顿，美术馆，1997年9月10日—1998年1月4日），玛丽莲·麦卡利（主编），华盛顿，国家艺术博物馆1997年版。

巴黎 2000
《毕加索雕塑家》（巴黎，蓬皮杜中心，2000年6月8日—9月25日），施皮斯·韦尔纳（主编），蓬皮杜中心出版社2000年版。

巴黎，蒙特利尔，巴塞罗那 2001
《情色毕加索》（巴黎，国立网球场现代美术馆，2001年2月19日—5月20日；蒙特利尔美术馆，2001年6月14日—9月16日；巴塞罗那，毕加索美术馆，2001年10月15日—2002年1月27日），居伊·科热瓦尔，多米尼克·迪皮伊-拉贝，热拉尔·雷尼埃等（主编），巴黎，法国国家博物馆联盟2001年版。

拉科鲁尼亚 2002
《年少毕加索》（拉科鲁尼亚，佩德罗·巴里埃·德拉·马萨基金会，2002年12月17日—2003年3月17日），玛利亚·特蕾莎·奥卡纳（主编），佩德罗·巴里埃·德拉·马萨基金会2002年版。

巴黎 2003
《“保存即存在！”毕加索文献》（巴黎，毕加索美术馆，2003年10月22日—2004年1月19日），劳伦斯·马德琳（主编），巴黎，法国国家博物馆联盟2003年版。

巴黎，渥太华 2004
《大游行：艺术家的小丑肖像》（巴黎，大皇宫国家美术馆，2004年3月12日—5月31日；渥太华，加拿大国立美术馆，2004年6月25日—9月19日），让·克莱尔（主编），渥太华/巴黎，加拿大国立美术馆/伽利玛2004年版。

巴塞罗那，马蒂尼 2006
《毕加索与马戏团》（巴塞罗那，毕加索美术馆，2006年11月15日—2007年2月18日；马蒂尼，皮埃尔·吉安纳达基金会，2007年3月9日—6月10日），多米尼克·迪皮伊-拉贝和玛利亚·特蕾莎·奥卡纳（主编），马蒂尼，皮埃尔·吉安纳达基金会2006年版。

克利夫兰，纽约 2006
《巴塞罗那与现代性：毕加索、高迪、米罗与达利》（克利夫兰美术馆，2006年10月15日—2007年1月7日；纽约大都会艺术博物馆，2007年3月7日—6月3日），威廉·H.罗宾逊（主编），纽黑文，耶鲁大学出版2006年版。

巴黎 2007
《毕加索立体主义》（巴黎，国立巴黎毕加索博物馆，2007年9月19日—2008年1月7日），安妮·巴尔达萨里（主编），巴黎，法国国家博物馆联盟/弗拉马里翁2007年版。

巴黎 2008
《毕加索与大师》（巴黎，大皇宫国家美术馆，2008年10月—2009年2月2日），安妮·巴尔达萨里（主编），巴黎，法国国家博物馆联盟2008年版。

奥尔塔德圣乔安 2009
《毕加索：年轻时的加泰罗尼亚朋友》（奥尔塔德圣乔安，毕加索中心，2009年9月19日—11月15日），爱德华·瓦莱斯（主编），奥尔塔德圣乔安，毕加索中心2009年版。

巴塞罗那 2010
《毕加索VS鲁西诺尔》（巴塞罗那，毕加索美术馆，2010年5月27日—9月5日），爱德华·瓦莱斯（主编），巴塞罗那市政府，文化局2010年版。

威廉斯敦，巴塞罗那 2010
《毕加索看德加》（威廉镇，马萨诸塞州，克拉克艺术中心，2010年6月13日—9月12日；巴塞罗那，毕加索美术馆，2010年10月14日—2011年1月16日），伊丽莎白·考林和理查德·肯德尔，威廉斯敦，克拉克艺术中心2010年版。

阿姆斯特丹，巴塞罗那 2011
《毕加索在巴黎：1900—1907》（阿姆斯特丹，梵高美术馆，2011年2月18日—5月29日；巴塞罗那，毕加索美术馆，2011年6月30日—10月15日），玛丽莲·麦卡利（主编），阿姆斯特丹/巴塞罗那/布鲁塞尔，梵高美术馆/毕加索美术馆/墨卡托基金2011年版。（英文版包含出自巴塞罗那的插页：《毕加索在巴黎，1900—1907：吞火者》，墨卡托基金2011年版）。

巴黎，旧金山，纽约 2011
《马蒂斯，塞尚，毕加索……斯坦因的冒险》（巴黎，大皇宫国家美术馆，2011年10月5日—2012年1月22日；旧金山，旧金山现代美术馆，2011年5月21日—9月6日；纽约，大都会艺术博物馆，2012年2月22日—6月3日），珍妮特·毕肖普，塞西尔·德布雷，瑞贝卡·拉比诺和盖瑞·丁特罗（主编），巴黎，法国国立博物馆联盟2011年版。

纽约、华盛顿 2011
《毕加索的素描，1899—1921：重新发明传统》（纽约，弗里克收藏，2011年10月4日—2012年1月8日；华盛顿，国家艺术博物馆，2012年1月29日—5月6日），苏珊·格蕾丝·加拉西和玛丽莲·麦卡利（主编），纽约，弗里克2011年版。

克利夫兰，巴塞罗那 2012
《毕加索与生命的秘密：生命》（克利夫兰，克利夫兰艺术博物馆，2012年12月12日—2013年4月13日；巴塞罗那，毕加索美术馆，2013年10月10日—2014年1月19日），威廉·H.罗宾逊（主编），克利夫兰/伦敦，克利夫兰艺术博物馆/吉尔斯2012年版。

巴塞罗那 2013
《蓝色之旅：生命》（巴塞罗那，毕加索美术馆，2013年10月10日—2014年1月19日），雷耶斯·希门尼斯（主编），巴塞罗那，巴塞罗那市政府2013年版。

巴塞罗那 2013
《我毕加索，自画像》（巴塞罗那，毕加索美术馆，2013年5月31日—9月1日），爱德华·瓦莱斯和伊莎贝尔·森多亚（主编），巴塞罗那，巴塞罗那市政府2013年版。

伦敦 2013
《成为毕加索 巴黎1901》（伦敦，考陶德美术馆，2013年2月14日—5月26日），玛丽莲·麦卡利（主编），伦敦，考陶德美术馆与保罗·霍伯顿出版社2013年版。

巴塞罗那 2014
《卡萨吉玛斯：神秘的艺术家》（巴塞罗那，加泰罗尼亚国家艺术博物馆，2014年10月31日—2015年2月22日），爱德华·瓦莱斯（主编），巴塞罗那，加泰罗尼亚国家艺术博物馆2014年版。

纽约 2014
《立体主义：伦纳德·A.劳德收藏》（纽约，大都会艺术博物馆，2014年10月20日—2015年2月16日），纽约，大都会艺术博物馆2014年版。

拉科鲁尼亚 2015
《最早的毕加索在拉科鲁尼亚》（拉科鲁尼亚，拉科鲁尼亚美术馆，2015年2月20日—2015年5月24日），马伦·瓜尔·帕斯库尔（主编），拉科鲁尼亚市政府/拉科鲁尼亚议会2015年版。

巴黎 2015—2016
《我毕加索！诞辰纪念展》（巴黎，国立巴黎毕加索博物馆，2015年10月20日—2016年1月31日），艾米丽·布瓦尔（主编），巴黎，国立巴黎毕加索博物馆/法国国家博物馆联盟-大皇宫2015年版。

马赛 2016
《没有架子的天才：毕加索与传统民俗艺术》（马赛，欧洲与地中海文明博物馆，2016年4月27日—8月29日），马赛，伽利玛/欧洲与地中海文明博物馆2016年版。

巴塞罗那 2016
《毕加索传奇》（巴塞罗那，加泰罗尼亚国立艺术博物馆，2016年11月17日—2017年2月26日），胡安·何塞·拉韦尔塔和艾米莉娅·菲利普特（主编），巴塞罗那，加泰罗尼亚国立艺术博物馆2016年版。

伦敦，巴塞罗那 2016
《毕加索肖像》（英文版/西班牙语版）（伦敦，国家肖像馆，2016年10月6日—2017年2月5日；巴塞罗那，毕加索美术馆，2017年3月16日—6月25日），伊丽莎白·考林（主编），伦敦，国家肖像馆2016年版。

巴黎 2016
《阿波利奈尔，诗人的目光》（巴黎，橘园美术馆，2016年4月6日—7月8日），劳伦斯·德·卡尔斯（主编），巴黎，伽利玛/奥赛与橘园美术馆2016年版。

巴黎，布鲁塞尔 2016
《毕加索：雕塑》（巴黎，国立巴黎毕加索博物馆，2016年3月8日—4月28日；布鲁塞尔艺术宫，2016年10月26日—2017年3月5日）塞西尔·戈德弗鲁瓦和维吉涅·佩尔德里索（主编），巴黎/布鲁塞尔，国立巴黎毕加索博物馆/索莫吉/布鲁塞尔艺术宫2016年版。

马德里 2017
《毕加索，劳特雷克》（马德里，提森-博内米萨国立博物馆，2017年10月17—2018年1月21日），弗朗西斯科·卡勒沃·瑟拉雷和帕洛玛·阿拉尔科，马德里，提森-博内米萨国立博物馆2017年版。

巴塞罗那 2017
《1917：毕加索在巴塞罗那》（巴塞罗那，毕加索美术馆，2017年10月25日—2018年1月28日），马伦·瓜尔（主编），巴塞罗那，巴塞罗那市政府2017年版。

巴黎 2018
《毕加索：蓝色与粉色时期》（巴黎，奥赛美术馆，2018年9月18日—2019年1月6日），洛朗·勒邦，克莱尔·贝尔纳迪，史黛芬妮·穆兰，艾米莉娅·菲利普特（主编），巴黎，哈赞2018年版。

巴黎 2018
《立体主义》（巴黎，蓬皮杜中心，2018年10月17日—2019年2月25日），布丽吉特·莱亚尔（主编），巴黎，蓬皮杜中心出版2018年版。

Selected Bibliography

Referenced Works

01. Artwork Catalogues

Baer 1986-89
Baer, Brigitte. *Picasso, Peintre-graveur. Catalogue raisonné de l'œuvre gravée et des monotypes, 1899-1972* (8 volumes). Bern: Kornfeld, 1986-96.

Bloch 1968-79
Bloch, Georges. *Pablo Picasso. Catalogue de l'œuvre gravé et lithographié* (4 volumes). Bern: Kornfeld & Klipstein Editions, 1968-79.

Bozo 1985
Bozo, Dominique. *Musée Picasso. Catalogue sommaire des collections, volume 1: peintures, papiers collés, tableaux-reliefs, sculptures, céramiques*. Paris: Réunion des Musées Nationaux, 1985.

Daix, Boudaille, Rosselet 1988
Daix, Pierre; Boudaille, Georges; and Rosselet, Joan. *Catalogue raisonné de l'œuvre peint. Picasso, 1900-1906: les années de formation, le préfauvisme, la période bleue, la période rose, le classicisme rose, le précubisme.* Neuchâtel: Ides et Calendes, 1988 (first edition Neuchâtel: Ides et Calendes, 1966).
Daix, Pierre and Rosselet, Joan. *Le Cubisme de Picasso, Catalogue raisonné de l'œuvre peint, des papiers collés et des assemblages, 1907-1916.* Neuchâtel: Ides et Calendes, 1979.

Leal 1996
Leal, Brigitte. *Carnets. Catalogue des dessins du Musée Picasso* (2 volumes). Paris: Réunion des Musées Nationaux, 1996.

Ocaña 1984
Ocaña, Maria Teresa. Picasso Museum: Catàleg de pintura i dibuix. Barcelona: Ajuntament de Barcelona, 1984.

Palau i Fabre 1998
Palau i Fabre, Josep. *Picasso vivant (1881-1907).* Paris: Könemann, 1998.
Palau i Fabre, Josep. *Picasso cubism (1907-1917).* Paris: Könemann, 1998.
Palau i Fabre, Josep. *Picasso. Des ballets au drame (1917-1926).* Paris: Könemann, 1999.

Richet 1988
Richet, Michèle. *Musée Picasso. Catalogue des collections, volume 2: dessins, aquarelles, gouaches, pastels.* Paris: Réunion des musées nationaux, 1988.

Spies 1971
Spies, Werner. *Les Sculptures de Picasso.* Lausanne: Clairefontaine, 1971.

Zervos 1932-70
Zervos, Christian. *Catalogue raisonné des œuvres de Pablo Picasso, volumes I-XXII.* Paris: Cahiers d'Art Editions, 1932-70.

02. Monographs, Testimonials, and Memoirs

Bernadac and Michael 1998
Bernadac, Marie-Laure and Michael, Androula, eds. *Propos sur l'art. Picasso.* Paris: Gallimard, 1998.

Brassaï 1964
Brassaï. *Conversations avec Picasso.* Paris: Gallimard, 1964.

Cabanne 1979
Cabanne, Pierre. *Le Siècle de Picasso. 1, La Naissance du cubisme (1881-1912).* Paris: Denoël, 1979.

Caizergues and Seckel 1992
Caizergues, Pierre and Seckel, Hélène, eds. *Picasso / Apollinaire: Correspondance.* Paris: Éditions Gallimard & Réunion des Musées Nationaux, 1992.

Cirlot 1972
Cirlot, Juan Eduardo. *Pablo Picasso. Naissance d'un génie.* Paris: Éditions Albin Michel, 1972.

Dagen 2008
Dagen, Philippe. *Picasso.* Paris: Hazan, 2008.

Daix 1977
Daix, Pierre. *La Vie de peintre de Pablo Picasso.* Paris: Éditions du Seuil, 1977.

Daix 1995
Daix, Pierre. *Dictionnaire Picasso.* Paris: Éditions Robert Laffont, 1995.

Daix 2012
Daix, Pierre. *Nouveau Dictionnaire Picasso.* Paris: Éditions Robert Laffont, 2012.

Gilot and Lake 1973
Gilot, Françoise and Lake, Carlton. *Vivre avec Picasso.* Paris: Le Livre de Poche, 1973.

Huelin Ruiz-Blasco 1975
Huelin Ruiz-Blasco, Ricardo. *Pablo Ruiz Picasso.* Madrid: Biblioteca de la Revista de Occidente, 1975.

Jacob 1927
Jacob, Max. "Souvenirs sur Picasso contés par Max Jacob." *Cahiers d'art* no. 6 (1927), pp. 199-203.

Jacob 1953
Jacob, Max. *Correspondance, tome I.* Paris: Garnier, 1953.

Jacob 1956
Jacob, Max. *Chroniques des Temps Héroïques.* Paris: Louis Broder, 1956.

Olivier 2001
Olivier, Fernande. *Picasso et ses amis* (introduction and annotations by Klein, Hélène). Paris: Stock, 2001.

Olivier 1988
Olivier, Fernande. *Souvenirs intimes, écrits pour Picasso.* Paris: Calmann-Lévy, 1988.

McCully 1981
McCully, Marilyn. *A Picasso Anthology: Documents, Criticism, Reminiscences.* London: Arts Council of Great Britain & Thames and Hudson, 1981.

McCully 2015
McCully, Marilyn, ed. *Picasso and Reventós: A Correspondence Among Friends.* Barcelona: Fundació Museu Picasso, 2015.

Palau i Fabre 1971
Palau i Fabre, Josep. *Picasso i els seus amics Catalans.* Barcelona: Editorial Aedos, 1971.

Parmelin 2013
Parmelin, Hélène. *Picasso dit.* Paris: Les Belles Lettres, 2013.

Penrose 1958
Penrose, Roland. *Picasso: His Life and Work.* London: V. Gollancz, 1958.

Penrose 1961
Penrose, Roland. *Picasso.* New York: Universe Books, 1961.

Reverdy 1999
Reverdy, Pierre. *Picasso.* Paris: Mercure de France, 1999.

Richardson 1992
Richardson, John in collaboration with McCully, Marilyn. *Vie de Picasso, Volume 1, 1881-1906* (English translation by Desmond, William O.). Paris: Éditions du Chêne, 1992.
Richardson, John in collaboration with McCully, Marilyn. *A Life of Picasso, Vol. 2: 1907-1917.* London: Jonathan Cape, 1996.
Richardson, John in collaboration with McCully, Marilyn. *A Life of Picasso, Vol. 3: 1917-1932.* New York: Alfred A. Knopf, 2007.

Sabartés 1996
Sabartés, Jaime. *Picasso. Portraits et souvenirs.* Paris: L'École des Loisirs, 1996.
Earlier version from a 1902 diary: Sabartés, Jaime. *Portraits et souvenirs.* Paris: L'École des Loisirs, 1996.

Sabartés 1954
Sabartés, Jaime. *Picasso. Documents iconographiques.* Geneva: Pierre Cailler, 1954.

Salmon 1955
Salmon, André. *Souvenirs sans fin, 1. Première epoque (1903-1908).* Paris: Gallimard, 1955.

Stein 1973
Stein, Gertrude. *Autobiographie d'Alice Toklas.* Translated into French by Faÿ, Bernard. Paris: Gallimard, 1973.

Stein 1984
Stein, Gertrude. *Picasso.* New York: Dover Publications, 1984.

Stein 1985
Stein, Gertrude. *Picasso: The Complete Writings.* Boston: Beacon Press, 1985.

Vollard 1948
Vollard, Ambroise. *Souvenirs d'un marchand de tableaux.* Paris: Albin Michel, 1948.

03. Studies and Essays

Apollinaire 1960
Apollinaire, Guillaume. *Chroniques d'art (1902-1918).* Paris: Gallimard, 1960.

Apollinaire 1965
Apollinaire, Guillaume. *Les peintres cubistes. Méditations esthétiques.* Paris: Hermann, 1965.

Barr 1946
Barr, Alfred H., Jr. *Picasso: Fifty Years of His Art.* New York: Museum of Modern Art, 1946.

Bernadac and Piot 1964
Bernadac, Marie-Laure and Piot, Christine (eds.). *Picasso: Ecrits.* Paris, Gallimard, 1964.

Blunt and Pool 1962
Blunt, Anthony and Pool, Phoebe. *Picasso: The Formative Years.* London: Studio Books, 1962.

Boncompte Coll 2016
Boncompte Coll, Concepció. *Picasso. De "Pageses d'Andorra" a "Demoiselles d'Avignon": un viatge romànic.* Andorra: Govern d'Andorra, 2016.

Crespelle 1991
Crespelle, Jean-Paul. *La Vie quotidienne à Montmartre au temps de Picasso: 1900-1910.* Paris: Hachette, 1991.

Daix 1987
Pierre, Daix. *Picasso Créateur. La vie intime et l'œuvre.* Paris: Seuil, 1987.

Daix 1994
Daix, Pierre. *Picasso au Bateau-Lavoir.* Paris: Flammarion, 1994.

Daix and Israël 2003
Daix, Pierre and Israël, Armand. *Pablo Picasso. Dossiers de la préfecture de Police: 1901-1940.* Paris: Éditions des Catalogues Raisonnés & Moudon/Acatos, 2003.

Daix, Moravia, Lecaldano 1980
Daix, Pierre; Moravia, Alberto; and Lecaldano, Paolo. *Tout l'œuvre peint de Picasso, tome 1: période bleue et rose.* Paris: Flammarion, 1980.

Earenfight 2011
Earenfight, Phillip J. *Picasso and the Circus: Fin-de-Siècle Paris and the Suite de Saltimbanques.* Carlisle: The Trout Gallery, Dickinson College, 2011.

Jacques Pi 2007
Jacques Pi, Jèssica. *Picasso en Gósol, 1906: un verano para la modernidad.* Madrid: A. Machado Libros, 2007.

Kaplan 1992
Kaplan, Temma. *Red City, Blue Period: Social Movements in Picasso's Barcelona.* Berkeley: University of California Press, 1992.

Le Morvan 2011
Le Morvan, Marianne. *Berthe Weill (1865-1951), la petite galeriste des grands artistes.* Orléans: L'Ecarlate, 2011.

Lieberman 1955
Lieberman, William S. *Picasso: Blue and Rose Periods.* New York: Abrams, 1954 (French edition: 1955).

Madeline 2006
Madeline, Laurence. *Van Gogh – Picasso.* Paris: La Martinière, 2006.

McCully 1978
McCully, Marilyn, ed. *Els Quatre Gats: Art in Barcelona Around 1900.* Princeton: The Art Gallery, 1978.

Rubin 1972
Rubin, William. *Picasso in the Collections of the Museum of Modern Art.* New York: The Museum of Modern Art, 1972.

Sabartès 1963
Sabartès, Jaime, ed. *Picasso. Les Bleus de Barcelone.* Paris: Éditions Au Vent d'Arles, 1963.

Starobinski 2014
Starobinski, Jean. *Portrait de l'artiste en saltimbanque.* Paris: Gallimard, 2014 (first edition Geneva: Skira, 1970).

Uhde 1928
Uhde, Wilhelm. *Picasso et la tradition Française.* Paris: Éditions des Quatre Chemins, 1928.

Vallès 2015
Vallès, Eduard. *Picasso i el món literari català 1897-1904.* Barcelona: Enciclopèdia Catalana, 2015.

Exhibition Catalogues

New York 1980
Rubin, William, ed. *Pablo Picasso: A Retrospective* (New York, The Museum of Modern Art, 22 May – 16 September 1980). New York/London: The Museum of Modern Art/Thames & Hudson, 1980.

Washington 1980
Carmean, E. A. *Picasso: The Saltimbanques* (Washington, National Gallery of Art, 14 December 1980 – 15 March 1981). Washington: National Gallery of Art, 1980.

Bern 1984
Glaesemer, Jürgen. *Der Junge Picasso. Frühwerk une Blaue Periode* (Bern, Museum of Fine Arts, 6 December 1984 – 17 January 1985). Bern: Museum of Fine Arts, 1984.

Barcelona, Bern 1992
Ocaña, Maria Teresa. *Picasso, 1905-1906: Période rose* (Barcelona, Museu Picasso, 5 February – 19 April 1992; Bern, Museum of Fine Arts, 8 May – 26 July 1992). Barcelona: Electa España, 1992.

Paris, Nantes 1992
Leal, Brigitte. *Picasso, jeunesse et genèse: Dessins, 1893-1905* (Paris, Musée national Picasso-Paris, 17 September – 25 November; Nantes, Musée des Beaux-Arts, 6 December

1991 – 16 February 1992). Paris: Réunion des Musées Nationaux, 1992.

Quimper, Paris 1994
Seckel, Hélène. *Max Jacob et Picasso* (Quimper, Musée des Beaux-Arts, 21 June – 4 September 1994; Paris, Musée national Picasso-Paris, 4 October – 12 December 1994). Paris: Réunion des Musées Nationaux, 1994.

Barcelona 1995
Ocaña, Maria Teresa. *Picasso i els 4 Gats. La clau de la modernitat* (Barcelona, Museu Picasso, November 1995 – February 1996). Barcelona: Museu Picasso/Lunwerg Editores, 1995.

New York, Paris 1996
Rubin, William, ed. *Picasso et le portrait* (New York, The Museum of Modern Art, 28 April – 17 September 1996; Paris: Galeries Nationales du Grand Palais, 15 October 1996 – 20 January 1997). Paris: Réunion des Musées Nationaux/Flammarion, 1996.

Barcelona 1997
Ocaña, Maria Teresa. *Picasso: la formation d'un génie, 1890-1904.* Dessins du Museu Picasso de Barcelone (Barcelona, Museu Picasso, 1997). Barcelona: Lunwerg Editores, 1997.

Paris 1997
Baldassari, Anne. *Le Miroir noir. Picasso, sources photographiques 1900-1928* (Paris, Musée national Picasso-Paris, 12 March – 9 June 1997). Paris: Réunion des Musées Nationaux, 1997.

Washington, Boston 1997
McCully, Marilyn, ed. *Picasso: The Early Years, 1892-1906* (Washington, National Gallery, 30 March – 27 July 1997; Boston, Museum of Fine Art, 10 September 1997 – 4 January 1998). Washington: National Gallery of Art, 1997.

Paris 2000
Spies, Werner. *Picasso Sculpteur* (Paris, Centre Pompidou, 8 June – 25 September 2000). Paris: Éditions du Centre Pompidou, 2000.

La Coruña 2002
Ocaña, Maria Teresa. Picasso Joven (La Coruña, Fundación Pedro Barrié de la Maza, 17 December 2002 – 17 March 2003). La Coruña: Fundación Pedro Barrié de la Maza, Conde de Fenosa, 2002.

Paris 2003
Madeline, Laurence. "On est ce que l'on garde!" *Les archives de Picasso* (Paris, Musée national Picasso-Paris, 22 October 2003 – 19 January 2004). Paris: Réunion des Musées Nationaux, 2003.

Paris, Ottawa 2004
Clair, Jean. *La Grande Parade. Portrait de l'artiste en clown* (Paris, Galeries Nationales du Grand Palais, 12 March – 31 May 2004; Ottawa, Musée des Beaux-Arts du Canada, 25 June – 19 September 2004). Ottawa/Paris: Musée des Beaux-Arts du Canada/Éditions Gallimard, 2004.

Barcelona, Martigny 2006
Dupuis-Labbe, Dominique and Ocaña, Maria Teresa. *Picasso et le cirque* (Barcelona, Museu Picasso, 15 November 2006 – 18 February 2007; Martigny, Fondation Pierre Giannada, 9 March – 10 June 2007). Martigny: Fondation Pierre Giannada, 2006.

Cleveland, New York 2006
Robinson, William H. *Barcelona and Modernity: Picasso, Gaudí, Miró, Dalí* (Cleveland Museum of Art, 15 October 2006 – 7 January 2007; New York, The Metropolitan Museum of Art, 7 March – 3 June 2007). New Haven: Yale University Press, 2006.

Paris 2007
Baldassari, Anne. *Picasso Cubiste* (Paris, Musée national Picasso-Paris, 19 September 2007 – 7 January 2008). Paris: RMN/ Flammarion, 2007.

Paris 2008
Baldassari, Anne. *Picasso et les maîtres* (Paris, Galeries Nationales du Grand Palais, 8 October 2008 – 2 February 2009). Paris: Réunion des Musées Nationaux, 2008.

Horta de Sant Joan 2009
Vallès, Eduard. Picasso. *Amics Catalans de joventut* (Horta de Sant Joan, El Centre Picasso, 19 September – 15 November 2009). Horta de Sant Joan: El Centre Picasso, 2009.

Barcelona 2010
Vallès, Eduard. *Picasso versus Rusiñol* (Barcelona, Museu Picasso, 27 May – 5 September 2010). Barcelona: Ajuntament de Barcelona Institut de Cultura, 2010.

Williamstown, Barcelona 2010
Cowling, Elizabeth and Kendall, Richard. *Picasso Looks at Degas* (Williamstown, Massachusetts, Sterling and Francine Clark Institute, 13 June – 12 September 2010; Barcelona, Museu Picasso, 14 October 2010 – 16 January 2011). Williamstown: Sterling and Francine Clark Institute, 2010.

Amsterdam, Barcelona 2011
McCully, Marilyn. *Picasso à Paris: 1900-1907* (Amsterdam, Van Gogh Museum, 18 February – 29 May 2011; Barcelona, Museu Picasso, 30 June – 15 October 2011). Amsterdam/ Barcelona/Brussels: Van Gogh Museum/ Museu Picasso/Fonds Mercator, 2011. McCully, Marilyn. *Picasso in Paris: 1900-1907.* Barcelona: Joaquim Sunyer, 2011.

Paris, Montreal, Barcelona 2011
Cogeval, Guy; Dupuis-Labbe, Dominique; Regnier, Gérard; et. al. *Picasso érotique* (Paris, Galerie Nationale du Jeu de Paume, 19 February – 20 May 2001; Montreal, Museum of Fine Arts, 14 June – 16 September 2001; Barcelona, Museu Picasso, 15 October 2001 – 27 January 2002). Paris: Réunion des Musées Nationaux, 2001.

Paris, San Francisco, New York 2011
Bishop, Janet; Debray, Cécile; Rabinow, Rebecca; and Tinterow, Gary. *Matisse, Cézanne, Picasso… L'aventure des Stein* (Paris, Galeries Nationales du Grand Palais, 5 October 2011 – 22 January 2012; San Francisco, Museum of Modern Art, 21 May – 6 September 2011; New York, The Metropolitan Museum of Art, 22 February – 3 June 2012). Paris: Réunion des Musées Nationaux, 2011.

New York, Washington 2011
Galassi, Susan Grace and McCully, Marilyn. *Picasso's Drawings, 1899-1921: Reinventing Tradition* (New York, The Frick Collection, 4 October 2011 – 8 January 2012; Washington D.C., National Gallery of Art, 29 January – 6 May 2012). New York: Frick, 2011.

Cleveland, Barcelona 2012
Robinson, William H. *Picasso and the Mysteries of Life: La Vie* (Cleveland, Museum of Art, 12 December 2012 – 21 April 2013; Barcelona, Museu Picasso, 10 October 2013 – 19 January 2014). Cleveland/London: The Cleveland Museum of Art/Giles, 2012.

Barcelona 2013
Jiménez, Reyes. *Journey Through the Blue: La Vie* (Barcelona, Museu Picasso, 10 October 2013 – 19 January 2014). Barcelona: Ajuntament de Barcelona, 2013.

Barcelona 2013
Vallès, Eduard and Cendoya, Isabel. *Yo Picasso: Self-Portraits* (Barcelona, Museu Picasso, 31 May – 1 September 2013). Barcelona: Ajuntament de Barcelona, 2013.

London 2013
McCully, Marilyn. *Becoming Picasso: Paris 1901* (London, Courtauld Gallery, 14 February – 26 May 2013). London: Courtauld Gallery & Paul Holberton Publishing, 2013.

Barcelona 2014
Vallès, Eduard. *Casagemas: El artista bajo el mito* (Barcelona, Museu nacional d'art de Catalunya, 31 October 2014 – 22 February 2015). Barcelona: Museu nacional d'art de Catalunya, 2014.

New York 2014
Naves, Mario. *Cubism: The Leonard A. Lauder Collection* (New York, The Metropolitan Museum of Art, 20 October 2014 – 16 February 2015). New York: The Metropolitan Museum of Art, 2014.

La Coruña 2015
Malen, Gual Pascual. El Primer Picasso a Coruña (Coruña, Museo de Belas Artes de Coruña, 20 February – 24 May 2015). Coruña: Ayuntamiento de A Coruña/Xunta de Coruña, 2015.

Paris 2015-16
Bouvard, Emilie. *¡ Picasso! L'exposition anniversaire* (Paris, Musée national Picasso-Paris, 20 October 2015 – 31 January 2016). Paris: Musée national Picasso-Paris/Réunion des Musées Nationaux du Grand Palais, 2015.

Marseille 2016
Gaudichon, Bruno. *Un génie sans piédestal: Picasso et les arts et traditions populaires* (Marseille, Musée des Civilisations de l'Europe et de la Méditerranée, 27 April – 29 August 2016). Marseille: Gallimard/MuCEM, 2016.

Barcelona 2016
Lahuerta, Juan José and Philippot, Emilia. *Picasso romanesque* (Barcelona, Museu nacional d'art de Catalunya, 17 November 2016 – 26 February 2017). Barcelona: Museu nacional d'art de Catalunya, 2016.

London, Barcelona 2016
Cowling, Elizabeth. *Picasso Portraits* (English version) / *Picasso Retrats* (Spanish version) (London, National Portrait Gallery, 6 October 2016 – 5 February 2017; Barcelona, Museu Picasso, 16 March –25 June 2017). London: National Portrait Gallery, 2016.

Paris 2016
Des Cars, Laurence. *Apollinaire, le regard du poète* (Paris, Musée de l'Orangerie, 6 April – 8 July 2016). Paris: Gallimard/Musées d'Orsay et de l'Orangerie, 2016.

Paris, Brussels 2016
Godefroy, Cécile and Perdrisot, Virginie. *Picasso: Sculptures* (Paris, Musée national Picasso-Paris, 8 March – 28 August 2016; Brussels, Palais des Beaux-arts – BOZAR, 26 October 2016 – 5 March 2017). Paris/Brussels: Musée national Picasso-Paris/Somogy/ BOZAR, 2016.

Madrid 2017
Serraller, Francisco Calvo and Alarcó, Paloma. *Picasso Lautrec* (Madrid, Museo Nacional Thyssen-Bornemisza, 17 October 2017 – 21 January 2018). Madrid: Museo Nacional Thyssen-Bornemisza, 2017.

Barcelona 2017
Gual, Malén. *1917: Picasso en Barcelona* (Barcelona, Museu Picasso, 25 October – 28 January 2018). Barcelona: Ajuntament de Barcelona, 2017.

Paris 2018
Le Bon, Laurent; Bernardi, Claire; Molins, Stéphanie; and Philippot, Emilia. *Picasso: Bleu et rose* (Paris, Musée d'Orsay, 18 September 2018 – 6 January 2019). Paris: Hazan, 2018.

Paris 2018
Léal, Brigitte. *Le Cubisme* (Paris, Centre Pompidou, 17 October 2018 – 25 February 2019). Paris: Éditions du Centre Pompidou, 2018.

致谢

Acknowledgments

一个展览的成功开幕，背后凝聚了无数人的贡献与努力，“毕加索——一位天才的诞生”的制作团队如下：

Behind the opening of every exhibition is the dedicated effort of countless partners and contributors. "Picasso – Birth of a Genius" was made possible by the following people:

展览 Exhibition

策展人 Curator
国立巴黎毕加索博物馆首席策展人
Head of Collections, Musée national Picasso-Paris
艾米利娅・菲利普 Emilia Philippot

项目总监 Project Manager
苏菲・哈塔扎克，国立巴黎毕加索博物馆
Sophie Ratajczak, Musée national Picasso-Paris

研究助理 Research Assistants
茱莉亚・亨利，国立巴黎毕加索博物馆
Julia Henry, Musée national Picasso-Paris
玛丽娜・埃维尔，国立巴黎毕加索博物馆
Marina Hervieu, Musée national Picasso-Paris

展览协调 Exhibition Coordination
Doors 门艺文化公司
Doors Art & Culture Agency
黎静 Bérénice Angremy
零零 Victoria Jonathan
汤绫子 Tang Lingzi
张斯琦 Nina Zhang

展览设计 Exhibition Design
阿德里安·卡迪 工作室
Studio Adrien Gardère
阿德里安·卡迪 Adrien Gardère
马克·萨拉赞 Marc Sarrazin

运输与搭建
Transport and installation
Chenue

艺术品修复与准备
Restoration and Preparation of the Works
帕斯卡・阿库耶团队
Restoration Pool, Pascale Accoyer
亚历山大・潘达佐普洛斯团队
Restoration Pool, Alexandre Pandazopoulos
奥利维耶・塔沃索团队
Restoration Pool, Olivier Tavoso

底座制作 Mount-making
阿里格里 Alighieri

画框制作 Production of the Frames
布莱斯・圣毛利斯 Blaise Saint-Maurice

出版物 Publication

文化艺术出版社
Culture and Art Publishing House
杨斌 Yang Bin
梁一红 Liang Yihong

26 Studio
冷静 Leng Jing
杨绍谆 Yang Shaozhun

UCCA

馆长兼 CEO
Director and CEO
田霏宇 Philip Tinari

首席运营官
Chief Operating Officer
朱玮琦 Windy Zhu

基金会理事长兼首席财务官
UCCA Foundation Chair and CFO
张朝卫 Ada Zhang

副馆长 Deputy Director
尤洋 You Yang

展览部 Exhibitions
卞卡 Bian Ka
杜帆 Duffy Du
关健 Edward Guan
郭希 Guo Xi
林鹭琪 Lin Luqi
栾诗璇 Luan Shixuan
施瑶 Shi Yao

公共实践部 Public Practice
杨紫 Yang Zi
安多英 Diane Dah-Young Ahn
韩馨逸 Liya Han
李艳 Lydia Li
林立 Wild Lin

研究部 Research
赖柏圣 Patrick Rhine
黄洁华 Huang Jiehua
黄明慧 Huang Minghui
黄文璇 Huang Wenxuan

品牌部 Communications
孔令祎 Kong Lingyi
西门・法兰克 Simon Frank
刘宇霆 Basha Liu
任立敏 Ren Limin
王继源 Wang Jiyuan
王可 Wang Ke
徐丹羽 Xu Danyu
袁嘉敏 Yuan Jiamin
张晴 Henry Zhang
朱若曦 Zhu Ruoxi

市场部 Marketing
王娟 Yolanda Wang
李思慧 Li Sihui
潘玲丽 Fatina Pan
孙晓雪 Sun Xiaoxue
钟世琴 Stephanie Zhong
周维 Zhou Wei

发展部 Development
游骁 Christina You
李琳 Li Lin
魏红箫 Ann Wei
张梦洋 Zhang Mengyang

观众部 Visitor Experience
杜英临 Joanna Du
郭昫辰 Guo Xuchen
李慧娟 Li Huijuan
李可人 Li Keren
刘新月 Liu Xinyue
刘莹 Liu Ying
闫笑 Lulu Yan
张睿 Zhang Rui
赵子慧 Zhao Zihui

UCCA 基金会 UCCA Foundation
陈睿 Alex Chen
江弋舟 Jiang Yizhou

馆长办公室 Director's Office
韩楠 Han Nan
张杨 Zhang Yang

UCCA Lab
李凡琪 Li Fanqi
刘雪丽 Liu Xueli
吴颜如 Wu Yanru

商业拓展部
Business Development
吴奕萱 Wu Yixuan
胡晓 Sam Hu
刘宇傲 Cynthia Liu
杨惠宇 Yang Huiyu

零售部 Retail
张曦 Aileen Zhang
周婷 Jennifer Zhou
毕卓异 Melo Bi
陈薇宇 Zoe Chen
丁雅超 Ding Yachao
关莹莹 Guan Yingying
贾逸铮 Jia Yizheng
姜茜 Jiang Qian
李贝贝 Li Beibei
李丹 Danae Li
李亚男 Li Yanan
梁媛媛 Liang Yuanyuan
刘亚洲 Rocker Liu
吕峥 Lü Zheng
潘超 Pan Chao
孙江涛 Sun Jiangtao
徐芬 Xu Fen
杨阳 Yang Yang
余慧敏 Auril Yu
岳爽 Claire Yue
张虹伟 Zhang Hongwei
张霞 Merry Zhang
张占春 Zhang Zhanchun
郑伟 Zheng Wei
周洋 Zhou Yang

教育部 Education
李晓晨 Betty Li
常力鑫 Chang Lixin
陈超伦 Chen Chaolun
程华 Cheng Hua
杜贺 Gabay Du
冯依琳 Feng Yilin
高毓鹏 Gao Yupeng
葛梦溪 Mia Ge
郭悦华 Guo Yuehua
李宣豫 Elsa Li
罗斌 Luo Bin
吕汇洋 Leticia Lv
秦雨晴 Ada Qin
宋晓茜 Song Xiaoqian
宿静 Su Jing
王梦怡 Wang Mengyi
王晴 Wang Qing
王晓玲 Wang Xiaoling
王艺潓 Wang Yihui
吴杭莹 Wu Hangying
王思思 Wang Sisi
许雯 Xu Wen
叶慧斌 Andy Ye
喻骞 Maggie Yu
张宝英 Zhang Baoying
张书轲 Lisa Zhang
章瑞波 Zhang Ruibo
张雪飞 Zhang Xuefei
赵梦颖 Zhao Mengying
郑艺 Helen Zheng
郑燕 Zheng Yan
周逸飞 Stella Zhou

人力资源部 Human Resources
孙侃 Sun Kan
韩晓萌 Han Xiaomeng
刘瑞 Liu Rui
刘伟东 Liu Weidong
王玉凤 Wang Yufeng

财务部 Finance
王志杰 Wang Zhijie
魏振玲 Wei Zhenling
蔡佩君 Cai Peijun
巩佳 Gong Jia
李宁 Li Ning
宋奎奎 Song Kuikui
王晓红 Wang Xiaohong
谢忱 Xie Chen

技术部 IT
李朗 Li Lang
李晔 Li Ye
朱昊 Zhu Hao

运营部 Operations
安闯 An Chuang
李洋 Li Yang

实习生 Interns
程婧 Cheng Jing
归熹溯 Nicholas Hall
余海杰 Marco Iu
张祎迪 Zhang Yidi

国立巴黎毕加索博物馆
Musée national Picasso-Paris

馆长 President
洛朗・勒邦 Laurent Le Bon

首席运营官
General Director
艾罗尔・欧克 Erol Ok

馆长业务负责人
Task Officer to the President
斯蒂范尼・穆兰 Stéphanie Molins

宣传与观众发展总监
Direction of Communication and Audiences Development
莱斯利・勒舍瓦利耶 Leslie Lechevallier

藏品、制作与公共教育总监
Direction of Collections, Production, and Mediation
克莱尔・卡尔尼尔 Claire Garnier

制作部 Production Department
苏菲・达伊尼 - 迪阿罗
Sophie Daynes-Diallo

人力资源总监
Direction of Resources and Means
马修・夏普龙 Matthieu Chapelon

建筑、开发、安全与信息系统总监
Direction of Building, Exploitation, Security, and Digital Resources
纪尧姆・加亚尔 Guillaume Gaillard

尤伦斯基金会理事会
UCCA Foundation Council

Jack Chen

仇浩然 Hallam Chow

高俊 与 徐月艺
Gary Gao & Paige Xu

江南春 Jason Jiang

乐拉 Ivy Le*

李琳 Li Lin*

刘珺珺 Liu Jun Jun*

刘兰 Liu Lan*

刘千里 与 秦致 *
Lily Liu & James Qin*

马寅 Ma Yin

茅矛 Jerry Mao*

沙烨 Sha Ye

苏丹瑞 与 梁琨如
Derek & Michelle Leung Sulger*

田军 Tian Jun*

涂雅芳 Carmen Tu

尤伦斯夫妇
Guy & Myriam Ullens*

杰克・沃兹沃思 与 苏茜・沃兹沃思
Jack & Susy Wadsworth*

王珺 Wang Jun*

谢伟 Alina Xie*

杨滨 Yang Bin*

曾宝宝 Baobao Zeng*

曾子墨 Zimo Zeng*

周航 Herman Zhou

尤伦斯当代委员会
UCCA Contemporary Circle

欧瑞思公主
Princess Alia Al-Senussi

郭佳鑫 Vince Guo

蒋霈铭 Peiming Jiang

林云松 Lin Yunsong

刘宏剑 Liu Hongjian

Dino Sadhwani

薛博中 BoBo Xue

张卫平 Tony Zhang

及其他不具名理事
标 * 者为基金会理事会的创始理事
按姓名首字母顺序排列

And those who wish to remain anonymous

Founding Members of the Council are designated by an asterisk

Names listed in alphabetical order

尤伦斯年度战略合作伙伴
UCCA Annual Strategic Partners

aranya

BARCO
睛彩艺术影像呈现

Bloomberg

多乐士
let's colour

展览支持
Exhibition Support

Morgan Stanley
摩 根 士 丹 利

Sotheby's | 蘇富比 EST. 1744

MARIE DALGAR

儿童教育项目赞助
Children's Education Program Sponsor

英氏
YEEHOO

合作方
Collaborators

RÉPUBLIQUE FRANÇAISE
AMBASSADE DE FRANCE EN CHINE

中法文化之春

TMALL天猫

Copyrights 版权信息

Photographic Credits 图片版权

本书出版于展览“毕加索——一位天才的诞生”在 UCCA 尤伦斯当代艺术中心举办之际（2019 年 6 月 15 日—2019 年 9 月 1 日）。

This catalogue is published on the occasion of the exhibition “Picasso – Birth of a Genius” at UCCA Center for Contemporary Art, 15 June – 1 September 2019.

本书由 UCCA 尤伦斯当代艺术中心与文化艺术出版社共同出版。

This book is jointly published by UCCA Center for Contemporary Art and Culture and Art Publishing House.

策展人及主编 Curator and Editor-in-Chief

艾米利娅・菲利普 Emilia Philippot

执行主编 Managing Editor

赖柏圣 Patrick Rhine

副主编 Associate Editor

黄洁华 Huang Jiehua

中文编辑 Chinese Editing

韩楠 Han Nan

作者 Authors

艾米莉娅・菲利普 Emilia Philippot
吴雪杉 Wu Xueshan

画册设计 Catalogue Design

冷静 Leng Jing
杨绍谆 Yang Shaozhun

翻译 Translation

李天 Sophie Jefford
李华 Li Hua
倪智刚 Brendan Nuse

封面 Cover

《自画像》（局部），巴黎，1906 年
布面油画，65 x 54 cm
国立巴黎毕加索博物馆 / 毕加索 捐赠，1979. MP8
Self-portrait (detail), Paris, a mn 1906
Oil on canvas, 65 x 54 cm
Musée national Picass ris / Pablo Picasso gift-in-lieu, 1979. MP8

印刷 Printing

雅昌文化（集团） 限公司 Artron Art (Group) Co., Ltd.

书号 ISBN： -7-5039-6713-9

艺术家、作者和出版方向允许他们在本书中使用版权所有材料的版权方表示感激。我们已竭尽所能地试图与版权持有人取得联系，以获得他们对材料使用的许可。出版方为书中可能有的错误或遗漏致歉，并向所有为此书提供勘误信息的读者表示衷心的感谢，我们将在本出版物未来的再印或再版版本中对其进行更正。

The artists, authors, and publisher gratefully acknowledge permission granted them to reproduce the copyrighted material in this book. Every effort has been made to contact copyright holders and to obtain their permission for the use of this material. The publisher apologizes for any errors or omissions and would be grateful if notified of any corrections that should be incorporated in future reprints or editions of this publication.

图书在版编目（CIP）数据

毕加索 ： 一位天才的诞生 / UCCA 尤伦斯当代艺术中心编. -- 北京 ： 文化艺术出版社，2019.6

ISBN 978-7-5039-6713-9

Ⅰ. ①毕… Ⅱ. ①U… Ⅲ. ①毕加索 (Picasso, Pablo Ruiz 1881-1973) —生平事迹—图录 Ⅳ. ①K835.515.72-64

中国版本图书馆 CIP 数据核字 (2019) 第 098927 号

毕加索——一位天才的诞生

主　　编　UCCA 尤伦斯当代艺术中心
执行主编　赖柏圣
副 主 编　黄洁华
责任编辑　梁一红
书籍设计　冷　静　杨绍谆
出版发行　文化艺术出版社
地　　址　北京市东城区东四八条 52 号　100700
网　　址　www.caaph.com
电子信箱　s@caaph.com
电　　话　（010）84057666（总编室）　84057667（办公室）
　　　　　（010）84057696—84057699（发行部）
传　　真　（010）84057660（总编室）　84057670（办公室）
　　　　　（010）84057690（发行部）
经　　销　新华书店
印　　刷　北京雅昌艺术印刷有限公司
版　　次　2019 年 6 月第 1 版
印　　次　2019 年 9 月第 3 次印刷
开　　本　889 毫米 ×1194 毫米　1/16
字　　数　80 千字　160 余幅图
印　　张　15.5
书　　号　ISBN　978-7-5039-6713-9
定　　价　268.00 元

毕加索为自己的“和平神庙”画鸽子
位于瓦洛里斯的城堡，卢西亚诺·埃米电影的拍摄期间，1953 年，国立巴黎毕加索博物馆，APPH2021
Pablo Picasso drawing doves for his Temple of Peace in the chapel of the manor at Vallauris, during the filming of Luciano Emmer’s movie, 1953.
André Villers, Musée national Picasso-Paris. APPH2021.

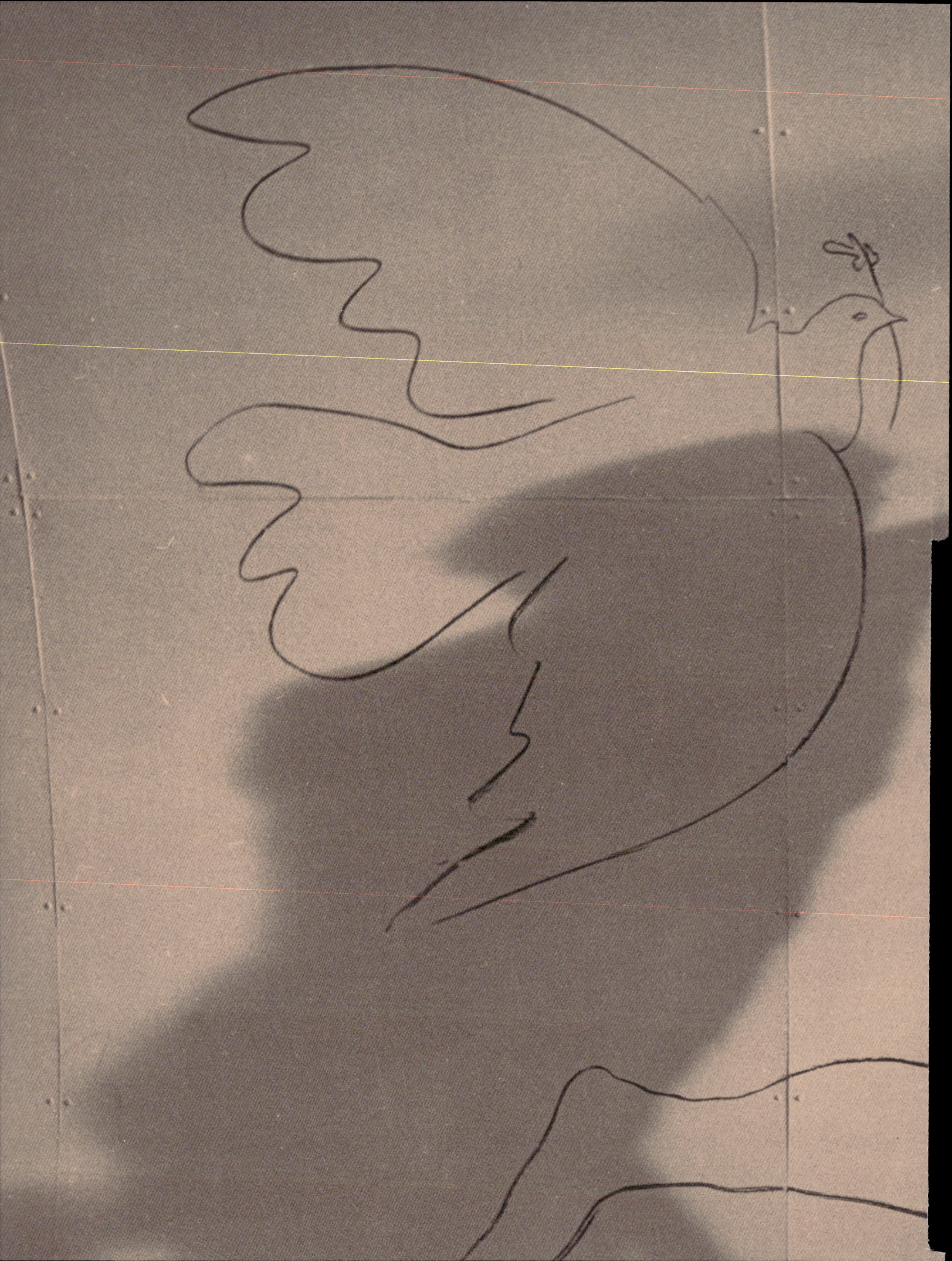